USING
ARTIFICAL INTELIGENCE (AI)
IN BANKING

Real-World Application, Use Cases in Banking, AI Technology, and Solutions

By

Dato' Arif Siddiqui

Copyright © 2024 by Dato' Arif Siddiqui

All rights reserved. No part of this publication may be reproduced, distributed, or transmitted in any form or by any means, including photocopying, recording, or other electronic or mechanical methods, without the prior written permission of the publisher, except in the case of brief quotations embodied in critical reviews and certain other non-commercial uses permitted by copyright law. For permission requests, write to the publisher at the address below.

Dato Mohammad Arif

ISBN: 9798339662983

First Edition
Published by Dato' Arif Siddiqui on 09-18-2024

The characters, incidents, and dialogue are products of the author's imagination and are not to be construed as real. Any resemblance to actual events or persons, living or dead, is entirely coincidental.

Disclaimer
The information provided in this book, including details about the status of AI implementation in banks, the features of solutions mentioned, or any other related data, is based on publicly available sources such as bank websites, industry reports, and other reputable publications. While every effort has been made to ensure the accuracy and completeness of the information at the time of publication, the author does not assume any liability for changes that may occur after publication, nor for the accuracy or reliability of third-party sources.

This book is intended for informational purposes only and should not be construed as professional advice. The author and publisher make no warranties, either expressed or implied, regarding the contents of this book. Any actions or decisions made based on the information in this book are the sole responsibility of the reader. The views and opinions expressed in this book are those of the author and do not necessarily reflect the official policy or position of any organization, financial institution, or company mentioned. All product names, logos, and brands mentioned are property of their respective owners.

CONTENTS

1. Innovation, strategy and governance are Reshaping Banking by AI
2. Enhancing Customer Experience through AI
3. Use of AI for Cross-Selling and Up-Selling in Banking
4. Use of AI in KYC in Banking
5. Managing Risk in Anti-Money Laundering (AML) with Artificial Intelligence
6. Using AI in Wealth Management
7. Use of AI for Loan Origination
8. Use of AI in Investment Banking
9. The Rise of Robo Advisor 4.0
10. Credit-Risk Prediction Using Hybrid Deep Machine Learning in Banking
11. AI-Driven Trade Finance: Transforming Global Commerce with Cutting-Edge Technology
12. AI is Shaping the Future of the Financial Market
13. Banks Adopting AI in Transaction Monitoring
14. Banking on AI: The Evolution from Simple Chatbots to Advanced AI Agents
15. Leveraging AI for Advanced Customer Segmentation
16. Use of AI for underwriting in Banking
17. Using AI and Smart Contracts for Contract Management in Banking
18. The Future of Trade: How AI and Automation Are Transforming Letter of Credit Issuance

About this book: Using AI in Banking: Real-World Application, Use Cases in Banking, AI Technology, and Solutions

By Dato Arif Siddiqui

Using AI in Banking is a comprehensive guide for banking professionals and tech enthusiasts eager to understand how Artificial Intelligence (AI) is transforming the banking sector. Written by **Dato Arif Siddiqui**, this book delves into how banks worldwide are adopting AI, implementing cutting-edge technologies, and reaping significant benefits in areas such as operational efficiency, fraud prevention, customer service, and risk management.

What's Inside the Book?

This book provides an in-depth look into the strategic application of AI across banking operations, offering over **150 real-world technology solutions** that have been used by banks to successfully implement AI. From **Machine Learning (ML)** to **Generative AI** and **Deep Learning (DL)**, readers will learn how these technologies are being applied to solve complex challenges and create new opportunities in banking.

The book explores:

- How global banks are using AI to streamline processes, reduce operational costs, and improve customer satisfaction.

- The practical benefits banks have achieved through AI-driven fraud detection, credit scoring, risk management, and regulatory compliance.

- Real-world examples of AI technologies used to personalize banking services, automate back-end operations, and forecast market trends.

With over **100+ use cases**, this book showcases how leading institutions like **JPMorgan Chase, Bank of America**, and **HSBC** are successfully implementing AI to enhance everything from customer interactions to back-office functions.

Who Should Read This Book?

This book is perfect for professionals working in the banking sector, fintech experts, and AI enthusiasts who want to learn how banks are adopting AI to drive growth and innovation. Whether you are a banker looking to explore AI implementation, or a tech enthusiast interested in financial technologies, **"Using AI in Banking"** offers the insights and strategies needed to navigate the rapidly evolving world of AI in finance.

Technology Insights

Dato Arif Siddiqui breaks down more than **150 cutting-edge AI solutions** used by banks, explaining how technologies like **cloud-based infrastructures**, **AI-powered fraud detection systems**, and **AI-driven credit risk models** are transforming the banking landscape. These insights will help readers understand the technical and operational aspects of AI implementation.

Bonus with book: List of 500+ references used by Author for the book, the PDF file can be downloaded by scanning barcode at back page of book.

About Author

Dato' Arif Siddiqui is a seasoned banking executive with over **30 years of experience** in the industry. As the **Chief Information Officer (CIO)** of **Standard Chartered Bank Malaysia**, he leads the bank's technology and operations, overseeing the development and support of retail and wholesale banking systems. Previously, Dato' Arif was the **CEO of Scope International Malaysia**, Standard Charterer's Global Shared Services Centre, where he managed a large global team and developed more than 100 banking applications. Renowned for his expertise in **digital transformation, blockchain, RPA, Customer experience, fintech,** and **innovation**, Dato' Arif's leadership has spanned multiple countries, driving change and success across the banking industry.

Introduction

Chapter 1: AI in Strategy and Governance

This chapter explains how AI transforms strategies in banking, drives higher customer engagement and deposits, makes the bank more efficient in operations, and enables new business models. Using AI technology — machine learning (ML), natural language processing (NLP) — banks can customize their financial products and services using data analytics. JPMorgan Chase, for example, uses COiN (Contract Intelligence) to automate document review and contract management. This AI-based assistant for legal documents uses NLP to process documents that were once manually compiled and regulated before execution, reducing human errors by thousands of hours. By improving risk assessment, guaranteeing security lines and ensuring compliance, AI assists banks in the growth.

15 bank use cases and **12 technology solutions** discussed and mentioned in this chapter.

Chapter 2: Enhancing Customer Experience through AI

In this chapter particularly, we would see how AI tools like chat bots and virtual assistants are now improving customer interactions with a use case. Erica is an AI assistant created by Bank of America, which delivers secure, personalized financial guidance and support to customers in real time. Looking after the customers, AI algorithms can effectively monitor every single customer issued credit card to find fraudulent activities and potential fraud cases, benefiting both sides — for example, banks like HSBC. AI boosts the satisfaction and reliability of your customers by improving response time and offering them personalized financial products.

15 bank use cases and **12 technology solutions** discussed and mentioned in this chapter.

Chapter 3: Contract Management in Banking

In this chapter, we would study this use case in detail, where AI tools like chat bots and virtual assistants are enhancing customer interactions. ERICA is a registered trademark of Bank of America Corporation it is their AI assistant provide secure, printable financial guidance and help customers in real time Monitoring every credit card issued to customers for fraudulent activities and potential fraud cases, AI algorithms can help the banks (e.g. HSBC) as well as the people >> A Win-Win situation, taking care of the customers on one side. Improves Your Customer Satisfaction and Reliability: AI elevates the response time and provides tailored financial products to your customers.

6 bank used cases are discussed, including JPMorgan Chase, HSBC, and Santander, and 7 technology solutions are mentioned, including smart contracts, natural language processing (NLP), and blockchain technologies.

Chapter 4: Risk Management in Banking Using AI

How AI improves risk management by examining extensive data sets to predict more unknown HSBC and Deutsche Bank - AI to monitor credit risks, market fluctuations and helps Standard Chartered to be more compliant from identifying regulatory risks beforehand. Lenders can leverage AI-driven models for enhanced risk assessments that allow them to respond swiftly and mitigate financial losses. Using machine learning and predictive analytics allows banks to detect risk early.

15 banks used cases are discussed, 12 core technology solutions are highlighted in use cases, including AI-powered document verification, smart contracts, NLP, machine learning (ML), blockchain, automated compliance checks, and AI risk assessment.

Chapter 5: Managing Risk in Anti-Money Laundering (AML) with Artificial Intelligence

This chapter focuses on the integration of AI into the Anti-Money Laundering (AML) processes of banks. Money laundering detection — More and more banks are using AI to spot suspicious behavior, with a view of cracking down on financial crime. It helps sort thousands of transaction trails, identify potential differences and make recommendations (for example, HSBC does this —"Fighting financial crime with artificial intelligence"). The AI solution adopted by JPMorgan Chase similarly allows the bank to be more secure in its AML compliance tests and risk reduction for financial crimes. AI technologies, such as natural language processing (NLP) and blockchain, make compliance checks more efficient, enabling quick identification of fraud. These are tools that allow banks to adhere to regulatory requirements without spending money and resources on manual processes.

10 banks are discussed, including HSBC, JPMorgan Chase, Deutsche Bank, and Bank of China, among others. 8 key technology solutions, including OCR (Optical Character Recognition), RPA (Robotic Process Automation), AI-driven document validation, blockchain for trade finance, and predictive analytics for risk management.

Chapter 6: Using AI in Wealth Management

We are going to see what effects artificial intelligence is having on wealth management by providing a step-by-step guide of how AI has taken over the personalized financial planning; the investment strategies, as well as its use in advising everything. For example, banks such as UBS and Morgan Stanley have used AI to offer tailored investment but structured along customers' financial ambitions and willingness to take risks. Wealth managers can make more informed investment determination, as AI can examine patterns in the financial data and movements of the market for them with no hiccups. AI powered Robo-advisors are also being developed and used more, giving clients automatic financial advice. Not only does it increase customer satisfaction, but the effects of AI are clear in wealth management, as it can cut out Human Error and deem itself a massive time save.

8 banks Used cases are discussed, focusing on banks such as JPMorgan Chase, HSBC, and Standard Chartered. 9 technology solutions are explained, including AI-powered document processing, blockchain for trade finance, predictive analytics for risk management, AI-driven fraud detection, machine learning models for credit scoring, and automated compliance checks.

Chapter 7: Use of AI for Loan Origination

In the chapter, we delve into how banking leverages Artificial Intelligence (AI) to streamline loan origination. AI applications have significantly improved the processing duration, quality of information examined before granting loans, and the longevity of both, transforming a previously slow and manual process. AI is now in play at banks to evaluate credit risk and, for auto document recognition, loan servicing algorithms that take about how much income a borrower makes versus the amount of debt they are going into. The chapter moreover explains how global banks like ICBC and DBS, use AI solutions to optimise their workflows. Thus, AI plays an important role in improving customer experience. This automatically leads to a decrease in errors and hence it sets the base for the emergence of Banking Innovation.

20 banks use cases are discussed, including HSBC, DBS Bank, ICICI Bank, Bank of China, and Citi, among others. 24 key technology solutions are discussed, including AI-based document verification, machine learning for predictive analytics.

Chapter 8: Use of AI in Investment Banking

AI changes the game as it enhances decision making, market analysis, and trade execution. Citibank and Morgan Stanley apply AI to evaluate big data pools, creating more profitable investment ideas and speeding up trading dealings. Automated trade execution and real-time market insights that are offered by AI-powered systems like Marquee and Sentieo, which help traders throughout. In addition, investment banks use AI in debt risk assessment and fraud detection to manage themselves against financial risks. It gives deep learning algorithms insights to predict market trends and give better advisory services. Investment banks can now use AI-driven solutions to enable easier trading of complex trades.

25 banks are discussed, including HSBC, DBS Bank, Rakuten Bank, UnionDigital Bank, and WeBank. 24 technology solutions are discussed, including biometric verification, document verification, transaction monitoring, fraud detection, compliance management, and AML screening.

Chapter 9: The Rise of Robo Advisor 4.0

AI-powered platforms automating the delivery of financial advice and portfolio management. Firms like UBS and Charles Schwab have implemented Robo-advisors that use customer data to develop tailored investment strategies. Basically, the concept behind a Robo-advisor is that they utilise AI and algorithms to assess your risk tolerance, financial goals and market trends to give you advice on investments custom made for you. Low-fee, aka low-cost trading and more streamlined access are reasoning these platforms are gaining popularity—most among young people opening retail investment accounts or first-time investors. Robo-advisors that are powered by AI can monitor portfolios and automatically rebalance investments, offering a more streamlined and still very useful investment experience.

3 banks are discussed, including Wells Fargo, Vanguard, and Charles Schwab. 6 technology solutions are highlighted, such as machine learning for credit risk evaluation, predictive analytics, AI-powered loan underwriting, cloud-based AI platforms, NLP for document processing, and real-time fraud detection.

Chapter 10: Credit-Risk Prediction Using Hybrid Deep Machine Learning in Banking

This chapter discusses how AI and machine learning models redefine banking credit-risk prediction. Banks — Capitec, Starling Bank has used AI to improve the quality of credit risk evaluations based on analyzing complex data sets and predicting default risks. Proof of solvency: AI tools like XGBoost and deep learning to predict customer solvency, external solutions with TransUnion / H2O. AI improves credit scoring models. It helps make the process of assessment of credit risk much more efficient, allowing these banks to reduce loan default rates whilst increasing loan approval rates, even in populations with non-traditional financial backgrounds.

15 bank use cases are discussed, including HSBC, Citi, ICICI Bank, DBS Bank, and others. 17 key technology solutions are highlighted.

Chapter 11: AI-Driven Trade Finance

This chapter describes the radical changes trade finance operations can bring to life by empowering regulation compliance, control of frauds, and validation of documents using AI technologies. HSBC, and Standard Chartered uses blockchain coupled with AI-powered automation for secure trade document handling. Ai tools for Tackling Frauds and Errors in a Trade Finance AI is used to auto-process trade finance documents by verifying the document veracity using OCR (Optical Character Recognition) as well as NLP (Natural Language Processing). The tech providers use these technologies to bolster operational efficiency, compliance and transparency in trade finance.

10 banks Used cases are discussed, including HSBC, Deutsche Bank, Bank of China, Standard Chartered, and MUFG.13 technology solutions are highlighted.

Chapter 12: AI is Shaping the Future of the Financial Market

AI is having a profound impact on financial markets; it provides advanced market predictor tools, fraud detection algorithms, and personalized investment strategies. Banks use AI-based platform (Marquee) to deliver traders' real-time intelligence and predictive analytics, like Goldman Sachs, Citibank. AI can also handle very large datasets at rapid speeds, so financial institutions can make data-driven investment decisions and improve profitability simply by reducing trading risks.

9 technology solutions discussed.

Chapter 13: Banks Adopting AI in Transaction Monitoring

Banks in this chapter are already applying AI to improve transaction monitoring, a vital factor in the fight against fraud and money laundering. For example, JPMorgan Chase and HSBC use AI-based IT systems to monitor transactions for irregularities in real time. Machine Learning and Anomaly Detection models are leveraged to identify outliers' transactions, thus reducing the amount of manual workload for reviewing them. AI tools: These use AI to help assess the risk and detect money laundering in real-time besides complying with AML laws.

10 Banks have been discussed; 14 technology solutions covered.

Chapter 14: Banking on AI: The Evolution from Simple Chatbots to Advanced AI Agents

In this chapter, we shall see how AI in banking started with a mere chatbot and graduated to an advanced AI agent capable of handling more complicated tasks from forests. For example, Bank of America relies on AI-driven systems for personalized financial advice, customer support, and transaction monitoring via its AI assistant Erica. These AI agents are far more advanced, like using NLP and machine learning, which helps in driving truly fluent interaction with customers, resulting in increased customer engagement and reduced operational costs.

10 Banks use case was discussed and 8 technology solutions.

Chapter 15: Leveraging AI for Advanced Customer Segmentation

By studying the behaviors and interests of their customers, banks can conduct more advanced customer segmentation with AI. HSBC and Citibank segment their customers based on spending behaviour through AI algorithms, which helps in personalized marketing and offer tailor-made financial products. Segmentation driven by AI will cause improved customer targeting and higher engagement and conversion rates.

5 banks use cases were discussed.

Chapter 16: Use of AI for Underwriting in Banking

Through the automation of data analysis and risk assessment, AI has revolutionized the underwriting process. Banks such as Wells Fargo deploy AI models to process loan applications at a faster pace, with ministries analyzing not only the financial information and credit report. This eliminates the need for this time-consuming work and processes with improved accuracy in risk assessment, faster underwriting, which results in quicker loan approvals leading to reduced defaults.

10 Banks used cases is discussed, and 16 technology solution.

Chapter 17: Using AI and Smart Contracts for Contract Management in Banking

Artificial Intelligence (AI) and Blockchain based Smart Contracts in Contract Management for Banking JPMorgan Chase and HSBC have both found success using smart contracts for automating trade finance agreements minimizing human error and increasing workflows efficiencies. The AI solution simplifies contract management for banks with automated document drafting, risk assessment and compliance monitoring.

Chapter 18: The Future of Trade: How AI and Automation Are Transforming Letter of Credit Issuance

AI and automation are redefining Letters of Credit in trade finance Case in point: BNP Paribas and DBS Bank are turning to AI-driven platforms (they recently introduced LC Nexus) to automate the Letter of Credit process, eliminating errors and speeding up verification. Leveraging these technologies speeds up the time to issue an LC while enhancing security and compliance, making global trade more productive and visible.

ONE

Innovation, strategy and governance are Reshaping Banking by AI

Future Business Model

This will redefine the future of banking for BSP from a business model perspective with AI. Applying this AI technology to achieve sustainable operational efficiencies and financial optimization. Banks need an AI-transformed business model that will start with the identification and prioritizing most affected immediate use cases. By developing more income streams, boosting customer engagement, and optimizing data monetization, banks can keep a powerful position in the market.

Banks strive to use AI capabilities and powers to realize efficiency and business growth. Banks can employ AI in product and service design; this makes it possible for them to deploy tailored financial services solutions while using the insight gathered from live data. For example, which may feature customized investment advice and personalized lending options or other savings strategies based on a person's attributes and behavior, which all can help in enhancing customer satisfaction and loyalty.

With AI, a bank can use data like customer transaction patterns, income levels, and financial goals. With this analysis, a bank could provide personalized investment portfolios according to the financial aspirations of the customer and create more trust and engagement. The bank can increase its competitive strength by mining customer data for additional earnings via tailored financial products.

1. How AI, Machine Learning and Deep Learning Can Empower Finance & Banking Sector

The banking and financial services industry is in turmoil because of the lighting progress made in Artificial Intelligence, Generative AI, Machine Learning, and Deep Learning. These technologies are transforming financial institutions, empowering them with unparallel opportunities to enhance customer experience, optimize processes and create innovation. Fitting these tech advances within the realm of well-established, and often decrepit legacy systems will need navigating while dealing with compliance, data privacy and ethical questions as well.

1.1. Generative AI in Banking: A New Era.

Generative AI is becoming a driver of innovation within the banking sector. This type of AI can produce added content like text, pictures, and even whole finance models. The capacity of AI to produce novel outputs is a distinguishing feature that makes it valuable for more complicated problem solving, such as risk modelling/fraud detection or tailored customer responses.

1.2. Machine Learning: The Backbone of AI in banking.

We will talk about Machine Learning (ML), which is the essential part of AI and has long been used to progress technology in banks for many years. Machine learning algorithms learn with the help of data and then they find out patterns in it and predict to determine decide no human explicit programming. Given machine learning's ability to tailor behavior, it would seem the perfect complement through much of this space in banking.

1.3 Detection and prevention of fraud activities.

ML has influenced fraud detection, making it one of the most crucial fields. Keeping up with developing fraud tactics is a challenge for traditional rule-based systems.

ML algorithms can examine large datasets in real-time, detecting unusual patterns that may show fraud. For instance, Banks used ML algorithms to process millions of transactions per day to detect suspicious patterns that may show fraudulence. By analyzing factors such as location and time of transaction, transaction amounts, and users' behavioral patterns, this ML system allows the machine to identify fraudulent transactions, leading to far fewer losses from fraud.

1.4 Guide on how lenders make lending decisions.

The novelty of ML is that it can change the shape of credit scoring and lending decisions, which grants us improved risk assessments. In conventional credit scoring models, evaluating credit worthiness is based on static data points like credit history and income levels. ML algorithms can train additional data like social media, spending habits, or smartphone utilization to create a more comprehensive and accurate credit rating.

Zest AI — a FinTech company — has developed ML-powered credit scoring models that incorporate alternative data sources when assessing credit risk. This is effective in low file, because these models allow the lenders to connect with credit invisible target populations and deliver a low default rate.

1.5 The power of deep learning: opening new possibilities.

Check out how Deep Learning (DL), a subset of ML, reshapes AI in banking by attempting to imitate the mind processes and structure of the human brain with the help of neural networks. Models created with DL are very in unstructured data, like images, text and audio, to perform more complex functions, for example NLP (Natural Language Processing), image recognition, and sentiment analysis.

1.6 The intersection of NLP and chatbots.

Banking customer service gets support from advanced chatbots and virtual assistants: AI-powered NLP services can read and respond to communication; they can provide the right context-aware response.

Chatbot boosted with NLP using DLT is a virtual assistant activates via text and voice. It helps manage customer accounts and respond to financial questions, providing actionable financial tips. With the enhanced natural language capabilities of virtual assistants, customer service efficiency and satisfaction has been increasing.

For example, deep learning models are useful in identifying nuanced patterns within vast datasets that are often overlooked using more traditional banking analytics and forecasting techniques. Using historical data, market trends and other variables, these models can piece together the future as it pertains to moving markets, behavior of customers, and financial success.

A top-tier investment bank employs DL models to interpret market data and generate trading strategies. The DL system uses deep learning to analyze massive amounts of unstructured data, which enables the bank to identify market trends and fosters better decision making while trading.

1.7. Ethical considerations

Although using AI, ML, and DL in banking enables various advantages but implementing them is quite problematic. Institutional banks will have to grapple even more with privacy, compliance and ethics for responsible deployment of the technology.

1.8. Data Privacy and Security

Because of handling massive funds and sensitive data of customers, the biggest concern for AI being used in banking is security and privacy. Banks should uphold strict security measures and abide by data protection regulations, such as GDPR, to keep customer data safe.

One prominent example was a European bank with strict GDPR regulations who found that using DL models becomes complex because of regulation restrictions. The bank implemented sophisticated encryption and anonymization techniques to secure customer data, enabling effective operation of AI.

1.9. Ethical AI and Bias

In AI implementation, QUALITY is determined ONLY by the training data they receive — AI or ML or DL., if the training data we feed to this AI system has a bias in it, then the outcomes created by this AI will have bias and might harm certain customers. Banks must therefore focus on extensive testing and validation to reduce bias in their AI systems and ensure proper functioning.

In the United States, a financial institution constructed a lending model using machine learning that experts discovered discriminated against minority applicants. To ensure fairness in lending decisions, the bank addressed bias in the model by retraining it using data that was more representative and putting extra controls in place.

1.10. Future of AI in The Banking Sector.

Banking integration of AI, ML and DL is still in its infancy but can be a game-changer for the industry. The industry embarks on an increasing journey of AI exploration and investment. We will see applications blossom to redefine the way financial institutions operate.

1.11. AI-Driven Financial Planning

Robo-advisors can also come of age, offering Robo AI advice that is personalized and adjusts in real-time based on the customers' situations and market conditions are likely to see fast adoption.

One of the largest financial services companies is working on an AI enabled financial planning tool based on DL models for accessing customer data and market trends. It provides you with only the best financial advice to help maximize your goals.

1.12. Autonomous Banking

In the future, there are plans for AI systems to handle all banking operations with minimal human involvement. Autonomous banking has the potential to be a significant change, providing customers in real-time insights into their financial well-being and offering access to banking services on an on-demand basis.

One FinTech startup is developing an AI platform that performs account management and investment decisions, making autonomous banking a reality. AI and DL powered. This platform adapts to customer preferences while providing an experience tailored to them; keeps the banking process as minimal friction and automated as possible.

Generative AI, Machine Learning, and Deep Learning are transforming the banking and financial services industry with exciting potential to transform customer experiences, drive operational efficiency, & spur innovation. Adopting those technologies requires thoughtful preparation, strong governance and a commitment to practicing ethical AI.

This can change the competition landscape for banks as well, if they implement AI. It will be interesting to see where this goes because we are just on the brink of what AI banking can do.

How AI, Machine Learning and Deep Learning are transforming banking — We plan to flip the above diagram upside down.

The ever-develop Artificial Intelligence, Generative AI, taking over the banking and financial services industry. Entities like Microsoft Co-pilot, Google Gemini and solutions such as Agenting, RAG, AI APIs are pulling this. These new opportunities are better customer experiences, more efficient processes, and further acceleration of digital transformation. This adds to the complexity of integration, data privacy, and regulatory compliance.

2. Generative AI in Banking: There will be More Than Traditional AI

Generative AI, which was first used to develop applications for banking services, has created opportunities to generate new types of content and handle broader customer interaction, decision-making capabilities constraints. Using tools and platforms such as Google Gemini, which have already integrated with third-party AI providers, banks can now easily use AI capabilities without having to build them themselves, thus fostering rapid implementation in this area.

2.1. Personalize experiences with customer engagement from Agenting and Google Gemini.

By utilizing Autonomous Agents, agenting can hyper-personalize customer experience and act on behalf of a user. Agenting isn't just another run-of-the-mill service people use; Agenting integrates with Google Gemini, an innovative AI model, to provide users with tailored financial services on the fly.

Customized Understand of Financial Planning used by HSBC for Agenting with Google Gemini with the use of these AI agents, creating custom investment strategies and savings for one individual regarding his/her spending patterns and life goals, depending on personal financial histories is done. By incorporating the Agenting and AI within banking has immense potential to support customer engagement being a responsive component, offering a level of adaptability as needed to maintain and exceed customer satisfaction, since an approach based on individual requirements seems promising.

2.2. RAG with Microsoft Co-pilot (enhanced risk management)

One such method for extra risk management in banking is Retrieval-Augmented Generation (RAG) that combines AI generative capabilities and retrieval systems. Integrated with RAG, Microsoft Co-pilot supports financial institutions to create comprehensive risk models made possible by using real-time data from different sources to inform smarter decision-making.

At Barclays, a RAG-powered risk management system is now run by Microsoft Co-pilot. Barclays leverages the platform for real-time access to market data and develops predictive risk models to lead balance sheet credit, market and operational risk management. The pipeline mentioned earlier, which combines RAG and AI tools like Co-pilot, generated significant savings by minimizing financial losses because of unanticipated market events revealing the true transformative power of them.

2.2. How machine learning contributes to AI in banking, backstopped by AI APIs

Banks use ML to analyze data, predict trends, and automate their decision making, even though it is not yet a central banking technology. This has improved ML capacities by introducing AI APIs (which makes it easier to add new AI features for banks into their existing architecture).

2.3 Prevent Fraud — AI APIs for fraud deduction

Getting AI APIs has set a new standard for fraud detection in banking that is now the benchmark use case of an ML implementation. These APIs can allow the bank to use pre-built AI models for real-time fraud detection, with no need for extensive in-house development.

By using AI APIs, JPMorgan Chase applies machine learning based algorithms for fraud detection on top of their existing infrastructure. These API help the bank in monitoring millions of transactions every day and catch any suspicious patterns, mitigating risks of Fraud. By integrating AI APIs, the firm has observed a decrease in fraud losses and enhanced security.

2.4. Credit Scoring and Third-Party AI Lending Decisions

Third-party AI platforms are using AI to generate dynamic risk assessments that revolutionize making credit scoring and lending decisions. Using powerful machine learning technology, these platforms can now analyze a greater scope of information, including alternative data points which allow for more accurate credit scoring.

Zest AI–An outstanding AI platform that applies machine learning to create specialized credit scoring models. These models look at other data sources to determine credit risk. AI APIs enable these models to be integrated by lenders and offer credit to the underserved population without a long credit history but provide a high-accuracy default rate.

2.5. New Horizons in Deep Learning via Microsoft Co-pilot & AI APIs.

DL is pushing forward the horizons of AI in banking by training it in unstructured data such as images, text, or audio. Banks can now also leverage the latest breakthroughs in natural language processing (NLP), image recognition, and sentiment analysis by incorporating platforms such as Microsoft Co-pilot and AI APIs.

2.6. Co-pilot for chatbots and Natural Language Processing (NLP)

Innovative chatbots and DL-based NLP-driven virtual assistants turning customer service to banking.by incorporating DL models with these tools, Microsoft Co-pilot enhances them and provides even more accurate and context-specific responses.

By linking Microsoft Co-pilot to its existing artificial intelligence-powered virtual assistant, Wells Fargo can now use the AI capabilities for client accounts and also answer questions and provide financial recommendation through text and voice communication. In banking, a live chat co-pilot has showed its might by increasing customer service efficiency and fun.

With AI APIs, banks can embed DL models for advanced analytics and forecasting to study massive data sets and predict.

Developing Deep Learning Models for Market Analysis Implementing DL model with AI APIs in an investment bank for conducting market analysis and trading strategy creation. The AI system of the bank, based on many unstructured data streams, such as news articles, social media and economic reports, allows for predict forecasting market trends. Working to make traders able to at least better believe...

2.7. Obstacles and Moral Concerns

While integrating AI, ML and DL with Microsoft Co-pilot, Google Gemini they seem a beneficial approach to offer the better financial services on the other side it is not lacking to encounter some issues as well. For responsible deployment to occur, these need to be addressed by the banks for data privacy, regulatory compliance, and ethical use of AI.

2.8 Third-Party AI and Data Security/Privacy

Third-party AI platforms require them to be equipped to handle large amounts of sensitive customer data, which can create concerns about data privacy and security. Banks have the duty to make sure these types of platforms comply with data protection legislation and high level of security.

One European bank faced issues with implementing third-party AI platforms because of stringent GDPR regulations. Using the capabilities of the AI platform enabled the bank to implement advanced techniques for securing and safeguarding customer data through encryption.

The accuracy of this data is very important for AI systems when combined with the fact that comprehensive AI training needs to be combined with AI API actioning on top and agenting technologies below. An AI system can treat customers if the training data is biased. These need to be tested and validated for fairness as well, if the bank is focusing on ensuring that its AI practices are following ethical guidelines.

One American finance institution that you discovered bias in its AI credit scoring models employed Agenting and API for the lending decision source mapping — Image Source: From the author. In response, the bank had to retrain models with more illustrative data and implemented further controls to ensure fair lending practices.

3. Future of AI, ML, DL, and AI APIs in Banking

Enabling AI, ML, DL in banking with some initial adoption using platforms like Microsoft Co-pilot or Google Gemini or AI APIs. Potential of the technologies to be industry disruptors.

AI-powered financial planning can dominate future banking services. On platforms like Google Gemini and AI APIs, customers could continue to consume personalized financial advice that meets their ever-changing financial circumstances and market conditions.

A financial services institution is building a tool for financial analysis with Google Gemini and AI APIs. Providing real-time financial advice by analyzing customer data and market trends, this tool renders benefits to customers focusing on attaining their respective finance goals.

3.1. Agenting and Artificial Intelligence in Autonomous Banking

And in the long run, autonomous banking (with very little human intervention) will become a reality as AI handles all bank transactions. This amalgamation of technology in agenting and AI could cause on-the-fly banking services that are automated. It would provide personalized services on-demand.

It can automate anything from account management to investment decisions and is being used by a FinTech startup to power the world's first autonomous bank. The Agenting and AI adapt the platform to customer preferences so that the banking journey becomes unique, self-service and personalized /automated.

RAG & AI APIs are transforming the Banking & financial services industry by infusing Generative AI, Machine Learning, Deep Learning and agenting. These technologies offer new possibilities in customer experience, operations and innovation. Proper planning, governance, and ethics of AI are the key factors to consider for successful deployment.

The banks that are going to be leading the way in this industry will implement these technologies. This is just the beginning of the era of AI delivered banking and there are infinite possibilities that lay ahead.

4. Rebalance the Innovation

Examples show the relationship between automation and cost savings. I believe that is not where the true value of AI lies.

Businesses can use this AI to improve their customer acquisition and retention with personalization. From social media posts to transaction history and customer feedback, there is a wealth of data for banks to analyze and, in doing so, detect the critical needs and demands of their customers. Banks offering hassle-free products and services delight customers and strengthen their loyalty.

AI allows the banks to consider transactional and social data around a person and predict major life events like buying a house or having children. Servicing the customer by providing specialized financial products such as personalized mortgages or education savings plans that reduce churn.

5. Create a center of excellence (CoE)

Banks should establish a Centre of Excellence for AI focused on AI implementation. As a center of excellence, it will be the central force for driving innovation, knowledge sharing and improving capabilities in AI. As AI capabilities scale, the CoE can shift to a control tower which directs the entire bank's AI strategy while ensuring its laser-focused on long-term objectives.

A CoE can help drive AI adoption across the organization, as it enforces a structured approach to experimentation, development, and deployment. This structured form of experimentation, build and deploy ensures that AI work aligns with the strategy of the bank by having its gaze on high while still being atm. for the business requirements. A CoE helps the bank stay ahead of the competition in moments like these, where innovation and learning never stop being important.

A large bank could build an AI CoE to support chatbots and conversational interfaces to serve customers.

6. Governance and controls

Given the potential damage, good governance frameworks need to be in place to ensure that embedding AI in banking does not magnify existing systemic risks. Banks must devise smart models and controllers for managing these sorts of risks, especially in compliance, ethical & data privacy-oriented areas.

Regulatory compliance is a partial approach to AI governance. Banks should develop explicit AI principles, especially in the more sensitive domains, such as AI credit scoring and customer profiling. The decisions made by AI in these areas have far-reaching consequences for individuals, so it is essential that there be human input on them.

Banks can avoid discrimination by using AI models in automated lending decisions, which must be rigorous, ensuring it is void of inadvertent biases. A bank, for instance, could put in place controls to audit AI models themselves to prevent them from affecting specific groups—whether defined by race, gender or socioeconomic class. Well compliance with regulations leads to the trust and confidence (between customers and regulators) that a bank wants.

7. AI is playing a leading role in Banking

The progress of AI is not just a trend in technology; it is escalating around us every day. The benefit for banking and financial institutions is that they ride this transformation. AI is playing a leading role in effecting this change — developing new content and analyzing huge datasets for operations optimization. Financial institutions struggle to fit AI into their current business models to drive innovation, enhance customer experiences, and keep up with the changing competition.

Based on the latest studies and news from sector blogs, below, I summarize AI in banking and AI in financial services.

7.1. Reinventing how customers engage and experience.

AI, through managing customer engagement, can turn banking into experience. These solutions are transforming traditional banking models by eliminating face-to-face interactions and manual operations with personalized services in real-time.

7.2. Custom Financial Products and Services

AI allows banks to provide tailored financial services that cater to each customer. Through the analysis of huge datasets, including the transactional history, spending behavior, and social media habits of consumers, AI can predict customer demands and propose customized solutions. With AI, banks can offer tailored investment advice, lending and savings plans, which were impossible until now.

A customizable investment advisory platform created using AI — as portrayed by a top bank in McKinsey report Instead, it uses AI to analyze customer data and market trends as inputs into personalized investment portfolio recommendations that lead to 30% higher customer satisfaction and a 20% increase in cross-selling opportunities.

7.3. Enhanced Customer Support

AI will change customer support by developing more advanced chatbots and virtual assistants. From checking account balances to complete complex loan applications, these AI tools can handle many customer queries and give immediate, accurate, and personalized information.

Erica, a virtual assistant for Bank of America, demonstrates the power of AI. In just 2 years since her debut, Erica has handled over 100 million customer requests, including everything from day-to-day transactions to financial guidance. The story of Erica shows just how much AI can elevate customer support while boosting customer satisfaction.

7.4. Improving productivity and decreasing costs.

AI can improve customer engagement and streamline banking operations with profound cost reductions and efficiency improvements. Artificial intelligence enhances the operations of the bank by automating routine tasks, optimizing workflows and analytic processes.

7.5. Automating Routine Tasks

AI excels at carrying out repetitive tasks with ease. In the banking sector it can be sentiments/compliance checks, transaction processing and reporting, etc.

According to a recent **PwC** study, **banks could reduce costs by up to 20% through automation of repetitive tasks using AI.** For example, when a European bank requested compliance reporting, the automation team completed the task on the same day, sparing four compliance analysts from working overtime. The AI system cut the time required to generate reports by 80 percent.

7.6. Optimizing Workflows

AI can analyze data to suggest effective strategies and pinpoint areas that need improvement. This feature comes in handy for loan origination and servicing, risk management, identity verification and fraud prevention.

8. HOW A LEADING U.S. BANK USED AI TO IMPROVE ITS LOAN PROCESSING EFFICIENCY:

The AI system reviewed past loan applications and identified root causes for slowdowns, suggesting process improvements. It sped up the bank's loan approval times by an average of 40%, improving customer satisfaction and providing operational efficiencies.

9. Improving the Risk Management and Fraud Detection

A List of Banking Areas Where AI Can Benefit-risk management fraud detection AI can analyze huge data in real-time, which provides capability to banks to recognize potential risks and threats such as frauds.

9.1. Advanced Risk Management

Using historical data, the actual movements in the market and real-time analytics allow banks to gain predictive insights with AI that lead to superior risk management. They do, however, take care of credit, market and operational risks.

Using AI allowed a Global Investment Bank to create an AI predictive risk management tool that analyzed market data and trading patterns and which could expect any potential risks and remediate them. AI helped the bank cut trading losses by over 15 percent.

9.2 Fraud Detection

Fraud Detection: Fraud detection is also a domain where AI thrives. Advanced fraudsters, who are always a step ahead of these technologies, can trick the rules and patterns that traditional fraud detection systems rely on. AI can analyze a vast quantity of transaction data and rely on automated processes to detect fraudulent transactions happening on the open network.

Powered by AI, JPMorgan Chase is using real-time transaction data with a fraud detection system integrated. The platform uses auto machine learning models to detect anomalies and flag suspect transactions. After instituting this, the bank saw a 50% reduction in fraud losses.

10. How to Innovate with AI Driven Products & Services

The power of AI is not just about making current processes better. AI-Investing Platforms.

In banking, the AI implementation we find most interesting is highly likely to be the use of artificial intelligence within investment platforms. These platforms can offer customized investment advice, portfolio management and trade executions using real-time data and market analysis.

A leading FinTech firm announced the launch of an AI-driven investment platform based on machine learning in understanding both market trends and customer data and giving recommendations on where to invest. It could also capture more customers in its shop as the platform outperforms traditional investment funds each year — by 10%.

10.1. Digital Banking Solutions

AI is also innovating their digital banking solutions. AI enables banks to offer sophisticated digital services, such as tools for personalized financial planning, AI-driven credit scoring models, and automated wealth management.

Spanish bank BBVA embedded AI into its own digital banking app so users can get behavioral analysis and custom financial planning features in their day-to-day account management. The app uses AI technology to offer personalized financial advice based on an advanced analysis of customer data, making it easier for customers to reach their financial goals. As a result, customer engagement with the app has grown by 25%.

11. Regulatory Compliance

Regulatory compliance is a factor banks consider AI technology cannot afford to overlook. For example, in lending, AI is often consequential enough for a legal and regulatory compliance measure to be put in place.

In financial services, the UK FCA released a paper with guidelines to ensure transparency, accountability, and fairness in AI-generated decisions. To avoid any legal complications, banks will need to ensure such AI complies with regulatory requirements.

AI & ITS UNDENIABLE IMPACT IN BANKING and FINANCIAL INSTITUTIONS.

AI provides banks with unprecedented opportunities to reshape their business models and stay ahead of the competition in a rapidly strengthening industry by transforming customer engagement, improving operational efficiency, strengthening risk management capabilities, and fostering innovation. To operationalize AI, however, it is an essential plan to establish robust governance and focus on ethical AI practices. The next Fortnite will be a game being deployed by one of the world's top online conquistadors who wanted it, but right now every bank with AI in farming has a competitive edge for its customers and shareholders. The institution that will make use of it, win in the digital finance area, ai is future banking.

Reference- Further reading - Chapter 1

1. How can generative AI add value in banking and financial services? McKinsey
   https://www.mckinsey.com/featured-insights/lifting-europes-ambition/videos-and-podcasts/how-can-generative-ai-add-value-in-banking-and-financial-services
2. Finding value in generative AI for financial services – Technology review
   MIT-UBS-generative-AI-report_FNL.pdf (technologyreview.com)
3. The future of banks: A $20 trillion breakup opportunity – McKinsey
   https://www.mckinsey.com/industries/financial-services/our-insights/the-future-of-banks-a-20-trillion-dollar-breakup-opportunity
4. Artificial intelligence: Transforming the future of banking
   https://www2.deloitte.com/content/dam/Deloitte/us/Documents/process-and-operations/us-ai-transforming-future-of-banking.pdf
5. AI: Flipping the coin in financial services – FCA
   https://www.fca.org.uk/news/speeches/ai-flipping-coin-financial-services
6. JPMorgan Deploys AI Chatbot To Revolutionize Research And Productivity
   https://www.gfmreview.com/banking/jpmorgan-deploys-ai-chatbot-to-revolutionize-research-and-productivity
7. HSBC and AI
   https://www.hsbc.com/who-we-are/businesses-and-customers/hsbc-and-ai
8. Wells Fargo's New Virtual Assistant, Fargo, to Be Powered by Google Cloud AI
   https://newsroom.wf.com/English/news-releases/news-release-details/2022/Wells-Fargos-New-Virtual-Assistant-Fargo-to-Be-Powered-by-Google-Cloud-AI/default.aspx
9. Interview: Wells Fargo's Kevin Cole on how banking assistant 'Fargo' is more personalised than ever
   https://www.retailbankerinternational.com/features/banking-assistant-fargo-more-personalised-than-ever-kevin-cole/?cf-view

TWO

Using AI in banking to enhance customer experience

Introduction.

The main reason the banking business is reforming enormously is that of how quickly AI (Artificial Intelligence) has been covering our daily life. AI is how banks are keeping up with the ever-increasing demands of customers for personalization, speed, and security. This comprehensive research explores ways in which AI enhances customer experiences across various banking categories, complete with case studies and input from the biggest banks.

How AI Revolutionizes the Customer Experience

Banks thus leverage AI to process data accurately and effectively at a massive scale, enabling them to tailor services for individual customers, playing an important part in advancing this transformation.

1. Personalization at Scale

The power of AI in banking overwhelmingly lies in its capacity to deliver targeted services at scale. Personalized financial advice, product recommendations and services — AI analyses customer data like transaction history, behavior patterns and preferences. BBVA provides tailored financial advice and budget recommendations through AI-powered analytics, allowing consumers to better manage their money. Individualizing client experiences fosters loyalty and appreciation, as customers are more likely to continue doing business when they feel valued and heard.

2. 24/7 Customer Support

AI chatbots and virtual assistants are changing the way customer support operates 24/7. With AI in place, AI systems replace human efforts and take care of regular inquiries and transactions and provide immediate help to guarantee help on time for a customer. The Royal Bank of Canada (RBC) is a case in point. A unique AI-driven virtual assistant named NOMI provides financial insights, along with real-time help, to give a much-improved customer service. This automation reduces wait times for customers and allows human agents to focus on more complicated matters.

3. Transaction Speed and Security Improved

AI is essential for speeding up the transaction and ensuring data security. It analyses the data from transactions in real-time, enabling AI to discover any fraudulent activity and automates authentication processes, helping to reduce time taken for a single credit transaction. AI also helps HSBC closely monitor transactions to detect unusual patterns, mitigate potential fraud risk, and inspire customer trust. AI powered security also covers biometric authentication that uses AI to confirm customer identification by the means of voice, facial or fingerprint, enabling a safe banking experience.

4. Optimizing Customer Services — A Case Study on Data Analysis

Banks, for example, can predict customer needs and provide tailored answers using AI tools. By analyzing your past transactions, spending habits, and significant life events, AI can predict your future needs, loans, investments or sometimes maybe a financial difficulty. Lloyds Banking Group is using AI to predict customer behavior and deliver tailored financial planning, helping customers achieve their financial ambitions. It follows this initiative that helps in improving customer satisfaction and creates stronger relationships with clients for the bank.

5. Improved Customer Insights

With AI-tools, banks can gain insights into customer preferences and behaviors, enabling them to develop informed marketing strategies, design products, and engage with customers based on their needs. By utilizing AI to unlock insights into U.S. Bank customer spending, they can offer more accurate and real-time recommendations for both life events (weird) and banking products. With this analysis, banks can offer their services based on what the customer wants — thus keeping them happy and growing their business.

> *"Generative AI can help create personalized product recommendations, reduce risks in underwriting, and enhance customer service, enabling banks to offer more tailored experiences."*
>
> *"Sixty-six percent of financial services executives say their organizations are likely to use generative AI for more advanced chatbots and virtual assistants, enhancing customer support and personalization."*
>
> Source: KPMG's Report "Generative AI Advantage in Financial Services"

AI to Improve Customer Experience

AI is making customer experience better in different banking sectors: customer support, marketing with individual approach & etc. The following are some of the key areas where its high impact is being determined in AI:

Swati Bhatia, Head of Marcus by Goldman Sachs, highlighted the importance of personalization in banking:

> *"Customers will choose their winners based on personalized experiences and 'transcendental magical experiences,' not just functional ones."*
>
> Source: The Financial Brand

1. Customer Support and Service via AI

Because AI-driven chatbots and virtual assistants form a vital part of customer support today, responsible for the handling of a wide variety of inquiries and transactions. AI systems automate repetitive work, increasing productivity and freeing up human agents to handle more complex tasks. The AI assistant called Erica from Bank of America does more than just simple questions and can even advise the customers on better financial decisions to increase customer experience. By decreasing wait times for customer service and providing customer support 24/7, AI-powered solutions can improve overall user satisfaction.

Aarushi Chopra, Senior Consultant at WNS, emphasized the role of generative AI in customer experience:

> *"Deploying the right Customer Experience (CX) strategy with generative AI harnesses data to deliver highly personalized banking experiences in real-time to greater customer retention and satisfaction."*
> Source: WNS's report on "Generative AI in Banking"

Tushar Bhatia, an AI expert at Enthu.ai, shared insights on AI

> *"AI-powered chatbots enable 24/7 customer support, streamlining operations and enhancing customer satisfaction by offering seamless, immediate solutions."*
>
> Source: Enthu.ai's article on AI applications in banking.

MMA Global report "The State of AI in Marketing and CX"

According to the MMA Global report, personalization is the predominant use case for AI, with 44% of organizations scaling it to tailor customer experiences and anticipate needs, bolstering loyalty and engagement.

2. Fraud Detection and Prevention with AI

Banks, for example, have been able to improve their fraud detection systems significantly through the deployment of AI that can analyze a vast set of transaction data instantaneously. For example, Artificial Intelligence programs could recognize aberrant patterns and behaviors by which banks used to protect their customers from fraudulent activity as fast as possible. By using AI to review complex legal documents and scan for fraud in real time, JPMorgan Chase's COiN platform even gives way to improved customer security. In using this approach, the bank not only strengthens trust and confidence in its security measures but also increases the customer's peace of mind that their funds are safe.

3. AI in Loan and Credit Scoring

Using AI has transformed the credit scoring process by evaluating loan requests and enabling the use of algorithms. By patenting the application of AI in analyzing financial data, credit history, economic figures, and social network risk factors, like Lenddo Credit, SMBSs and business loans, can be facilitated. This automation speeds up loan approvals, and it increases transparency in the decision-making process. Wells Fargo — for example, uses AI to speed up its loan application process, which enables quicker decisions and less time waiting around for customers. With AI-based credit scoring models, it will fit the customers, which are usually left out by traditional systems.

4. Targeted ads and promos

Banks use AI to analyze customer behavior, preferences, and transaction history, resulting in personalized marketing campaigns and product offers.

Citibank is a notable example of using AI to develop personalized investment recommendations and campaign materials that incorporate customers' financial goals. The custom experience will increase your user engagement — and hence usage of the bank services — which improves end-customer satisfaction and loyalty.

5. Voice / Biometric Authentication

Voice and biometric authentication in your AI Chatbots drastically improve security and convenience for the customer experience. Using AI, banks can have friction-free login with excellent data safety since the wizard will be on voice (or face or fingerprint) and already under scrutiny for biometrics. Standard Chartered Bank has unveiled a new service that will allow account holders to gain access to their accounts and carry out transactions by voice command. So, it allows customers to have better financial management.

6. Predictive Analytics and Financial Projections

Since AI can predict the financial requirements of customers, it is easier for banks in order that they can give guidance, which is financial. To predict future needs such as loans, investments, or financial hardships, AI can leverage historical transactions, spending styles, and life events. Through the use of AI, Lloyds Banking Group can predict customer behavior and offer highly tailored financial planning services which help guide customers towards their financial goals. What this does is that it not only provides a booster shot to the customer's financial world, but also scales the boundaries of Bank customer relationships.

7. Enhanced Customer Insights

For banks, AI offers insights into customer behavior and preference that can feed marketing, product design, and customer engagement. U.S. Bank uses AI-based insights to identify how customers spend and then offers these actionable patterns that are available as personal finance products and services. These insights power business growth and customer satisfaction because the needs of the users can get aligned with what businesses offer.

8. Automated Financial Advising

With AI, Robo-advisors are taking the millennial sector by storm and providing them fully personalized investment advice through automation.

Using the enormous stores of market data, customer risk profiles and financial goals, these advisors create their own portfolios with individualized investment advice. Vanguard Personal Advisor Services, for example, employs artificial intelligence and human advisors to deliver individual investment advice at scale, democratizing elite-level financial advising.

9. Live Financial Management

Real-time Finance: AI helps in tracking finance in real-time, which also provides customers a quick view of how they are spending and saving. It can categorize purchases like Mint, alert you to new or recurring expenses and suggest spending adjustments on the fly. With apps like Mint, users get their full financial picture and insights into how to save or not waste money. This helps customers make more financially responsible and informed decisions, leading to enhanced overall financial wellness.

10. AI-Driven Product Innovation

Banks are using AI to churn out consumer-centric financial products for the emerging demands. Goldman Sachs and Marcus are one example of a consumer lending and savings platform. They offer competitive interest rates and personalized loan offers using AI. Banks can differentiate by adopting AI to recognize market trends and customer preferences, enabling them to constantly innovate their products.

11. Compliance and risk mitigation

To help manage risk programmatically and pre-emptively, banks can use AI to discover problems before they become a threat. Take the help of AI risk management tools to predict market trends, estimate credit risks and comply with laws associated with it. Banks such as HSBC also use AI to improve security and confidence by automating the compliance process and reducing regulatory risks. The bank can enhance its reputation and provide better assurance to the end customer with a risk management technique.

12. Omnichannel Integration

It is a crucial factor that enables customers to have smooth experiences across various platforms, such as applications, social media, mobile apps, and physical stores. By leveraging AI, the bank can unify data across various touchpoints of interaction and offer customer service that is seamless and personalized, irrespective of where the customer interacts with them. Its system uses AI to weave together a customer's interaction with the brand across multiple touchpoints, allowing its customer relationship management "to be truly one-to-one," said the official.

> *"Banks are cautiously optimistic about the future and ready to leverage AI in new use cases to create a more personalized, enriched, and long-term customer experience that supports customers through life events."*
>
> Source: KPMG's "AI and the Orchestrated Customer Experience".

Gianna Maderis, Principal Customer Experience Manager at Zendesk, shared insights on AI's efficiency gains in customer service:

> *"AI tools enhance agent efficiency and productivity by simplifying workflows, handling requests, and automating processes, allowing agents to focus on high-value tasks."*
>
> Source: Zendesk's report on AI for customer experience

Case Studies of Top Banks Using AI in Customer Services

Artificial intelligence (AI) has supported many top financial institutions in the fast-growing banking industry to improve customer experience. Through this, they are setting new industry standards as their AI-powered solutions improve efficiency, enable more personalized services and increase security. In our last blog, we discussed how top banks are using AI to transform customer experiences and improve satisfaction.

1. JPMorgan Chase

1. COiN (Contract Intelligence): JPMorgan Chase has launched an AI-driven platform called COiN that standardizes how it reviews complex legal agreements. Legal agreements, including loan documents, that users had to review and interpret in the past sometimes ran for hours or even days. COiN leverage machine learning algorithms to read through documents at a fast pace and extract key ones raking risks out. The significant reduction in processing time allows details of transaction to be updated much faster and enables JPMorgan Chase simultaneously enhance speed and frequent feedback to clients. This allows legal teams to spend more time working on business-critical, strategic activities and provides a better experience to their customers by streamlining operational workflows with COiN.

1.1. AI-Powered Chatbots — JPMorgan Chase has integrated AI-powered chatbots to help customers seek solutions for routine requests and transactions. They provide immediate help with functionalities like account balance checks, funds transfer requests, & standard Q&A. The bank has implemented them across its digital platforms, and the chatbot's AI understands natural language processing capabilities, allowing customers to interact with it with no restriction of a format. This leads to a seamless, more user-friendly experience that cuts down on waiting times and overall increases consumer satisfaction. Chatbots escalate to more complex issues for humans, so the customers get the level of support they need.

2. Bank of America

1. Erica -Bank of America, which is incidentally the first financial institution to use AI for customer service by inventing Erica. Erica debuted in 2018 and helps customers better manage their finances. The AI-driven assistant based on your financial behavior gives you personalized insights, reminders and recommendations. This way, for example, Erica can help customers by warning them soon about upcoming bills or helping save.

Money and how to deal with credit scores. Though, what puts it in the category of financial management is its holistic approach towards money related matters through features including bill payments, credit score monitoring and fraud detection on Erica. Bank of America customers love the convenience and personalization that Erica provides, which has led to increased engagement and satisfaction.

Bank of America (BofA) has also used AI to improve fraud detection. They leverage advanced machine learning algorithms to track transactions in real-time and identify signs of potential fraud. These AI systems analyze millions of transactions for patterns or anomalies that show fraud, helping the bank to identify and mitigate fraudulent activity to protect their customers. By implementing this security method, the bank ensures the safety of customers' assets, fostering trust and confidence in our bank's commitment to protecting their financial information. Bank of America is Safety & Assures a lower bank risk for consumer banking.

3. Wells Fargo

Wells Fargo: AI-Driven Personalization — Wells Fargo has used AI to deliver a more personalized solution to its banking consumers. The bank's AI systems provide personalized financial advice and product recommendations by analyzing customer data, including transaction histories and spending patterns. Wells Fargo introduced an AI that can suggest customer-tailored savings or investment options or loans, depending on what the individual's financial goals are. Tailored services: The personal touch the bank brings to its business helps in improving customer relationships through more custom services that cater to their unique needs.

3.1 Improved Security: As security is a major concern for Wells Fargo, it has implemented AI to improve its fraud detection and prevention. Wells Fargo uses AI to scan over transactions and detect when patterns are not the norm in order to act quickly against security breaches. AI powers its facial recognition and fingerprint-scanning that helps offer customers safe log-in to their account. So, such additional security features make it easier for customers to trust your business, as they know their financial data is well protected.

4. HSBC

AI in Customer Support — As an example, for routine inquiries and transactions towards a high volume of them, HSBC integrated AI-powered chatbots into its customer service operations4. These chatbots serve two roles: assisting customers with requests such as password resets and account balance checks and providing information on the bank's products and services. By automating these interactions, HSBC can provide faster responses and free up human agents for more complicated customer issues. AI in customer support has helped HSBC to increase service efficiency and foster remarkable improvements in the level of customer satisfaction.

4.2 Artificial Intelligence for Regulatory Compliance: Aside from customer-facing use-cases, HSBC also leverages AI capabilities for regulatory compliance. The bank uses AI-based systems to analyze transactions and customer data for potential risks of money laundering or fraud. However, by detecting issues with compliance processes sooner and acting quickly to resolve them by automating compliance, HSBC can reduce the risk of fines and reputation damage. In this process of regulatory compliance, the bank protects itself and makes a quality environment for clients to trust in their institution.

5. Citibank

5.1 AI-Powered Investment Advice: Citibank has adopted Artificial Intelligence technology to provide its customers with tailored investment advice. The AI tools in the bank analyze the customer's goals for profitability, attitude towards risk and the state of the market, and then offer customized investment plans. For instance, Citibank's AI can recommend targeted stocks, bonds, or mutual funds based on the investment objectives of the customer. Citibank has created an initiative focused on helping people understand how Guys banking can empower investor clients through personalized advice. This includes offering individual investors more support to enable them to make better-informed investment decisions that improve their overall financial well-being. Yes, investment management AI allows Citibank to provide tailored investment advice that suits a diverse customer base and at all levels of expertise.

5.2 Voice Recognition Technology: Citibank has also deployed an AI-powered voice recognition technology in its customer care services for convenient and safer consumer access to their accounts. Callers can use voice commands to engage in conversational transactions, inquire about accounts or balances and learn account details with banking industry-leading voice recognition (also automatic speech recognition) techniques. While it makes the bank may be easier to operate, it also adds a level of security. Voice Recognition: Voice recognition is the automated process of converting spoken words into text, which then identifies a user and authenticates that identity based on their unique voice patterns.

AI is reshaping the banking sector by improving customer experience with customized services and quicker computing methods, besides increasing security. Top banks like JPMorgan Chase, Bank of America, Wells Fargo, HSBC and Citibank have used AI to add more value to the consumer space. Investment in AI-led solutions is empowering these banks to cater better services while ensuring greater customer delight and loyalty, both by detecting potential frauds at the earliest and reading behavior. It is AI technology will lead to an increased contribution to customer experience in banking — which means banks need it. With those markets strengthening, so do firm requirements for personal interaction and support. These successful case studies of the top banks exhibit the power of AI to empower banking experiences through personalization, security, and productivity.

A Customer Experience Boost for the Asia-Pacific Banks: Case Studies

Most of these banks in the Asia-Pacific region are using artificial intelligence (AI) for seamless services to their customers. Competition is increasing and customer expectations are rising, therefore banks in this region are using artificial intelligence to provide customers with better personalization, service delivery and security. Learn how 5 leading Asia-Pacific banks are using AI to transform customer engagement and satisfaction.

1. DBS Bank (Singapore)

Innovative Financial Planning: Singaporean giant DBS Bank is one of the first to have experimented with an AI that performs banking services better than a human. The AI-driven financial planning tool of the bank, 'NAV Planner', which empowers clients to do a better job at managing their finances. The NAV Planner gives this personalized advice regarding investment and insurance based on the financial information of a customer. Helps customers make informed decisions: besides providing real-time insights into spending habits and future financial needs, this tool also assists customers in making the best possible decision. This allows DBS to provide customized advice at scale, making it the customers' top choice for full-scale financial planning.

Customer Support with Conversational AI: DBS also leverages AI-powered chatbots on its digital channels to help customers get immediate answers to common queries. These chatbots leverage natural language understanding and processing to help customers check balances, transfer funds and send payment reminders. For more complicated issues, a chatbot can easily transition the conversation to a human agent so that customers receive the right amount of help. Using AI in customer support, DBS has shortened response times to the customer and provided better service, which means more convenience for banking customers.

2. Commonwealth Bank of Australia

The Commonwealth Bank of Australia has developed an artificial intelligence-driven virtual assistant called "Ceba." Ceba can answer questions on over 500,000 common banking requests, such as checking a balance or transferring funds between accounts. Looking at a customer's transaction records and behavior, Ceba can make personalized suggestions and reminders — recommending the best savings strategies, reminding customers about their next bill payment. By providing these personalized services, CBA has boosted customer engagement and loyalty.

Real Time Fraud Detection: CBA has implemented AI into its fraud detection systems to help prevent customers from falling victim to any fraudulent activities. The bank uses artificial intelligence to monitor transactions and analyze them for potential signs of fraud. By stopping incoming transfers within seconds of them being processed, the bank can now reduce the window during which any fraudster would have wreaked havoc, while also sending out customer alerts as quickly. The security method has increased transparency among the customers by making use of AI. This not only increased customer trust but also made banking safer.

3. ICICI Bank (India)

AI-Powered Virtual Banking Assistant "iPal": ICICI Bank, the country's largest private sector bank by merged assets has developed an AI-based virtual assistant, who addresses all banking related queries and services of customers The chatbot helps on-boarding new customers with their various banking services 24*7, providing an improved customer experience. Other than reporting customer account balances, transferring funds, and monitoring transactions, iPal also assist customers. It offers tailored financial advice based on spending patterns and financial ambitions. AI integration has made it easier for millions of people who previously could not have or afford to access banks and helped in increasing service efficiency, ICICI Bank stated.

ICICI Bank has also implemented the use of Artificial Intelligence to incorporate credit scoring and loan approval processes. AI algorithms at the bank assess a variety of inputs from financial history to credit behavior, and even social media activity to decide on whether an applicant is worthy of credit. By taking this stance, ICICI has granted faster loan approvals and extended credit to a larger number of potential customers that have never had a mainstream line of credit. The bank uses AI in credit scoring, allowing for better lending decisions and a smoother loan application process for customers.

4. Bank of Tokyo-Mitsubishi UFJ (MUFG) — Japan

MUFG Provides Personal AI Investment Recommendations: Japan, MUFG, the country's most extensive financial group, launched an AI-powered investment recommendation service in its wealth management. Using this information along with macroeconomic data and customer preferences, the bank AI-platform offers customers better strategies for investing outside the home. With MUFG, an AI platform developed by Promote will recommend a unique investment portfolio with details, such as customer risk profile and financial objectives. By meeting their customers' needs through such a personalized approach, the bank can deliver superior investment results while increasing customer financial welfare and satisfaction as part of its services.

AI Voice Recognition for Secure Banking: To improve security and convenience in banking, MUFG has adopted AI voice recognition tech. A customer can have a voice, authenticated with transactions (and accessing account information, amongst other banking actions). This further improves security and increases customer convenience, banking occasionally, which they try to do away with. The businesses who value their banking customers in terms of safety alongside humane interaction have loved this move.

5. Commercial Bank of China Merchants (CMB)

One most advanced digital banking service, China Merchants Bank (CMB), offers AI-assisted mobile banking experience. CMB mobile uses AI to provide personalized services in the finance area, so that the user can achieve the purpose of investment advice, consumer fingerprint analysis, and interest customization. The algorithms within the app analyze customer behavior and financial data, then offer personalized services based on individual requirements. For example, the app can help tailor investment products for the customer based on her risk profile and financial goals, extending the reach of wealth management to a wider demographic.

Secure Transactions with Facial Recognition Technology: CMB has gone a step further by integrating AI-based facial recognition technology within its mobile banking app for greater security and unsurpassed customer convenience. Customers can log in and allow a transaction, too, which also enables them to enter the entire spectrum of banking services using facial recognition. This tech not only offers security and convenience but also eliminates the need for passwords or PINs. Facial recognition in digital banking has ensured a smooth customer experience and trust at Chinese CMB.

Banking experiences are where the Asia-Pacific region uses AI most aggressively for customer experience. Banks such as DBS, Commonwealth Bank of Australia, ICICI Bank, MUFG, and China Merchants Bank are using AI in various parts of the world. This enables them to offer personalized services, protect against fraud, and improve their internal systems. They are setting higher standards for competition, and their ability to do so directly results from using artificial intelligence in their operations. The trajectory of AI technology presents a real significant change in customer experience for banks looking to differentiate themselves in the hotly contested but lucrative Asia-Pacific financial environment.

We also look at some case studies of small banks using AI to improve customer experience.

While the attention is on the powerhouses of finance, smaller banks are also realizing the potential of using AI to improve customer service. These providers have still implemented AI to create personal, effective, and secure banking. Find out how five community banks are using AI to disrupt the customer experience and drive their satisfaction scores higher.

1. Radius Bank (United States)

How AI is transforming the way companies understand their customers Bank /Powering Customer Insights with AI Driven by the belief that technology can make things more human, we focus on creating secure and seamless experiences... Understanding Humans AI-driven systems can provide Radius Bank deep insights into customer preferences and needs by analyzing transaction data, social media activity, among other customer behavior metrics. The bank can utilize this information to provide personalized financial advice, targeted product offers, and service alerts. Examples include bill pay reminders, savings opportunities, and suggestions for improvement. Because Radius Bank is smaller on the depositor scale side, it has a bevy of benefits for consumers such as customized service that has built solid trust in its customers.

AI Chatbots: Radius Bank also uses AI chatbots for improved customer service. The chatbots are available 24/7 to field an array of inquiries from account balances to loan information. Customers can interact with these chatbots in the same way they would engage in discussing a human agent, as the chatbots can understand natural language. They escalate the conversation to a live representative for more complex cases, assuring customers get the help they need! Radius Bank is using AI to improve account opening times while keeping low costs and offering a more responsive experience for customers.

2. Axos Bank (United States)

AI-Driven Lending: Based in San Diego, the digital-first banking platform Axos Bank also uses AI to improve its lending operations. Using its AI-based lending platform, the bank assesses the creditworthiness of loan applicants on parameters, including credit history, income pathways and spending behavior. Faster Loan Approvals — Get Lower Rates through Axos Bank's AI Powered Lending Platform. The bank includes credit cards, pay slips, and expenditure to assist people who conventional lenders exclude. Beyond just reducing wait times and easing the process for customers, adopting AI in lending has led to broader credit accessibility to reach more customers.

Axos Bank leverages AI to deliver tailored digital financial management tools. Customers receive tailored budgeting advice and spending insights, as well as saving recommendations through their financial activity. For example, the banks' AI algorithms can track a customers' spending and provide recommendations on how they might reduce costs or save more. The better a bank aids its customers in managing their own financial situation, the higher satisfaction and loyalty to that same bank it will achieve.

3. Live Oak Bank (United States)

Live Oak Bank, a community bank in Wilmington, North Carolina that focuses on small business lending, uses AI technology to streamline the process. The bank's underwriting system uses AI to examine data from multiple sources, including private business performance statistics, industry trends, and macro-economic indicators, to assess loan applications. Using this method, Live Oak Bank can more quickly approve small business loans and meet the number one need for entrepreneurs–capital when they need it. It helps the bank automatically identify risks and opportunities that arise, improving its small business customer service.

AI-Assisted Customer Support: This is where Live Oak Bank has well used AI, by creating an assistant for the customer support team. Its chatbots automatically manage most workload questions for business customers, such as asking for account information and inquiring about a loan status using AI. The chatbots process the natural language, which results in immediate responses and lesser waiting time for customers. Chatbots seamlessly hand off conversations to a human representative for more complex issues. Providing human support and integrating AI means that Live Oak Bank can continue the high standard of service without having expensive associated costs.

4. N26 (Germany)

Personalized Financial Insights AI has empowered N26, a Berlin artificial bank, to provide its customers with personalized financial insights. Personalized budgeting, saving, and investing suggestions are provided by the bank's AI-led lending platform, which leverages customer data. Sorting transactions, analyzing monthly spending behavior, and offering financial health tips are just some features the N26 app has. The insight the bank provides to customers through its mobile app helps them to stay financially fit on-the-go. The bank has built out a large audience of younger, digitally native customers around its personalized insights.

N26 uses AI for Fraud Detection too: To improve security for its customers and secure them from fraud N26 also uses AI. The banks utilize AI algorithms to analyze user transactions, detecting unusual activities like large purchases from distant locations or repeated requests. The AI system can detect fraudulent behavior and prevent fraud in real-time by blocking the transaction and automatically notifying the customer. Indeed, this security scarcity has endeared N26 to customers wary of the risks of digital banking.

5. Monzo Bank (United Kingdom)

Monzo Bank (London): a digital bank that has been using AI to improve customer engagement and experience. Using AI, the bank looks at customer data and interactions to communicate information or deals that are relevant. AI from Monzo can spot low balances to prevent overdraft fees and offer help with budgets if spending rises to AI for client engagement. Fraud prevention prompts new plans for AI-enhanced communication.

AI in Financial Wellness Tools: Monzo offers the customers an AI tool that helps guide you by providing tips on how to better manage your money. These AI-driven tools that aim to provide personalized advice and analysis of the data on their customer base usually come with budget type features, spending trackers, savings goals, etc. For instance, if Monzo customers notice they are close to reaching their specified savings goal, the app may suggest making a small transfer to achieve completion. Many customers relate to Monzo's financial wellness message and find value in the app helping them achieve their financial goals.

Big banks are not the only ones taking advantage of AI to increase their customers' experience, so do smaller banks to compete. Smaller financial institutions like Radius Bank, Axos Bank, and Live Oak Bank, as well as digital banks such as N26 and Monzo, are using AI to enhance security, streamline operations, and offer personalized services. The success of these banks teaches smaller banks a valuable lesson - technology allows even smaller players in the banking industry to provide excellent customer experiences and foster loyal relationships. It will be interesting to see how AI continues to improve and, as smaller banks develop, what kind of wonderful new customer offerings will they come up with?

AI is revolutionizing the banking industry, offering better customer experience, security, operational efficiency, and more. AI helps banks to know more about their customers, predict needs, and deliver bespoke solutions, which boosts their overall levels of satisfaction and loyalty. AI technology development will build pressure on banks to use artificial intelligence technology for customer experience in banking for a competitive edge in transforming market landscape. Frontrunner banks like JPMorgan Chase, Bank of America, Wells Fargo, HSBC and Citibank have proven that by utilizing artificial intelligence (AI), you can drive tremendous customer experience benefits.

Reference – Further Reading – Chapter 2

How AI Is Transforming the Banking Industry, *Forbes*, available at Forbes Banking AI
https://www.forbes.com/councils/forbesbusinesscouncil/2023/03/20/the-future-of-ai-in-banking/

Capturing the full value of generative AI in banking – McKinsey
https://www.mckinsey.com/industries/financial-services/our-insights/capturing-the-full-value-of-generative-ai-in-banking

Banking in the age of Generative AI
https://www.accenture.com/us-en/insights/banking/generative-ai-banking

How JPMorgan Chase Is Using AI to Improve Customer Experience," *Harvard Business Review*
https://hbr.org/2022/03/customer-experience-in-the-age-of-ai

Bank of America's Erica: A Case Study in AI-Powered Virtual Assistants," *Business Insider*
https://www.businessinsider.com/bank-of-america-artificial-intelligence-tool-banker-assist-2023-6

Fraud, productivity are top of mind for AI thought leaders in banks
https://www.americanbanker.com/news/fraud-productivity-are-top-of-mind-for-ai-thought-leaders-in-banks

Artificial intelligence has the potential to reshape banking – Wells Fargo
https://stories.wf.com/artificial-intelligence-has-the-potential-to-reshape-banking/

Fighting money launderers with artificial intelligence at HSBC
https://cloud.google.com/blog/topics/financial-services/how-hsbc-fights-money-launderers-with-artificial-intelligence

DBS – AI-Powered digital transformation
https://www.dbs.com/artificial-intelligence-machine-learning/artificial-intelligence/dbs-ai-powered-digital-transformation.html

Meet Ceba, Commonwealth Bank of Australia's intelligent virtual assistant
https://whatsnext.nuance.com/en-au/customer-engagement-en-au/financial-services-ai-au/major-au-bank-services-customers-with-ai-virtual-assistant/

ICICI Bank offers voice banking via Amazon Alexa and Google Assistant
https://www.retailbankerinternational.com/news/icici-bank-voice-banking-amazon-google/?cf-view

Japan's MUFG Bank taps AI to triple online small-business loans
https://asia.nikkei.com/Business/Finance/Japan-s-MUFG-Bank-taps-AI-to-triple-online-small-business-loans

Radius Bank: This Virtual Bank Wants to Be The Engine Behind Fintech Brands
https://thefinancialbrand.com/news/fintech-banking/virtual-bank-fintech-digital-deposits-api-application-program-interface-87175/

Axos Bank Streamlines Lending with AI
https://www.axosbank.com/personal/mortgages/

N26 uses Rasa to handle complex back-and-forth conversations
https://rasa.com/customers/n26/

Monzo: how the bank of the future uses AI
https://tbtech.co/innovativetech/artificial-intelligence/monzo-how-the-bank-of-the-future-uses-ai/

THREE

AI Applications for Cross-Selling and Up-Selling in Banking

Introduction

Banking Industry is getting advance the competition is overwhelming and non-stop. The expectations of the consumers are at their peak. Innovation to stay ahead of Cross-Sell/Up-sell: This is the Beretta of strategies. Cross-selling or upselling by selling more products/services to existing customers. Far too often, though, conventional grounding methods fail. Artificial Intelligence (AI) and Machine Learning (ML) to the rescue — Technology has essentially transformed interactions between banks and customers. We know AI (Artificial Intelligence) and ML (Machine Learning) can predict customer needs like never through analyzing huge data. I will cover how the top 7 banks are using AI and ML to drive cross-selling and up-selling, amongst other use cases in this article. What technologies are involved, both from the vendor's side and customer and expert perspectives? data-driven approaches to success; and the latest in vendor solutions that make it possible.

1. AI for Cross-selling and Up-selling

AI and ML are revolutionizing cross-selling, up-selling in banking. However, the bank could only make suggestions based on age, income, and account activity data. However, this method was not very flexible. Most of the offers were generic and therefore had low conversions. AI/ML are significant changes. The figures are typically based on a system which processes large sets of data, such as history, spending habits and even social media. The result? custom product recommendations.

2.1 Predictive Analytics- the significant change Artificial Intelligence can predict the next thing a customer might need. One such idea could be a high-yield savings account if the customer saves enormous sums of money. Artificial intelligence, If another type of customer were to travel, recommend pet rewards credit card. To make the most of these opportunities, use this personalization to increase conversions.

2. 2 Timing is another vital aspect. AI can find out the opportune time when an offer should be presented. For example, receiving a bonus will always make someone consider investing it. With the help of machine learning, the AI, by analyzing real-time data, makes sure that offers should reach the customer when required.

AI and ML features empower banks to be more focused and maintain a closer alignment to the original products for cross-selling or up-selling. It results in better conversion rates and overall revenue.

2. Customer focus selling

Customers can view AI-driven cross-sales and up-sales as a suit of both good hope and apprehension. On the bright side, customers are receiving welcome deals at just the right time for them. They see this as being valued by your business. Consider the fact that a customer who travels often would find it appealing to be presented with a credit card full of travel rewards. For example, if a customer is part of a growing family, an offer for life insurance might be well-timed.

But there are also doubts. Privacy is a big issue. Because customers are worried about banks knowing their information. The personalization needed for advanced offers can make many uncomfortable. Half of banking customers like personalized offers, but personalization faces trouble when **32% worry about whether their data is private and secure, according to the survey conducted by Accenture.** This signifies the importance of being transparent. Chat about this web app right here Banks Must Explain to Customers Just What They Are Doing with Their Data Offer options to opt-in or opt-out of personalized offers.

AI-Driven suggestions do not work universally for all customers. Some may find them intrusive. Despite that, some may take comfort in a human advisor. This raises the question: where to draw the line for banks. While AI improves efficiency and personalization, making it valuable for many day-to-day financial decisions, human interaction is still crucial — especially for more complicated choices.

Using AI for cross-selling and up-selling can benefit both customers (who buy more relevant products) and banks (who earn more profit from each customer).

Amazon founder **Jeff Bezos** puts it simply:

"The price of cookies is up — a box costs about the same as it always has but now there are only 16 cookies in it instead of 24."

Jeff Bezos believes our relentless focus on customer experience is why we rarely fail and why we are the best. He emphasizes that the best way to grow your business is through putting customers first & in digital powered world, where people talking about you has amplified effect. (CustomerThink).

What will that tell the customer? When deciding. In a SaaS environment, customer satisfaction is crucial to retain customers and prevent churn.

3. AI and ML as powerful tool

Many in the sector share this view. AI can manage extensive databases beyond human capacity. Elements like financial advice or customer service still require humans.

As expected, experts also underline the importance of data quality. The ALV is at the mercy of the training data it possesses. However, incomplete, or biased data can cause wrong prophecies. To take yet another example, an AI system that is trained on biased data could make incorrect recommendations designed to ensure a certain demographic never gets proper representation. Banks need powerful databases to sustain and fulfil the same processes. This comprises information updated and cleansed to the highest level.

A second important area is the transparency of algorithms. There is some expert consensus that banks should be able to explain how their AI systems decide. For regulatory compliance, this becomes especially important. With the increasing integration of AI systems into various banking operations, regulators also anticipate investigating how they function. More transparent banks in how they develop and use AI will ultimately position themselves to respond accurately to those regulations.

AI For Improving Customer Service-Quality-Satisfaction-experts, **A McKinsey report found that banks have seen profit gains of 10% to 15% with personalized interaction and have achieved customer satisfaction improvement by as much as 20%. These statistics highlight the importance of AI in delivering better customer experiences.**

To conclude, AI and ML are potent weapons when utilized, it can supercharge the cross selling/ up-selling effectiveness per the experts.

One of Industry expert said that.

"While the report confirms that businesses are embracing these technologies, it also warns businesses need to implement them in a way that prioritizes data quality and transparency — and does not forget the human aspect"

Name-Data Based Approach and Analysis

AI and ML rely on data. These systems become more accurate the more data a business has, and the better they can predict specific customer demands. But not every data is precious. Banks should prioritize finding data analysts to make AI work.

> *"By applying data-driven strategies, sales leaders achieve up to 2-5% incremental uplift in their sales from improved decision-making and cross-functional coordination, which can help the latter earn another potential 5-10%. Centralized analytics allow companies to make data-driven decisions, which can help better coordinate sales efforts with what customers need rather than what has historically worked"*

Transactional Data is Gold for banks. Each transaction a customer completes provides clues to their spending patterns, financial goals, and future consumer needs. Alternatively, a customer who always spends money each week with an online retailer might want to consider a cashback credit card. A client that moves money into a brokerage account might be a referral for wealth management.

> *Transaction data provides personal lifestyle and preference landscape of customer unlike anything else. He elaborates, noting that tracking how their customers spend helps banks develop customized products and services to cater to changing needs. This is an enormous advantage in competition.*

3.3 Behavioral Data: Behavior data is another crucial ingredient for your likelihood of employment. Customer behavior data, such as how customers engage with the bank's digital channels. Such as, do they look at the balances of their accounts? Do they use budgeting tools? Banks can learn product importance to the customer from this data.

In the banking world, for example, you need behavioral data to explore customer habits, preferences and financial behaviors. This way, banks can present the data and provide tailor-made services like targeted credit cards or loan products to drive customer engagement and eventually sales. He also states that by tracking customer behavior, banks can provide services that are not only real-time and relevant but will also help them build a strong bond with the consumers.

3.4 External Data may Sometimes be of Use This could be anything from social media data, public records or even through 3rd party providers. For instance, if a customer writes travel-related content on social media, then the bank may conclude that this person is also may be interested in products such as travel insurance.

According to Deloitte, banks that sell products through AI for cross-selling and **up-selling techniques have a 20 percent increase in customer retention.** AI-driven offers being personalized in nature attribute to this improvement. Offers that apply to the current needs and circumstances of customers have a higher engagement.

A separate **Accenture report** insisted on valuing data in harnessing the AI productivity. According to the report, banks that **use AI to analyze customer data and offer a personalized package can increase acceptance rates by 30% higher than traditional methods.** But the report also underscores transparency as a factor. People are more likely to agree to personalized offers when they understand how their data is used and can trust that companies will process their personal information with care.

You will fail in AI-driven cross-sell and upsell if you do not follow a data-driven model. Instead, banks need to concentrate on gathering data that is accurate and then analyzing it so they can develop custom offers for the customers.

Banking AI/ML & Vendor Software Global Leaders

The biggest financial organizations have incorporated AI and ML into their banks to change the way they originate cross-selling and up-selling. Banks can later analyze customer data in greater detail and cater to custom products and services based on specific individual requirements by utilizing these technologies. How the world's top five banks are managing successful cross-selling and up-selling strategies with AI, ML & external vendor solutions.

1. JPMorgan Chase (USA): AI powered personalized banking

Use Case — Perhaps one of the world's large bank JPMorgan conveys to utilization of AI & ML for cross-selling efficiently. In real-time, the bank AI algorithms analyze customer data to predict what product a customer might need next. For instance, if a customer uses the tab for more; it may suggest a different credit card or loan product which matches your financial behavior.

Predictive analytics: JPMorgan Chase employs ML models to analyze customers' data of transactions and their behaviors on spending, helping the banking sector in anticipating future financial requirements as well. They are a tool in rendering customized financial products such as opportunities for investment, loans or dedicated accounts.

JPMorgan Chase partners with Salesforce and Adobe to provide advanced customer relationship management and digital marketing solutions. These solutions use artificial intelligence to enhance the personalization of customer engagement strategies.

This has brought the cross-selling conversion rate to a **20% increase through the AI/ML approach increased customer satisfaction by providing an Upsell offer in time and context.**

2. Bank of America (USA): Erica, the AI-powered Virtual Assistant

Bank of America has integrated a virtual assistant, Erica, into its digital banking services to recommend personalized products and manage user finances. Erica examines patterns in customer transactions, spending and account balances to custom financial advice.

Erica will use the ML algorithms to assess customer data and give personalized recommendations for products such as credit cards, savings accounts and investment opportunities. Those suggestions can relate to the financial goals and habits of customers, ensuring personalized purchases based on their own financial habits and goals.

Solution providers: Bank of America has teamed with IBM Watson to bolster the efficacy of Erica as a virtual assistant, it can provide financial advice accurately and dynamically.

Erica's introduction led to a **20% increase in customer engagement and significantly improved acceptance rates for cross-sell offers.** This resulted in overall growth for product uptake by the bank.

> *"Erica is the definition of how Bank of America is delivering personalization and individualization at scale to our clients," said David Tyrie, Chief Digital Officer and Head of Global Marketing at Bank of America. "We expect the second billion to come even more quickly as we continue to evolve Erica's capabilities, providing clients with the shortest route to the answers they need about their financial lives."*
>
> *Source: Newsroom, Bank of America*

3. Wells Fargo (USA)- AI and ML for better Customer Engagement

Use Case: Wells Fargo is using ML/AI to improve its cross-selling by presenting personalized offers relevant to their customer's financial behavior & life events/purchase milestones. The AI system at the bank recognizes certain trigger points, for example, when a customer receives a paycheck and recommends a particular financial product.

Behavioral: Wells Fargo uses AI to analyze customer behavior — such as spending habits and financial activity — to recommend products that meet the demand of a user in their current context. For example, Wells Fargo's AI could sell a customer on opening a high-yield savings account or signing up for an investment product.

Credit Card Offers: The bank will run targeted marketing campaigns based on AI-powered insights to provide credit card authentic offers at the best time that has maximum chances of acceptance.

Vendor Solutions: Wells Fargo works with Oracle and SAP to power its data analytics, adding AI/ML techniques into CRM and marketing systems.

The AI and ML push led to an increase in conversion rates by **about 25% for Wells Fargo cross-selling campaigns.** Better customer satisfaction through relevant offers.

4. HSBC (UK): AI-powered financial solutions

Use Case; HSBC employs AI and ML for customer financial services to deliver individualized and approachable solutions. Income, spending behaviors, and market conditions are factors that the bank's AI systems analyze to provide customers with financial products like loans, credit cards, and investments.

With ML models, you can personalize every customer offering, such as data-driven personalization. HSBC utilizes comprehensive datasets and thousands of features from structured and unstructured sources to recommend products tailored to your financial situation and goals. The imitated approach ensures that the suggestions not only match applicable criteria but are also uniquely generated to fit the specific financial path of their customer and prospect.

Dynamic Segmentation: The AI also helped HSBC segment their customer base so the bank could target each group with more relevant offers.

The Bank collaborated with Google Cloud to enhance its data analytics and AI capabilities through Vendor Data Solutions. This enabled the bank to deliver more accurate and timelier product offers to its clients.

HSBC's personalized cross-selling strategy has resulted in a 15% increase in conversions, showcasing the effectiveness of targeted banking to drive customer activation and sales.

5. Citi Bank (USA) — AI & ML for Real-Time Customer Interaction.

Case Study: Citi Bank used AI and ML in product recommendations through customer interactions (up to real-time) The bank uses AI to analyze real-time data around customer transactions so it can offer the customer products and services.

AI/ML Implementation:

With real-time data processing, Citi Bank's AI-driven systems monitor customer transactions and spending habits, enabling them to provide various products such as loans, credit cards, and investment options. In this way, your offers are never out of place.

Customer Journey Mapping: The AI system also helps Citibank map each customer's journey and highlight the touchpoints where a personalized offer could provide even more value in their customer experience.

Vendor Solutions: Citi Bank has collaborated with Microsoft Azure to offer cloud computing and AI features that empower its high-volume data processing of AI & ML systems.

AI and ML initiatives at Citi Bank contributed a 15% uptick in recommended product choice. Real-time offers provide great convenience and apply to the customers.

Leading global banks like JPMorgan Chase, Bank of America, Wells Fargo, HSBC and Citi Bank are adopting AI/ML for cross-selling and up-selling. Peer-to-peer data affinity analysis and personalized products and services tailored for everyone make these technologies possible. To ensure high-quality, long-term strategies that are both effective and scalable, these banks partner with top-tier vendors to up the AI game. Their results have been substantial, with a significant increase in customer engagement and increasing conversion rates and overall satisfaction. As AI and ML advance, they are on a strong path to redefine banking with the best solutions in the world as market leaders.

Case studies on AI/ML in banking and use of vendor software in

banking: Asia-Pacific region

The banking industry in the Asia-Pacific region has picked up AI and ML solutions to its core structures. This is enabling greater cross-and up-sell tactics for banks, as customers are demanding tailored financial services. This article will explore how five of the biggest banks in Asia-Pacific are harnessing the power of AI, ML and other third-party solutions to power their cross-selling and up-selling strategies.

1. DBS Bank Singapore: AI-Powered Personalization and Customer Insights

Case Study: DBS Bank, one of the largest banks in Southeast Asia, has led the way in digital transformation. The bank uses AI and machine learning (ML) to involve customer behavior, automate customer scorecards and drive-up sell rates. DBS can provide banking products (credit cards, loans and investments), that are personalized based on the life stage of customers and transactional data demographic insight.

AI powered Insights: DBS leverages ML models to analyze customer data as spending patterns and financial goals. For example, the bank's AI system tells customers their next best action or product, ensuring that all offers are timely and relevant.

Customer Journey Mapping: With the help of AI, DBS has achieved a holistic view of customer journeys and identified pivotal touchpoints for initiating targeted offers

DBS has collaborated with Adobe Experience Cloud to refuel its digital marketing strategies with the role of AI-based recommendations in customer engagement and personalization.

Results: The bank reports the AI solutions have boosted customer engagement and increased cross-sell conversion rates by 20%; accurate timing for when to reach a specific customer is key.

2. Commonwealth Bank of Australia (CBA):

Use Case: The Commonwealth Bank of Australia (CBA) has leveraged AI and ML to offer intelligent product recommendations from what it learns about customers. AI-Based Platform of The Bank Tracks Transactions & Spending of Customers To Provide Personalized Offers On Products Including Home Loans, Insurance & Credit Cards.

Behavioral Analysis: The AI models at CBA analyze customer interactions too, such as transaction histories and other financial activities and responses with the bank to propose suitable products. For instance, if a customer is paying off a mortgage regularly, CBA's AI models could advise whether that customer needs insurance or investment products.

Real-Time Engagement: The AI system also shows the optimal time to engage customers so that offers are made when they have the highest likelihood of being accepted.

Vendor Solutions: The CBA works with Microsoft Azure for cloud computing and artificial intelligence capabilities that let the bank crunch huge datasets and get customers real-time, personalized recommendations.

Result: The team achieves a 25% increase in acceptance of offers through AI and ML processes. This leads to improved customer satisfaction and loyalty.

3. OCBC Bank (Singapore): AI-driven financial planning

Case Study: OCBC Bank Revamps Financial Planning Using AI/ML Using AI, the bank evaluates customer-level financial data and provides individual recommendations all the way from savings to investment or retirement planning. Using this data-driven aim, OCBC could cross-sell products optimized for the financial needs of each customer.

Personal Financial Plans: Using customer data such as income, expenses & long-term financial goals, AI models at OCBC provide personal financial plans. This then lets the bank offer the customer specific savings accounts, investment opportunities, or insurance products.

Interactive Tools: OCBC is using AI to power, interactive financial planning tools that give customers real-time insights and suggestions, helping increase their engagement with the bank.

Vendor Solutions: OCBC works with IBM Watson to fuel its AI-driven financial planning tools, allowing the bank to provide correct recommendations based on customer needs.

AI implementation for financial planning has led to a 22% increase in consumption of suggested products. Clients perceive it as a personalized approach to managing their finances.

4. ICICI Bank (India): AI and ML Customer Segmentation

Case Study: India's leading private sector bank ICICI is an AI-ML enabled use case that segments their customer base and delivers on targeted product recommendations for the customers. Using customer data such as transaction history and financial behavior, ICICI Bank segments customers based on these similar characteristics to custom craft marketing campaigns.

ICICI Bank's Artificial Intelligence system divides the customers into real-time data such as income levels, spending patterns and credit history through real time segmentation. This helps the bank tailor its product offering, like personal loans, credit cards or investment plans.

The bank uses ML to predict which products would be most appealing to each segment, allowing them to focus their marketing efforts.

Vendor Solutions–ICICI Bank partners with SAS to deliver advanced analytics and AI-based solutions, enabling the bank to strengthen its customer segmentation and targeting strategies.

Customer Segmentation: 30% increase in conversion rate when AI and ML used the personalized marketing efforts and customers.

5. ANZ Bank (Australia):

ANZ Bank — The bank has applied AI and ML algorithms in its wealth management services to analyze individual investment profiles and provide unique investment advice and recommendations. The bank's AI systems use various data, such as transaction history, investment preferences and financial goals, to offer customized financial services.

Investment Profiling: ANZ's AI based wealth management platform builds a deep, detailed profile of a customer considering their risk appetite, history of investment and financial goals. As a result, the bank can provide tailored made investment products and services.

The asset management capabilities of AI watch the market conditions and portfolios of clients, leading to recommendations for suitable investments or products based on the client's requirements.

Vendor Solutions: ANZ Bank collaborates with IBM Cloud to provide the AI and ML backing up its wealth management services which feed on real-time data on Vendor Solutions lines.

By utilizing data and analytics to introduce AI into ANZ's wealth management service business, customer engagement with investment products has increased by 20% and satisfaction among wealth management customers has improved.

The Asia-Pacific region is its forerunner with the application of AI and ML in the banking sector. Banks (DBS, CBA, OCBC), other institutions (ICICI) and ANZ to achieve hyper-personalized cross-selling and up-selling strategies use these technologies. With the help of AI and ML, banks can provide personalized financial products and services that meet their customers' unique needs, resulting in increased satisfaction, loyalty, and revenue. They benefit from the expertise of working with external vendors, which helps them stay competitive in an emerging market. These technologies will improve both optimization and customer-facing use-cases alike — enabling banks in the Asia-Pacific to both pioneer innovative banking services such that no other region can.

AI/ML & Vendor Software in Banking — Small Banks Lead the Way

Big banks are not the only ones innovating with AI and ML tech for improved cross-selling and up-sell; small banks, despite their size, are making big moves. These firms have been adopting sophisticated technologies with an emphasis on tailoring financial products and services for individual customers, enhancing the customer experience, fostering growth. Five Smaller Banks Leverage AI, ML and External Vendor Solutions.

1. Bank of Hawaii (USA): AI for Customer Engagement

Bank of Hawaii found that machine learning models can serve as an AI-powered growing channel by analyzing customer behaviors and offering tailored products for specific market segments. Based on past transactions and financial behavior of the customers, the bank may predict when the customers can go in for new products like saving accounts, loans or insurance policies.

Predictive modelling: The bank uses ML models to understand aspects of customer data, like their transaction history and spending habits. This model enables the bank to recognize which customers are most probably also looking for other financial products.

Deals: AI decides when to show these offers, ensuring a relevant, optimal experience.

Bank of Hawaii has partnered with FICO to provide predictive analytics solutions that enable the bank to improve their ability to predict customer needs and deliver timely, tailored offers-Vendor Solutions.

Result: AI/ML led to gains in new product sales by 15% as customers find more value with a personalized pitch

2. Metro Bank (UK): AI and ML for Real-Time Customer Insights

Use Case: Metro Bank is a challenger bank in the UK using their piece to offer real-time and your specific financial products with AI, AC. The bank can drive higher acceptance by using this customer behavior and transaction data to make relevant offers at the right time.

Metro Bank uses AI to analyze customer transactions and behavior in real time. This allows the bank to sell products such as loans, credit cards or savings accounts.

Such as that of customer journey mapping, where AI allows the bank to build rich customer profiles that ensure the product recommendations are accurate and tailored to a specific client.

Vendor Solutions: Metro Bank works with, among others, on an AI-enabled core banking platform and supports real time analytics and customer profiling.

Result: With integrating AI and ML, cross-selling campaigns of Metro Bank have witnessed an increase in conversion rates of 22%, delighting customers with the right offers that matter.

3. Australia — Bendigo and Adelaide Bank (Ranked 5th) with AI innovation in personalized financial services.

Example: Australia-based community-focused bank Bendigo and Adelaide Bank use AI-Based Machine Learning Software to Customize Financial Products and Services process. The bank utilizes AI-powered tools and machines to analyze customer data. Based on this analysis, tailored offers such as home loans, investment products, and retirement accounts are made to clients in line with their financial goals.

Very personalized recommendations: the bank uses AI to analyze customer data such as income, spending and financial goals to show each client relevant products.

Targeted Marketing—Bendigo and Adelaide Bank use AI to create targeted marketing campaigns that deliver offers directly to the customers at the ideal time.

Vendor Solutions: Oracle — The bank uses the AI and ML capabilities of Oracle to scale data analytics effectively, offering customers tailored financial services.

Results: AI used in financial services-driven personalization has uplifted customer engagement by 20% and boosted product recommendation consumption.

4. Umpqua Bank (USA) — AI-Powered Financial Planning and Recommender

Use Case; Umpqua Bank (a regional US bank) ML/AI Applications: Personalized Financial Planning, and Product Recommendations. Bankers expect the bank's AI to be as skilled in money management as it is in chess. The AI analyses customer data to suggest appropriate savings accounts, loans, or investment products based on their financial goals.

Financial Planning Tools: Umpqua Bank makes use of AI-driven financial planning tools to offer personalized advice and product recommendations that are based on a customer's financial behavior.

Mobile App (AI): The bank uses their AI platforms to interact with customers via mobile banking and offers them "real-time advice."

Vendor Solutions: Umpqua Bank uses NCR for their digital banking solutions, including AI, to improve customer engagement and personalization.

Result: Tailored advice closer to customer needs has led to a 12% spike in product recommendations uptake, boosting advisor productivity while providing a convenient service for customers.

5. Starling Bank UK AI and ML for customer onboarding

Use Case; Starling Bank, a UK-based digital-only bank is using AI and ML capabilities to allow faster customer onboarding and enhance opportunities for cross-selling. Automation of identity verification and KYC processes using AI systems carried out by the bank facilitates swift account opening for new customers.

Automated Onboarding: Starling Bank uses AI-driven systems for onboarding, to ensure a faster process of verifying user identity and running KYC checks so customers can open an account in minutes.

The AI then optimizes this profiling data for cross-selling analysis of customers who successfully onboard. It would then prompt them with loans, savings accounts or budgeting tools.

Vendor Solutions: Verification of identity with Jumio powered by artificial intelligence to enable 100% customer onboarding seamlessly and safely.

Processing time for accounts by up to 60% besides delivering a 30% increase in account openings and over 20% to adopt other banking products via the AI-driven onboarding process. Customers today have minimal friction and tailored banking experience.

In short, banks that are tech-savvy, — Bank of Hawaii, Metro Bank, Bendigo and Adelaide Bank, Umpqua Bank, (also Starling) — demonstrate size really is no barrier to innovation. Using AI and ML, the campus-based business improvement solutions tailor to students' financial needs by offering personalized financial products and services, which help boost customer satisfaction and grow more business. The combination of their partners' superiority in technology makes them more ready and able to compete at the highest level in digital banking. With the ongoing development of AI and ML, these little bank innovators have the potential to create even more customized-banking experiences.

Reference – Further reading - Chapter 3

The future of personalization—and how to get ready for it - McKinsey
https://www.mckinsey.com/capabilities/growth-marketing-and-sales/our-insights/the-future-of-personalization-and-how-to-get-ready-for-it

McKinsey Teams Up with Salesforce to Deliver on The Promise of AI-powered Growth
https://www.biia.com/mckinsey-teams-up-with-salesforce-to-deliver-on-the-promise-of-ai-powered-growth/

Personalizing the customer experience: Driving differentiation in retail
https://www.mckinsey.com/industries/retail/our-insights/personalizing-the-customer-experience-driving-differentiation-in-retail

Banking of on AI – Top 10 Trends for 2024
https://www.accenture.com/content/dam/accenture/final/industry/banking/document/Accenture-Banking-Top-10-Trends-2024.pdf

The future of AI in banking - From experimentation to full-scale deployment
https://www2.deloitte.com/us/en/pages/consulting/articles/ai-in-banking.html

Banking IT services and solutions - Unlock value with AI you can bank on
https://www.ibm.com/industries/banking-financial-markets

FICO. (2022)-*Predictive Analytics for Better Decision-Making in Banking*FICO Financial Services
https://www.fico.com/blogs/what-decision-intelligence-platform

Temenos : Real-Time Campaigns
https://www.temenos.com/products/digital-banking/customer-retention-and-marketing/

Jimio - Online Identity Verification for Fast, Secure User Onboarding
https://www.jumio.com/use-case/user-onboarding/

How Do I Perform Customer Segmentation with SAS Intelligent Decisioning?
https://www.sas.com/en_us/webinars/customer-segmentation-sas-intelligent-decisioning.html

JPMorgan Chase - Leading with AI
https://www.jpmorgan.com/technology/news/leading-with-AI

Bank of America - How to generate sales leads for your business
https://business.bankofamerica.com/resources/how-to-generate-sales-leads-for-your-small-business.html

HSBC - How HSBC Transformed Its Customer Experience
https://hbr.org/sponsored/2024/03/how-hsbc-transformed-its-customer-experience

DBS empowers its Customer Service Officers with Gen AI-powered virtual assistant to reduce toil and enhance customer experience
https://www.dbs.com/newsroom/DBS_empowers_its_Customer_Service_Officers_with_Gen_AI_powered_virtual_assistant_to_reduce_toil_and_enhance_customer_experience

How OCBC is building a customer-centric bank powered by personalisation and AI
https://www.thecorporatetreasurer.com/article/how-ocbc-is-building-a-customer-centric-bank-powered-by-personalisation-and-ai/493091

ICICI Bank's AI chatbot iPal empowers customers with information and financial s ..
Read more at:
https://cio.economictimes.indiatimes.com/news/enterprise-services-and-applications/icici-banks-ai-chatbot-ipal-empowers-customers-with-information-and-financial-services/61118452

FOUR

Use of AI in KYC in Banking

1. Introduction

Introducing Artificial Intelligence (AI) into Know Your Customer (KYC) processes has revolutionized how banks confirm identities, screen customers, and continuously monitor them. Banks could use AI to navigate these complex processes, implement regulatory requirements effectively, and improve customer experience.

Banks call the regulatory and compliance process to let them comply with the KYC in banking. It includes due diligence on the identity of clients, their financial risks, and monitoring transactions for any suspicious purchase. These processes are crucial to fight against money laundering, terrorist financing and fraud.

2. The Role of AI in KYC

The process of KYC is more efficient and effective with the aid of AI in specific verticals.

Customer Onboarding- AI driven input collects and verifies detailed customer information in 24 hours, forcing account opening times down. AI systems can confirm identification documents and compare all the information against databases, as well as determine the risk levels of new customers via machine learning algorithms.

KYC focused tasks with predefined rules and increasing customer experience could be well handled by AI as the integration shortcuts in a defined processing layer. This streamlined KYC process with tools like portals will replace the custom of traditional practices. But to fully leverage AI and

Generative AI (Gen AI), banks need to create a strong digital fabric that has defined automation processes and quality data to deliver greater context about the customer.

Gen AI Rises It's not going to replace KYC analysts, but what it is going to do is accelerate those processes and make it more efficient for them to be able to identify these financial crime risks. KYC is not straight-forward even for the banking sector, least of all where new risks associated with AI are present. Like any FinTech, banks need to develop an understanding and manage control over it!

One of the bigger problems for banks is they are just drowning in data. The key to addressing this issue is the very specific data attributes that change KYC risk ratings. One way data is captured and then analyzed to determine which attributes are the most important by technology. There will be accompanying growth in global regulations fueled by multiple triggers.

This is where FinTech delivers technology-driven data handling and decision making. This is expected to lead to more frequent exception-based case reviews by humans and therefore better KYC process delivery.

There are a lot of global forces pushing for more regulations next year, including those that are geopolitical, legal and economic. Meanwhile corporate and commercial banks must evolve their systems with agility based on technology.

2.1 Customer Due Diligence (CDD):

Automated tools allow to do CDD, which can identify high-risk customers and ensure complete background verification of the customer. AI systems can uncover hidden relationships, beneficial ownership and other risk indicators manually unseen through countless data analysis.

2.2 Continuous monitoring:

AI continuously monitors customer transactions to identify fraudulent activity. By identifying patterns and behavior, AI models can detect suspicious transactions on real-time basis as well, ensuring swift response, reducing the chances of financial crime.

2.3 Enhanced Due Diligence (EDD):

AI facilitates EDD by triggering further analysis and activation of more granular information in high-risk customers. Although, as it always is with such things, first you must get a complete understanding of the resulting risks (and bring regulatory standards in line.)

3. Top Features in KYC Tools/Systems for Banks

The expanding financial landscape put pressure on banks to implement a mandatory and effective KYC process due to operational demands. Here, the top five key features modern KYC tools and systems should concentrate on:

3.1 Automated Identity Verification

Automated identity verification automates this process and simplifies the onboarding experience, allowing a quick and secure way to verify customer identities. This includes proprietary technology like biometrics, facial recognition, and optical character recognition (OCR) to validate passports, driver licenses, national IDs and other similar documents.

3.2 Biometrics:

Using distinct biological characteristics, such as fingerprints, eye designs or voice prints, biometric systems provide a greater level of safety than the conventional kinds. They reduce the risk of identity fraud by making sure that the person presenting the ID is the owner of the identity.

Facial recognition technology compares the user's live image/video with the photo on their official ID. Adding a second layer of security, it is proof that the person with the document in their hands is really the owner of this. same. document.

3.3 OCR stands for Optical Character Recognition:

It is a technology that extracts text from images of documents. Users can compare this extracted text with existing information in databases. They also reduce the time required for customer onboarding, which enhances security and betters the overall experience of customers.

3.4 Transaction Monitoring and Machine Learning

ML is also key in facilitating the adequate transaction monitoring processes to enhance the KYC process. Natural Language Processing NLP algorithms can automatically analyze transactions in seconds and detect deviations as well. Anomaly detection Machine learning models can identify changes in normal transaction behaviors that may show malicious behavior. For example, if a customer who mostly makes small, local purchases suddenly starts moving lots of money around, the system could flag this as a possible risk.

3.5 Rule-Based System False Positives:

Traditional rule-based systems will often create a high number of low-risk false positives which translates into compliance teams being overwhelmed. These mechanisms ensure ML models adapt and reduce the number of false alerts from historical data, without compromising on identifying genuine threats correctly.

By utilizing machine learning for transaction monitoring, banks can proactively detect financial crimes such as fraud and money laundering, even before they happen and in real-time.

3.6 Scoring and Profiling for risk-based

With risk-based scoring and profiling, banks can provide the precise risk levels of every customer on account of utilizing transactions, behavior dynamics, geographic positions besides occupation. Essential for making resource allocation decisions and targeting efforts towards high-risk customers.

Risk-based KYC eliminates one-size-fits-all due diligence by determining the level of risk and adjusting the intensity of due diligence. This is the process where we conduct a more in-depth check on high-risk customers, while we onboard low-risk customers almost instantly.

Banks can calibrate the risk scoring model to match their specific risk appetite and regulatory demands by customizing the risk parameters. Different banks can modify the scoring system by assigning varying weights to factors, such as transaction volume, source of funds (individual or corporate), and customer type (personal or corporate).

Risk-based scoring — allocating resources and increasing KYC accuracy = efficiency + proper risk management.

4. Integration with Regulatory Compliance

This activity not only requires running a mile but also implies that regulatory compliance becomes something of a moving target as laws and guidelines update in response to new threats. KYC tools with regulatory compliance integration make sure banks are on par with the most recent requirements.

This software automates laws and regulations updates, updating of protocols in real time by linking with global regulatory databases. It mitigates non-compliance risk and a heavier fine and reputation ally damaging.

4.1 Cross-Border Compliance:

Banks working in multiple geographies can use these solutions to tailor KYC processes per the corresponding regulatory requirements. This is of significance to international banks, who must navigate the maze of global regulation.

Automating compliance within KYC systems helps banks avoid manual repetition and reduces human error, making it easier for them to comply with the law.

4.2 Verifying/ authenticating documents:

Customers should be able to give some information to the KYC system without manual intervention from a bank, but verifying and authenticating documents is a required element in compliance checking.

We use high-resolution scanning and AI to identify forgeries or modifications in documents. We look at the hologram, watermark and micro-text descriptions to contract security.

KYC tools connect to international databases, affirming the legitimacy and accuracy of customer documentation by comparing it with official records.

4.3 Prevent Fraud:

These tools verify documents against known data sources and leverage sophisticated forensic techniques to detect and stop identity theft before it happens.

This feature enhances securing the KYC process by ensuring that only genuine customers receive banking services.

5. The Advantages of Having a Comprehensive KYC Process in Place

There are many benefits that financial institutions can gain by deploying rigorous KYC processes. Introduction of a strong KYC process will function as the primary defense against financial crimes, especially money laundering, terrorist financing and fraud. This reduces the chance of people turning to crime and financial services.

Transparent and efficient KYC procedures help in building customer trust and satisfaction by showing dedication to security and compliance. The reason for this is that customers interact more with institutions they see as safe.

5.1 Operational Efficiency:

Automation and streamlining of KYC, AML, and compliance processes can help banks lower the operational cost for onboarding new customers or updating existing ones. And the best part of it is that making things more efficient and better using resources, all this time exchanging, keeps you in a virtuous cycle as well.

Global Compliance and Market Access: Secure KYC procedures create an environment for compliance with international rules, allowing banks to work in more than one jurisdiction without suffering legal backlash. This opened the door to global expansion and partnership.

KYC systems help financial institutions become more agile in the face of additional risks and regulatory changes. What makes this such an important feature, especially given the always changing regulatory environment, one that could mean meaningful penalties for non-compliance?

Top 10 AI and ML Solutions for KYC for Banks

1. JPMorgan Chase

Use Cases: Customer onboarding, compliance monitoring, transaction monitoring, block list screening, address and phone verification, picture verification, and risk scoring.

The comprehensive solution incorporates a variety of resources for this purpose. Jumio with biometric verification, Acuant with OCR, Nice Actimize for transaction monitoring and risk scoring, World-Check to check the blacklist of all individuals globally, Loqate to verify address and Twilio for next generation phone verification (Check more Live Working Example)

With benefits such as a 20% reduction in onboarding time, increased accuracy in identifying suspicious activity, higher global compliance and lower operating costs.

2. HSBC

Use case: KYC (KYC solutions from around the world), AML (risk management and blacklist screening), risk assessment, ID / address verification by photo, checking the photograph with documents.

Our technical solution incorporates a set of tools used in different crucial parts. It incorporates iProov for biometric authentication, IDnow again for OCR, BBA FICO TONBELLER for AML and transaction monitoring, Dow Jones Watchlist checking blacklist checks, Melissa Data to verify address details only, Telesign as the phone verification vendor and Socure for–PIP–Person In Person–verification.

Benefits: Automation tools offload over 35% work, better high-risk customer identification and a global compliance with consistent effectiveness on AML detection.

3. Wells Fargo

Possible applications: Transaction monitoring, fraud detection, customer onboarding, blacklist screening, address/phone/picture, risk scoring.

A technical Solution — Onfido for biometric verification, Jumio provides OCR, Actimize Transaction Monitoring / Risk scoring, World-Check Blacklist Screening, Location Address Verification, Tele Phone Verification. Advantages: Real-time fraud detection with 30% fewer false positives.

4. Standard Chartered

Use Cases — Customer onboarding, identity verification, compliance monitoring, fraud detection/black-list screening, Address/phone/picture verification, PIP Verification.

This is a technical solution: it combines different software tools. The system has a multitude of technologies for various purposes. Here are just a few examples of how Portier uses various APIs and external resources for biometrics, OCR (Optical Character Recognition), compliance, fraud detection, blacklist screening, address verification, phone verification and PIP verification: — Tek Entity has connected the global telecom operators to "Veridium" for the Bio-Metric Database Access. — IDology provides authentication solutions with high-tech tools that bankers need every movement while verifying any document scanned by them since it is based on OCR. Oracle Financial Services enables insurers to handle the compliance and fraud detection process easily from AML Screening servers.

This really paid off. The bank has got a 25% increase in onboarding speed, delivering far greater identity verification rates and fraud detection competing across all its regions.

5. Deutsche Bank

Use Cases: KYC, Identity verification Customer onboarding, Ongoing Risk Scoring Transaction Monitoring Continuous Compliance Blacklist Screening Address Verification Phone Number Validation Picture Verification

Technical Solution: That is the resolution consolidates some instruments for various functionalities. "BioID" for biometric verification, "Trulioo" API for OCR, SAS AML (for transaction monitoring and risk scoring), World-Check (blacklist screening) and Loqate (address verification), Twilio–Phone Verification.

Advantages: Reducing compliance costs by 20%, applying more accurate risk assessment, detecting fraud better, and improving resource allocation.

6. Silicon Valley Bank

Use Cases: Customer onboarding, identity verification, blacklisting check, address + phone + picture verification.

For example, one technical solution: Social Verification uses Socure for biometric verification, Mitek (OCR document scanning), Dow Jones Watchlist (blacklist checks), Melissa Data (address review) and Telesign (telephone feedback).

Benefits: The bank reduced onboarding time by 30%, increased the accuracy of verification, and improved fraud detection simply because they could visualize all data points affecting a particular relationship.

7. Cross Riverbank

Applicable use cases: Transaction monitoring, compliance management, blacklist screening, address and phone verification, picture verification (ID document matching) / PIP verification.

Technical Solution: "Chainalysis" for transaction monitoring, "PassFort" for compliance automation, "World-Check" Lists Screening and Monitoring, "Loqate" Data Validation - Address Verification APIs, "Telesign" Phone Verification API (2FA) And Voice Messaging Platform, IDology PIP Identity Verification System.

Benefits: Automated compliance process, 25% reduction in false positives and enhanced suspicious activity detection.

8. Radius Bank

Use Cases: KYC verification, monitoring updates, backlist screening, address photo and identification.

Technical Solution: Onfido for Biometric Verification Trulioo global ID verification Dowjones Watchlist Checking Melissa Data for address validation Telesign Phone number checking

Benefits: The bank improved its verification speed by 20%, lower costs and higher compliance with global regulations.

9. Live Oak Bank

Use Cases: Identity verification, fraud prevention, blacklist check, address verification, phone and image confirmation. PIP Verification.

Tech Solution: IDology (Document Verification), Kount (Fraud Detection), World Check (Blacklist Screening), Loqate (Address Verification) Twilio (Phone verification) and Socure (PII verification).

Benefits: Increased detection accuracy of fraudulent activities, faster onboarding, and 15% lesser need for manual compliance efforts.

10. Axos Bank

Use Cases: Customer onboarding, transaction monitoring, risk grading — apart from the blacklist screening and address/phone/picture verification.

The following components implement the technical solution: "Jumio" for biometric and document verification, "NICE Actimize" for transaction monitoring and risk evaluation, "Dow Jones Watchlist" for checking against blacklists, "Melissa Data" for verifying addresses, and "Twilio" for verifying phone numbers.

Benefits: As a result, these cohesive solutions decreased onboarding by 25 percent and were reduces which improved model accuracy in transaction monitoring and resource investment in compliance efforts.

AI and ML in KYC processes have changed the game for banks as it increases efficiency, accuracy, and compliance in their operations. Powered on state-of-the-art artificial intelligence (AI), automated identity verification, dynamic risk assessment capabilities combined with strong fraud detection enable faster customer onboarding and ongoing monitoring. Using such advanced technologies, biometrics/OCR, real-time transaction monitoring enables banks to handle regulatory demands more efficiently as well manage operational costs better and improvise customer journey. With AI strengthening as we speak, the grand world of finance hinges further on its paradigm associated with KYC.

10 smaller Asian banks and virtual banks.

1. Krungsri, Thailand - Bank of Ayudhya

Uses: Customer onboarding, transaction monitoring, identity verification.

Technical Solution: Trulioo for global ID verification, KYC-Chain for compliance management and SmartSearch for transaction monitoring.

Benefits: Increased fraud detection accuracy, a 25% reduction in onboarding time, automated systems facilitated more streamlined customer experience.

2. Rakuten Bank — Japan (Virtual Banks)

Sector focus: Digital identity verification, transaction monitoring, compliance management

Technical Solution (Issuer): Biometric verification through Onfido, document verification using Jumio and AML compliance with AMLSpotter.

Benefits: Improved security for digital transactions, a 30% reduction in KYC processing time, and friction-less custom onboarding experience.

3. DBS Bank India

Use Cases: CDD (Customer Due Diligence), Blacklist Screening, Identity Verification.

Tech Solution: Implements iComply, BioID and World-Check

Benefits: Eased KYC procedures, better fraud detection and increased compliance (meeting licenses).

4. Mox Bank–Hong Kong (Virtual Banking)

Use Cases: Customer onboarding Property Verification Transaction Monitoring

Technical Solution (using Socure for identity verification, Chainalysis for transaction monitoring and Comply Advantage for AML screening)

Benefits: Fraud decreases with the use of more advanced biometric solutions. Improved customer on-boarding time Improves accuracy of transaction monitoring.

5. CIMB Bank PH (Virtual Bank)

Use Cases, Identity Proofing, Transaction Monitoring, Compliance Management.

Technical Solution: using Onfido (facial recognition), Trulioo (global ID verification) and Sift (fraud detection).

Benefits: Faster onboarding, more fraud detection, and better KYC processes.

6. SBI Sumishin Net Bank - Japan

Use Cases: Digital Onboarding, Transaction Monitoring, Fraud detection

Tech Solution: Has "Jumio" for ID proofs verification, "Actimize" for filtering of fraudulent transaction and "Telesign.

Benefits: Operational cost savings, improved onboarding experience, more powerful fraud detection

7. UnionDigital Bank–Philippines (Virtual Bank)

Use Cases: KYC compliance, identity verification, Fraud detection.

However, it provides Technical Solution: Veridium (Biometric Authentication) + IDology (Document Verification) Trulioo (Compliance Checks).

Benefits: Focus on better customer onboarding, world class security and international standards compliance.

8. WeBank - China (Virtual Bank)

Use-Cases: Digital KYC, AML transaction monitoring, Regulatory Compliance management.

Technical Tools: Yitu for facial recognition, Ant Financial KYC based on blockchain technology and Chainalysis to monitor transactions.

Benefits: Streamline digital KYC procedures, shorter onboarding period, and better conformance to regulatory schemas.

9. Australia JudoBank (SME lending)

Areas of use: Identity verification, KYC, transaction monitoring and risk assessment.

Tech Solution: Uses Trulioo for global ID verification, Jumio for document verification and Actimize AML monitoring.

Benefits: Reduce risk, simplify KYC checks and improved client onboarding experience.

10. Name: Tovik Bank — Virtual Bank Philippines

Use Cases: Digital Onboarding, Identity Services, AML Compliance

Technical Solution: Introduces iProov for biometric identity verification, Onfido for document scanning, and Actimize for transaction monitoring.

Use case: Better customer onboarding experience because of enhanced AML compliance and decreased fraud.

A detailed analysis comparing banking tools used for KYC and AML processes, with a focus on their best practices, performance, and functionality.

Compression of various tools in its own area of specialization.

1. Biometric Solutions for Verification

Tools: Jumio, Onfido, Veridium, BioID, iProov, Socure

Jumio and **Onfido** both have strong facial recognition capabilities. However, Jumio has gained a reputation for its high accuracy in matching biometric data with government-issued IDs. This makes it the preferred choice for banks that need strict identity verification. Onfido has value for its flexibility and ease of integration, especially in mobile environments.

Veridium vs. **BioID**: Veridium excels in multi-factor biometric authentication, offering additional security layers beyond just facial recognition. BioID, however, is well-known for its advanced liveness detection, which ensures that the biometric data is being provided by a live person rather than a spoof.

iProov's exceptional liveness detection and resilience against deep fake attacks make it indispensable in high-stakes environments that demand robust fraud prevention measures. Socure, with its combination of AI and ML, provides robust fraud prevention and identity verification but shines in environments requiring rapid onboarding.

2. Text Extraction using OCR

Implemented tools: Acuant, IDnow, Trulioo, Mitek & Jumio.

Acuant vs IDnow: Acuant greater text extraction accuracy in a wide variety of fonts and low-quality images. However, IDnow offers a range of compliance tools and an excellent integration capacity with them, so that banks have a seamless end-to-end solution.

Trulioo vs Mitek: Trulioo is known for its global ID verification on a massive data set, which allows cross border verification with high accuracy. Mitek excels at the speed of document scanning and real-time processing, which is required for customer on-boarding processes that demand fast results.

Jumio, with its world-class OCR and biometric verification, is such a perfect fit for high-stakes environments where both a document-check and individual identity-verification are absolute requirements.

3. Fraud Detection and Transaction monitoring

Technology Stack: NICE Actimize, SAS AML, Chainalysis Actimize,, Kount AMLSpotter

NICE Actimize v/s SAS AML — Nice Actimze is known as the most trusted leader providing end-to-end solutions for transaction monitoring and fraud detection, implementing AI with predictive analytics and customisable financial action against various transactions. Their AS AML is the go-to option for banks with a larger scale of operations across the globe, primarily because of its impressive data integration prowess.

Chainalysis vs Kount: Chainalysis is the most widely used in the domain of blockchain analysis and a very reputable source for revealing frauds relevant to cryptocurrencies — perfect for banks that handle digital assets. Kount backs these machines learning models with more sophisticated ones for detecting traditional transaction fraud — which helps reduce false positives.

The firm founded itself as a start-up with a focus on providing smaller financial institutions with an affordable, yet effective solution equipped with strong transaction monitoring capabilities that rival the best solutions in the market. As with most SaaS AML offerings, the product is less configurable than NICE Actimize or SAS AML, but few banks truly need a bespoke solution.

4. Risk Scoring and Profiling

Instruments: FICO TONBELLER, NICE Actimize, SAS AML

FICO TONBELLER vs. NICE Actimize: More precise risk scoring algorithms benefit configurations that require highly detailed customer risk profiles, just the type already typical for existing FICO customers. NICE Actimize focuses on our RBA capability is second-to-none; we offer the most comprehensive views combining risk assessments with real-time transaction monitoring for Risk Scoring in the market today.

One of SAS AML best features is risk analysis updating customer risk profile over time based on the latest activities. It is popular in contexts such as for an unforeseeable, watched only content wrap to support customer action.

5. Blacklist Screening

Tool: World-Check, Dow Jones watchlist, Comply Advantage

World-Check vs Dow Jones Watchlist — World-Check has larger global watchlists for the world, making it suitable for banks operating in multiple jurisdictions. It also scored well at PEP blocking but was less reliable in this score. Though more limited, Dow Jones Watchlist is more up-to-date as it blends real-time news information and regulatory changes into its coverage, making it able to respond rapidly to market shifts across the world.

ComplyAdvantage — Cheeky slogan for unsexy solution to run-of-the-mill blacklist activities using AI and provides a less outdated compliance approach. Smaller banks or FinTech companies that require a cloud-based system are an ideal candidate.

6. Address; Phone Verification.

Useful Tools: Loqate, Melissa Data, Telesign, Twilio

Best Global Address Verification:

LoqateLoqate vs. Melissa Data: For banks that cater to a richly diverse customer base, particularly international customers, Loqate is perfect as it offers superior accuracy in global address verification. Melissa Data can handle more complex use cases in addressing standardization, which might make it a good choice for a bank that needs to keep the address data consistent across several systems.

Telesign vs. Twilio: Telesign can give you robust phone verification, plus several security features like device fingerprinting and behavioral analysis, which could also be helpful in fraud prevention. Where the need for better integration with other systems is critical, I find many choose Twilio simply because of its more extensible API.

7. Regulatory Updates and Compliance Management

Engines: KYC-Chain, PassFort, Oracle Financial Services, iComply

KYC-Chain and PassFort: Where KYC-Chain apps to provide blockchain-based but cropline compliance management where secure or transported In its immutable record conspiracy. Better User experience and compatibility with existing compliance setup make it a superb choice if banks are seeking to deploy the solution in a short time. PassFort is supportive and straightforward for businesses.

Oracle financial services: Oracle provides an end-to-end compliance management suite which is very scalable and works well with other Oracle products, making it a good fit for large financial institutions.

This is a viable product, particularly for small institutions or if you need to create a solution quickly to comply with new regularity requirements, then this could be an option.

8. Enhanced Due Diligence (EDD)

Software: Socure, iProov, Chainalysis

Socure vs. iProov: Socure is for the analysis of large data sets to find hidden risks and thus very suited for a bank with deep insights into customer backgrounds. For environments where seconds matter, and the decision is life or death, there is nothing more reliable than iProov with real-time liveness detection.

Chainalysis: Chainalysis is the best there is in cryptocurrency EDD, with their advanced blockchain transaction analysis. The go-to tool for banks interfacing with cryptocurrencies and the flexibility of emerging regulatory frameworks in this space.

9. Document Proof and Verification

Tools: Mitek, Acuant, IDology

The document scanning and verification speed of Mitek is the fastest one in high-volume environments where quick on-boarding is a need. That makes it the best solution. However, if you are looking for strong fraud detection, with the best ability to identify even the most sophisticated document forgeries, then Acuant remains unbeatable which makes it more suited for high security environments.

IDology: IDology is great for verifying document data against external databases — ensuring not only that the documents are real but also that they exist on file.

10. Detecting Fraudulent Customer Behavior

Sift, Kount and AMLSpotter

Some people enjoy the predictive analytics that Sift offers, allowing it to predict fraudulent action before it happens. Kount is built for real-time detection and works well on use cases when anything beyond the speed of light response time will be a bottleneck to your business / e-commerce transactions.

Smaller institutions often use AMLS Potter, which offers a more balanced introduction with cheaper but still reliable fraud detection capabilities, and they prioritize simplicity over complexity from advanced toolsets.

Keep in mind that each of these tools is very different and better suited to some use cases than others for the overriding needs of a bank. Certain tools like Jumio and Acuant are best suited for high accuracy, fraud avoidance only environments. Again, tools like Sift & Chainalysis can detect fraud in a way that prevents such actions from completing with same day verification checks and real-time compliance for crypto-related transactions.

Reference – Further reading - Chapter 4

Artificial Intelligence in Banking by Business Insider Intelligence. (2023)
https://www.businessinsider.com/ai-in-banking-report

Seven Insights Into The Future Of KYC Compliance
https://www.forbes.com/councils/forbestechcouncil/2022/12/14/seven-insights-into-the-future-of-kyc-compliance/

The new era for KYC processes-by Deloitte
https://www2.deloitte.com/content/dam/Deloitte/fi/Documents/risk/The%20new%20era%20for%20KYC%20processes.pdf

KYC Solutions – PwC
https://www.pwc.com/gx/en/news-room/assets/analyst-citations/chartis-kyc-2022.pdf

AI implementation - An overview of the use of AI Tech Stack in Banking
https://www.finextra.com/blogposting/26626/context-is-king-in-ai-implementation---an-overview-of-the-use-of-ai-tech-stack-in-banking

How AI transforms KYC into a continuous compliance powerhouse
https://member.regtechanalyst.com/how-ai-transforms-kyc-into-a-continuous-compliance-powerhouse/

JPMorgan's AI-Powered KYC Operations Boost Productivity by up to 90%
https://medium.com/vanguard-industry-foresight/jpmorgans-ai-powered-kyc-operations-boost-productivity-by-up-to-90-ae043f55c4c7

Standard Chartered Bank - KYC-Chain provides an on-boarding
https://kyc-chain.com/industries/

Deutsche Bank – Five KYC
https://flow.db.com/more/regulation/five-kyc-essentials

Difference between e-kyc- and v-kyc
https://www.axisbank.com/progress-with-us-articles/digital-banking/differences-between-e-kyc-and-v-kyc

Top 10 global KYC best practices
https://cdn.twimbit.com/uploads/2024/05/15144935/Top-10-global-KYC-best-practices1.pdf

WeBank pushes for biotech ID in China:
https://www.financeasia.com/article/webank-pushes-for-biotech-id-in-china/406173

Onfido auto KYC solution
https://onfido.com/use-cases/kyc/
Veridium Partners with Jumio to Deliver Groundbreaking Biometric Identity Verification
https://www.veridiumid.com/veridium-partners-with-jumio-to-deliver-groundbreaking-biometric-identity-verification/
iproov KYC verification
https://www.iproov.com/use-cases/know-your-customer-kyc
Socure Verify - Precise, accurate, and inclusive identity verification
https://www.socure.com/products/identity-verification
Acuant's Trusted Identity Platform provides AI-powered identity verification, regulatory compliance (AML/KYC)
https://support.pingidentity.com/s/marketplace-integration/a7i1W000000TQzbQAG/acuant-connector
Identity verification tech
https://www.idology.com/solutions/identity-verificati
idnow KYC solution
https://www.idnow.io/regulation/what-is-kyc/
KYC for Crypto
https://www.chainalysis.com/blog/what-is-aml-and-kyc-for-crypto/
KYC Xpress: Comply with Agility
https://www.niceactimize.com/data-intelligence/kyc-xpress/

FIVE

How do banks use AI for risk management in an Anti-money laundering effort (AML)?

Introduction

The financial services sector, like other industries, has seen a wave of innovation around Artificial Intelligence (AI). In this sector, one of the most important use cases is AI used for Anti-Money Laundering (AML). One widespread issue in the global economy is money laundering. Banks and other financial institutions need to deal with both the tough rules and cunning ways of organised crime. AI puts them in a situation to detect and prevent money laundering much more powerful.

But using AI in AML transcends even a technological upgrade; it represents a sea-change for how financial institutions look at risk management. AI can help improve informing banks to identify suspicious activities, operational efficiency and compliance level of AML processes. This change is not just mandatory, but also unavoidable as financial crimes become increasingly sophisticated, and regulators tighten their grip.

1. Overview of AI in banking

AI technologies are taking shape in various aspects of banking. AI has many applications, making it one of the most versatile tools that we have at our disposal.

PFM (Personal Finance Management): AI tools that help customers automatically manage their money, advising based on your spending habits and goals.

Location Intelligence: AI empowers banks to analyse where its customers go, 4 helping it understand customer behavior and optimize branch locations.

KYC & ID Management: AI simplifies the process of user identity verification, minimizing KYC procedures to a fair extent and thus indirectly minimizes efforts and time.

Anti-fraud System: The routing system directly analyses the behavior of transactions, finding abnormally fraudulent factors in real time.

Robo-Chat Customer Services: This is a 24/7 customer care service powered by AI-driven chatbots that answer questions and solve problems without human help.

AI revolutionizes loan applications and credit scoring in the lending industry. By analyzing vast amounts of data, AI enables banks to make faster and more informed lending decisions, ultimately mitigating credit risk.

Loan Quality Assessments: AI helps in the quality monitoring and assessment of loans, predicting defaults, managing loan portfolios, etc.

One of the key areas with a potential for AI to make a tremendous impact is AML and Compliance. Recently, there has been a significant evolution in methodologies for determining and applying AML solutions and Financial Crime & Compliance processes. Automation has played a crucial role in saving valuable time previously wasted on inefficient manual work. AI can automate these processes, improving them and enabling banks to respond to techniques of new money-laundering.

2. The Scope of Money Laundering

Global Issue — both an affluence and third world economy must face the challenges of money laundering. According to the United Nations Office on Drugs and Crime (UNODC), global money laundering amounts to $800 billion to $2 trillion, which is 2-5% of the world's GDP. This comes with about 2 trillion dollars of illegal money that moves around the financial system and funds criminal enterprises in drug dealing, terrorism, corruption.

3. Money laundering is a three-stage process.

Placement: The first step involves entering "dirty money" into the formal financial system, through cash deposits, currency exchanges, or the purchase of high-value goods.

Layering: Using various transactions to move the money and make it difficult to identify the original source of. The third stage is layering. This might entail transferring money through several accounts, jurisdictions or even turning it into distinct assets.

Integration is the final stage where criminals reintroduce laundered money into the economy as "clean" money through legitimate investments, purchases, or business operations.

Banks have a role in the fight against money laundering. They are the first to monitor and report suspicious transactions. Current AML practices have their limitations for facing the gargantuan nature of contemporary money laundering operations. With criminals continuously finding innovative ways to overcome existing controls, it is necessary for banks to adopt state-of-the-art technologies like AI as well.

4. Traditional AML Practices

Money laundering, for a long time, relied on traditional AML practices to prevent its occurrence in the banking and finance industry. These steps are as practices that help identify and remove risks from financial crimes. How do traditional AML processes work? Traditional AML working components.

Customer Due Diligence: Banks need to identify and verify the identity of who they are banking with at customer inception. This includes the collection and validation of personal information: names, addresses, dates of birth or ID numbers. This is crucial to validate the identity of the customer and reduce the possibility of identity fraud.

Customer Due Diligence (CDD) collects detailed information about a customer, including their identity, address, financial activities, and risk categorization. Banks need to know the nature and purpose of the relationship between their customers and themselves, deploy transaction surveillance systems, as well as conduct an AML risk assessment. Banks impose additional obligations and undertake Enhanced Due Diligence (EDD) for high-risk customers, such as Politically Exposed Persons (PEPs) or individuals from high-risk countries.

Transaction Monitoring: Banks have to track transactions of customers and monitor any changes that may look bizarre. This includes looking at transactional behavior and comparing it to predefined rules, as well as identifying anomalies. In contrast to this, traditional transaction monitoring systems work on rule-based mechanisms, according to which alerts are thin only in case of surpassed specific thresholds or criteria.

Payment screening checks transactions against watchlists like those from OFAC in the US or the EU's sanctions list. It is this step that prevents transactions from taking place between sanctioned entities or individuals and that they comply with the rules of international regulations.

Using customer screening: this is for identification of clients within databases like money launderers, terrorist analysts, PEPs, and high-risk individual lists. This enables banks to identify and mitigate the fraud risks on a per customer basis.

5. Challenges in Traditional AML

Traditional AML practices are of utmost importance. They also present multiple challenges that reduce their capabilities:

Manual Processes — Most of the AML processes are manual and require third-party intervention for the transactions. Therefore, they are time-consuming, labor-intensive, and error prone. Using manual forms of due diligence hinders AML efforts on a larger scale. This means banks cannot keep up with the growing number of transactions or the increasing regulatory burden.

False Positives: Legacy AML systems typically produce a high number of false positives—alerts that are wrongly identified as dubious, when they are innocuous. This places a heavy burden on compliance teams — they still need to look into every alert, which leads to inefficiencies and higher operational costs.

6. An Inability to Detect Complex Schemes:

This more adaptable approach than the rigid traditional rule-based systems of old put limits on their flexibility and ultimate effectiveness regarding identifying complex money laundering schemes. Saboteurs and criminals use these restrictions to their advantage; they changed how they operate to skirt the system alerts. They could, for instance, split up hefty purchases to escape notice–a practice called "smurfing."

Slow Response Time: Traditional AML processes are slow and those who would like to finance terrorism can act in the meantime. Criminals can move the funds through the banking system again before getting caught once they realize the delay, highlighting the importance of this delay.

7. The Role of AI in AML

AI has huge scope in solving myriad problems of traditional AML practices. AI can help improve the accuracy, efficiency, and efficiency of AML processes using sophisticated algorithms and machine learning techniques. Important features of AI in AML include:

Improved Risk Detection: By processing tremendous amounts of data simultaneously, artificial intelligence can recognize trends and spot red flags that legacy systems would never catch in the first place; while machine learning models can leverage their experience with historical data to better predict suspicious behavior. For instance, AI can detect small transaction patterns that may show money laundering and suggest suspicious activities like regular offshore transfers or atypical activity spikes.

A top Europe-headquartered bank went live with a next-GenAI-based AML solution, which immediately reduced false positives by 50% and increased true positive detection rates. — The AI system uncovered complex money laundering schemes that flew under the radar of traditional platforms.

Decrease in Operational Costs: Using AI to automate AML processes will reduce the need for manual reviews, reducing operational costs. Considering the great numbers of transactions, AI systems have the advantage of performing better where human teams would deliver on time.

HSBC's Google-supported AI-powered AML approach sped up the bank's transaction monitoring, slashed compliance costs by 20%.

Enhanced Governance and Compliance: AI gives the bank an improved mechanism to oversee and regulate AML. Regardless of role changes, AI-driven systems guarantee uniform AML procedures followed throughout the organization, mitigating the likely hood of human error and regulatory oversights.

Standard Chartered Bank uses AI to gain a holistic picture of customer risk, ensuring it meets Anti-Money Laundering legislation. The bank uses the AI system to detect high-risk clients and supervise more efficiently.

AI systems possess an unparalleled capability that surpasses that of humans, allowing them to learn and constantly develop. This is crucial in the ever-developed landscape of financial crime as criminals continue to adapt and discover new ways to avoid being caught out.

ING now has an AI-powered AML solution that learns from new data, detecting unknown patterns or behavior traditional tools may miss. The system has attributed many new patterns of suspicious activities.

Customer experience: Reducing false positives and the flow of unnecessary interactions with customers due to streamlining AML processes. This enhances the customer experience by enabling faster processing of genuine transactions and reducing compliance check overheads for customers.

One of the largest U.S. banks announced that customer complaints over AML processes decreased by 30%, after the bank reduced false positives using an AI system.

8. Implementing AI in AML

Applying AI to AML is a tricky task and needs well-crafted planning. Key steps include:

Data Quality Management — The power of AI in AML hinges on the quality of data it interacts with. Data is accurate, comprehensive and following standardizations — Banks have to make sure that their data should be accurate, complete and standardized. It depends on consolidating and aggregating data from many systems, as well as implementing effective data governance.

A global bank spent two years cleansing and normalizing its data to power an AI-driven AML solution. It turned out to be an excellent investment, because the AI system could analyze data more efficiently, leading to 40 percent gains in risk detection.

9. Explanation of transparency and accountability

AI systems need to explain their decisions — this is crucial for regulatory compliance. To avoid this, banks must also provide the clear reasoning from their AI models so that regulators know the logic behind them.

Explainable AI model for AML:

JPMorgan Chase developed an explainable AI model that provides a detailed explanation, revealing what reached a certain threshold. This approach has allowed the bank to remain compliant with regulations and yet realize some benefits that AI can offer.

Regulatory Compliance & Integration: AI systems should integrate seamlessly with current AML regulations. AI should help banks comply with all statutory or regulatory requirements for AML, and this is something they need to work on in collaboration with regulators. The work may involve integrating AI systems into operating established compliance regimes and ensuring that regulators audit and monitor their operation.

A top Asian bank partnered with regulators while building its AI-enabled AML tool. The top Asian bank partnered with regulators during the design phase of its AI-enabled AML tool, engaging them to ensure compliance needs were met and agreeing from regulatory authorities.

10. AI and human collaboration

Even though AI can automate a lot of tasks in AML, we still need human expertise. Banks have to hire teams who can work with AI systems, interpret them and make grounded decisions. However, for those AI-driven AML programs to succeed, a close collaboration between AI and human analysts is essential.

Also in Europe, a bank rolled out a combined human and AI anti-money laundering system. The software automation deals with most of the transactions and professional reviewers do them on a case-by-case human investigation. This more recent method has managed the efficiency and accuracy of the system by a lot.

Regulatory considerations:

We should ensure that AI systems allow their use for good and minimize bias and unfair procedures in decision-making. For instance, banks need to check their AI models and ensure that they can distinguish any bias in a dataset — if they identify biased data, they should neutralize it. Also, it is necessary to implement ethical considerations (and the associated repercussions on clients and society at large).

Our team successfully implemented the framework for detecting bias in the AI that drives an AML system at a North American bank. The framework flags existing biases with an AI model and then, using this information, corrects the algorithms to act on behalf of all customers.

Importance of AI in AML has been increasing:

The depth of that sophistication mirrors the need for AI in AML.

Real-Time Analysis:

AI can analyze many data in real-time, constantly updating its learning process to provide helpful insights for financial institutions. Financial institutions, which have an imminent requirement of firewalls against risks and hazards, will spearhead the global penetration of AI in AML.

> *MarketsandMarkets predict that the AI in the AML market will grow to $3.9 billion globally by 2025 at a CAGR of 22.5% from just $1.4 billion last year. IT is driven by growing regulatory pressure, the increasing complexity of financial crime, and the need for banks to reduce operation costs at the same time.*

Luckily, there is a way for banks to keep up with new threats. It is called AI. It is essential that AI can strengthen to keep up with introducing fresh red-flag patterns and tactics as criminals continue to find innovative ways to circumvent standard AML controls. With an AI-driven AML solution, the financial institutions have the power to identify financial crimes and prevent it along with keeping their customers safe and meeting the regulatory obligations.

The coming trends in AI driven AML.

AI is here to stay and will increasingly intertwine with the industry, defining the future of AML through key trends.

Integration with Blockchain:

We have integrated AI with blockchain technology for greater AML functionalities. Combining AI with the transparency and immutability of the ledger within a blockchain can bring more light into how funds are flowing. By using this integration, banks will have a more efficient way of tracing assets down the financial system, empowering authorities to catch and curb money laundering.

In Europe, a consortium of banks is working on a blockchain and AI based platform for real time AML transaction monitoring. It is to help provide a standard of recording transactions from the multiple banks in order that those doing evil can work together with each other more closely.

AI-based predictive analytics:

Predictive analytics are becoming an essential element in the AML procedure. By compiling historical records into the system, AI can provide information about potential money laundering activities that are yet to take place. Banks can proactively identify potential risks, take actions to prevent them, and reduce financial crime.

One of the largest global banks uses AI-driven predictive analytics to determine which customers are likely high risks for money laundering. It used different data sets alongside transactional history, customer behavior and other external factors to generate risk scores. These scores enable the company to identify leads, investigate, and react accordingly.

NLP in AML: NLP is being used to scan unstructured data such as customer emails, social media posts, and news for potential risks. Banks can harness this technology to inform decisions and draw conclusions about customer behavior, or information is available through unstructured data points.

A large bank in the USA uses an NLP system for tracking news and social media mentions of its clients. If the system detected articles linking a client to criminal activities, it may have prompted bank staff to launch their own investigation.

Regulatory reporting is a major stumbling block for financial institutions AI-Driving Regulatory Reporting. Banks can automate this process using AI, which allows them to comply with AML regulations faster. AI-backed reporting systems can also serve more granular information to regulators, adding another hammer over non-compliance.

An Asian bank plugged into an AI-based regulatory reporting solution which automatically produces AML reports for regulators. It also aggregates transactional data and customer information with risk scoring to provide full reports compliant with regulatory demands.

AI-Powered AML: Challenges and Implications

Though AI is helpful in several ways, it brings about some difficulties and aspects that the banks must solve when using AML systems powered by AI.

Secure Data and Privacy:

Watermark ensures it maintains the privacy of user data and security. Therefore, banks will have to build powerful defenses around their infrastructure to prevent any unauthorized access of the sensitive data available. This will have data encryption, secure communication channels and regular audits to ensure there are no security holes in the implementation.

Global bank licked its wounds over a data breach that had revealed customer details which were being used as part of its AI-driven AML system. After the breach, which showed vulnerabilities in security, the bank began using encryption and multi-factor authentication to ensure data safety.

Regulatory Compliance: The more intricate AI systems get, the harder it is to assure compliance with existing AML regulations. To ensure that AI-led AML processes of banks are legally safe, banks must partner with regulators. Such steps could be as far-reaching as getting regulatory approval for AI models adopted by banks and so on.

An Asian Bank — one leader in the country and globally — works on developing AI so that each time they go to a regulator, they clearly understand the expectations beforehand. The bank could involve regulators earlier in the process and use them to validate that the AI system complied with all requirements.

Ethical considerations: it considers limitations on the use of AI to reduce bias and decision-making fairness. To prevent discrimination or other ethical issues, banks must monitor their AI systems. For example, in this case, we should test the AI models on biases and prevent them with measures if society identifies any biases.

A North American bank deployed an AI-driven AML system with a bias detection framework. The rules also tell the framework of how to detect any bias in the AI model and change its algorithms so that all customers get treated fairly.

Price of Implementation:

Implementing AI-based AML systems can be costly, especially for smaller financial institutions. Banks need to weigh the benefits of AI against costs and returns. This could involve conducting a cost-benefit analysis and gradually implementing AI in stages.

Prior to implementing an AI-powered AML system, a mid-sized bank conducted a financial analysis to determine the system's cost over a few years and the required number of FTEs. The analysis showed that the bank would save money in the long run and improve risk detection, so it decided to proceed.

Collaboration is Key to AI-Driven AML

For AI to affect the AML process, all the networks involved in this should be able to collaborate effectively, which entails the financial institutions, technology providers and regulators. They can collaborate to create effective practices and methods, share information, and overcome common obstacles. The development and implementation of AI-powered AML solutions are being sped up through the collaboration of banks pooling resources and knowledge via industry consortia and partnerships.

A consortium of European banks and technology providers launched a project for building an AI-powered AML solution shared among all its stakeholders. The platform enables taking part in banks to access and jointly test risk identification data, which ultimately results in a more efficient AML process.

Enterprise AI solutions are revolutionizing banks' AML processes to deliver improved risk detection, reduced operational cost, a stronger compliance and regulatory relationship, ongoing learning capabilities and an enhanced customer experience. When banks deploy AI to AML, they must consider certain factors, such as data quality, explain ability, regulatory compliance, human expertise, and bias management. Tackling these challenges and capitalizing on the power of AI will enable banks to fight money laundering and related crimes, thus protecting their business and image.

As AI becomes increasingly advanced, it will be a critical part of the war against financial crime. Investing in AI during introduction gives financial institutions an advantage in detecting and preventing money laundering. Staying ahead protects customers and keeps regulators satisfied. With the complex competitive environment, AI integrated AML processes are imperative for banks beyond technology maturation.

USE CASES:

1. HSBC

Overview

HSBC, one of the world's largest banks and financial services organizations, has been leveraging technology to enhance its Anti-Money Laundering (AML) capabilities. This bank has leveraged a combination of Artificial Intelligence, Machine Learning, and Blockchain technologies for transaction monitoring, customer due diligence, regulatory compliance.

Challenges Addressed

Millions of Transactions: HSBC processes millions of transactions every day, making it difficult to keep track of and check each if they are involved in money laundering.

Complex Global Operations–Conducting business in multiple jurisdictions with its own regulatory requirements adds a layer of complexity to AML compliance.

High Number of False Positives: Traditional rule-based systems produced a high volume of false positives, which resulted in inefficiencies and higher operational expenses.

Data Silos: Different data systems, such as CRM, ERP, etc. made it harder to have a holistic view of customer activities across jurisdictions.

Transaction Monitoring: In collaboration with AI companies, HSBC has built machine-learning (ML) algorithms to run through huge datasets to identify anomalous transaction patterns showing money-laundering.

Machine learning models apply knowledge about past transaction records and known financial crimes to detect minute deviations that might otherwise slip through traditional methods.

AI-powered systems have automated the identification and risk evaluation phase of Customer Due Diligence (CDD) for customers.

Companies use NLP to analyze likely negative information related to customers in data sources, such as news articles, social media, and other unstructured outlets.

AI is used to performing Entity Resolution (ER), join the information of customers from different sources, and reduce duplication by reconciling details about customers.

Blockchain Technology

Shared Ledger for KYC: HDFC bank has explored the use of a block chain in enhancing the customer identification process, i.e. KYC (Know Your Customer).

The bank took part in trials using the R3 Corda platform (), a permissioned blockchain specifically built for enterprise-interior usage.

Functionality:

Immutable Records maintains a copy of customer identity data in the blockchain, enhancing security by providing and storing evidence that it cannot be altered.

Data Sanction: Institutions allowed to access verified KYC data will share the same through a centralized process, reducing both duplication of efforts and compliance effectiveness.

Auditability: The transparent nature of blockchain helps in better terms of auditing and the ease of tracking data access and data modifications.

Trade Finance: HSBC has finished the world's first trade finance transaction adopting blockchain technology; this solution decreases processing time and raises transparency.

AML: Because of the traceability and immutability element of transactions on blockchain, trade finance can be more transparent for regulators to monitor and follow accounting flows.

Integration and Workflow

We gather data here by taking transactions and customer information from different systems to feed the AI/ML engines.

Data Analysis:

AI/ML Processing: These systems analyze data as it comes in, looking for patterns and abnormalities that show potential illicit behavior.

Risk Scoring — assigns risk scores to transactions and customer profiles based on predefined criteria and learned patterns.

Alert Generation: If a particular transaction is high risk in nature, it triggers alerts which are then referred to by the compliance officer for subsequent investigation.

Blockchain Recording:

Where KYC Data Storage stores confirmed customer information on the blockchain for access by approved individuals only.

Blockchain registers important transactions, especially in trade finance, to make them transparent and traceable through transaction logging.

Investigation and Reporting:

Review: The compliance team checks alerts from AI, who compare them against the bank transaction on the blockchain.

Regulatory Reporting: We report all suspicious activities to proper authorities with detailed audit trails based on blockchain data.

Outcomes and Benefits

Lower False-Positive Rates: Roll-out of AI/ML reduced the rates by approximately 20% to allow compliance teams to investigate more actual threats.

Increased Efficiency–Both in automation & process optimizations, to handle several transactions faster with less cost.

Improved Compliance: The system of integrated compliance enabled better monitoring and reporting features, ensuring compliance with an improved global AML regulation.

More Transparency: Blockchain technology creates a record that is immutable, traceable and transparent, which makes auditing and investigations.

Reduced Onboarding times because of shortened KYC processes–Enhanced customer satisfaction.

By encapsulating AI, ML, and Blockchain technologies amongst others, HSBC is showcasing a collective lens towards technology adoption for modernizing AML endeavors. These technologies have helped the bank on two main fronts — the detection and prevention of financial crimes, management of ever-increasing compliance requirements and improvements in operational efficiency.

2. JPMorgan Chase

Overview

JPMorgan Chase, a major global financial services company, has used advanced technologies to improve its efforts in preventing money laundering and complying with regulations. It builds superior systems to locate and report money laundering using AI-ML Blockchain.

Challenges Addressed: Ledger processing: Sophisticated systems are required for monitoring read billions of transactions.

Creation of financial Crime Techniques: These involved wrongdoers will change their methods so a more dynamic vigilant style-based AML arrangements be required.

Managing Compliance Complexities: This could be one of the most significant challenges in adhering to various regulatory standards across different geographies.

Operational Inefficiencies: Manual AML procedures are resource intensive and prone to backlogs

Implementation: In-house AI models detect fraud by analyzing transaction data in real-time.

Capabilities:

Pattern Recognition: Different ML algorithms can identify intricate patterns and anomalies in a behavior which may indicate money laundering.

Monitoring and scoring: Systems monitor current data and feedback to better pinpoint attacks

Tools and Frameworks: Apache Spark, TensorFlow (For large-scale data processing & model development)

To Process Natural Language (NLP)

Capability: Extracts data, connects dots and identifies and flags risk indicators

Robotic Process Automation (RPA):

Aids in automating redundant works within an AML Process like Data entry and Report Generation & increases productivity and reduces the chances of human errors.

Blockchain Technology: Blockchain Platform JPMorgan developed its blockchain platform known as Quorum, which is an enterprise-focused version of Ethereum.

IIN offers a platform for participating banks to exchange data on cross-border payments, causing unease as the potential risks and vulnerabilities of sharing sensitive information arise.

The expedited payment system eliminates the need for time-consuming compliance checks and eradicates the nerve-wracking delays caused by interbank information requests.

AML Relevance: Recording transactions on a shared ledger enforces transparency, establishing clear sight and traceability for Anti-Money Laundering (AML) purposes.

Enhanced Compliance: Enables instantaneous verification of payment information with p watchlists and sanctions.

Contribution to AML:

Immutable Records provide clear audit trail capabilities for compliance and tracking purposes as they ensure that transaction information cannot be altered. Tokens will represent digital assets, enabling a view of asset movements.

AI/ML Processing:

Real-Time Analysis: The AI models analyze transactions in real-time and take a decision based on historical data with the contextual information of that transaction.

Criteria-Based Alerts System: The system assigns scores to risk levels and generates real-time alerts when the transaction is high risk for interrogation.

Blockchain Recording:

Transaction Logging is Secure: The Quorum blockchain logs all cross-border payments and related information for visibility by allowed parties.

Fast Information Sharing: Also, the IIN allows for a speedy response to compliance queries because of a cadre of banks collectively sharing relevant information.

Compliance Review:

Automated Controls: Tools like RPA and AI can do an initial review and highlight areas of concern along with required documentation.

Compliance officers review human review: AI alerts and blockchain records to confirm or escalate

Regulatory Reporting:

Detailed Reports: Advanced systems create full reports for regulators, and use results of the AI analyses, data from the blockchain records.

Outcomes and Benefits

Advanced Identification: AI/ML systems enhanced the detection of suspicious activities by as much as 50%, allowing for a more efficient discovery of intricate schemes for money laundering.

Lower Processing Time: The cross-border payment compliance checks time reduced from days to hours with a blockchain integrated.

Decrease in Operational Costs: Automation and effective data sharing meant a huge reduction in manual workload, therefore the cost reduced as well.

Better Regulatory Compliance: Strong systems catered to international AML standards imposition, which brought forth lesser regulatory fines.

More Effective Interbank Collaboration: IIN helped banks cooperate better among themselves, making the financial ecosystem more effective in fighting financial crime.

Conclusion: This indeed speaks to the holistic nature through which JPMorgan Chase has embraced AI, ML, and Blockchain technologies to modernize its AML processes. Through proprietary platforms and smart analytics, a bank significantly improved its ability to detect and deter money laundering. This also resulted in enhanced operational efficiency and reduced compliance costs.

3. Standard Chartered Bank

Overview

One of the leading international banking groups — Standard Chartered Bank — has opted to harness state-of-the-art technologies to enhance its AML compliance. Bank uses the solutions of AI, ML and Blockchain technologies to provide risk detection capabilities and compliance process automation — level of inter-industry cooperation is increased within the financial industry.

Challenges Addressed: Serving clients in both developed and emerging markets, with their varying risk appetites and regulatory environments, sent a shiver down the spine of the diverse buy-side.

The traditional software creaked under the weight of modern demands, its outdated infrastructure struggling to keep up with the ever-increasing need for efficient data processing and risk assessment.

The limited ability to share verified information across jurisdictions and within the industry makes us uneasy. It leaves us vulnerable to potential risks due to gaps in knowledge.

Relying too much on manual reviews made the team anxious, fearing critical errors and feeling physically affected.

Launched ML models which modelled the risk for our clients based on their transaction's behaviors and external data.

With its ability to analyze customer transaction patterns over time, the AI instils a sense of unease as it uncovers subtle deviations that could show potentially fraudulent activities.

Constant monitoring in real-time sends shivers down my spine, as every alert brings the lurking presence of deceit into sharp focus, demanding immediate action.

My excitement bubbled up as I imagined the limitless possibilities that come with utilizing scalable computing and cloud platforms like Microsoft Azure, envisioning the ease and efficiency it would bring.

Name Screening Optimization: Compliance officers rely on AI models to sift through customers, their spirits burdened as they strive to uncover hidden threats among the crowd.

Some of the key techniques used are fuzzy logic and contextual analysis to determine proper matches from ones which are suspect.

Document Analysis: Use case: During KYC onboarding, we automate the extraction and validation of information from unstructured documents using NLP technologies.

CryptoBridge Accounts: in the ongoing KYC Chain project over Hyperledger Fabric blockchain Landbox Platform took part in building a private blockchain platform, called SagaChain.

The designers aim to use a decentralized database with Shared Customer Information so that taking part in financial institutions can share their verified KYC data.

Enhanced Data Security — Uses cryptographic methodologies for maintaining data privacy and integrity.

Regulatory Compliance: Generates provable records that are consistent with a variety of different regulatory requirements.

Trade Finance Digitization: Developed blockchain solutions to digitize trade finance processes (Letters of credit and supply chain financing)

Chainyard: Engaged with TradeLens and Contour (Specific Blockchain Platforms for trade finance).

The use of blockchain makes it simple to track and verify trade financing transactions, providing a complete record from start to finish. This way, planning for a threatened financial scam will be very challenging.

Efficiency: simplifies document verification and prevents fraud in trade finance.

Customer and Transaction Data — This includes both banking through one of its many services/small business/SME/corporate banking, co-branded products or from external sources.

Recording and Sharing of the Blockchain: KYC Data Management stores unloader's KYC details on the blockchain that helps to prevent duplicity and provides an uploaded customer data access to specific institution.

Trade Transaction Logging: The logging of trade finance transactions, allowing for all traceability and full information.

Compliance and Investigation:

Alert Handling–Compliance teams review alerts with high-risk levels generated by AI systems using combined analysis data and blockchain records.

Automated Compliance Reports: A full report on your compliance with digital records powered by data directly from the blockchain.

Outcomes and Benefits

Better Risk Detection: Ability to identify even complex money-laundering schemes with its dynamic and intelligent analysis.

Operational Efficiency Saves on processing times for KYC and transaction monitoring up to 30%, cutting costs.

Fewer/Reduced False Positives: AI-powered screening processes helped in reducing the cases of false-positives, so compliance teams could focus on tackling the genuine threats.

Secondary Features enhanced collaboration blockchain-based KYC utilities enabled banks to share the information quickly, securely and significantly improved industry-wide AML initiatives.

Compliance: Strong systems that kept the company to be compliant globally and locally at the same time with AML strictures, preventing possible fines and image issues.

CX: Quicker and streamlined onboarding and transaction processing improved customer satisfaction.

By incorporating AI, ML and Blockchain technologies into their conduct risk system, Standard Chartered Bank has showed a holistic approach in tackling AML. Now, driven by innovation and collaboration, the bank has built a wall against financial crime and streamlined its processes — demonstrating to the industry what best-practice compliance can achieve.

4. Banco Santander

Overview

The global bank headquartered in Spain took advanced technological measures to strengthen its AML functionality — Banco Santander. Bank Uses AI, ML and Blockchain to enhance its transaction monitoring capabilities, verified customers and compliance efficiency.

Common Example: Global Operations managing AML compliance in multiple countries with different regulatory requirements

Large Transaction Volume: Sent a lot of transactions per day, requiring scalable and efficient monitoring systems.

As a solution for this Use Case, the customer turned to: Legacy Infrastructure — The existing systems were not capable of real-time analysis and could not integrate data across multiple regions.

Resource shortages: Manual procedures created large operating expenses and resources went uncollected.

Advanced Transaction Monitoring: Advanced transaction monitoring feature can intercept any of your incoming or outgoing transactions and you will need to do the manual approval for each transaction.

Manufacturing ML models enables us to detect white-collar crimes more effectively.

Real Time Analytics-process the transaction as they occur to detect and react immediately to suspicious activity.

Self-Learning Systems: updates new data and emergent patterns detection algorithms.

Platforms and Tools: IBM Watson services, learn open-source framework for building models.

The Customer Due Diligence (CDD) module provides detailed training on the specific requirements of the 2001 USA Patriot Act, going beyond a bank's policy mandates for employees.

In NLP, it pulls and understands information from external data sources, such as legal documents and public records.

Transparent Transactions: Consumers get transaction alerts and confirmations immediately to make payments, which increases the trust level of users.

Secure Onboarding: New customer onboarding is seamless and secure thanks to biometric verification.

Outcomes and Benefits

Raised Detection Precision: Criminal AI/ML products improved the precision detection of criminal activities, hence **lowering False-Positive by 25%.**

Operational Efficiency: Regarding automation and the simplification of processes that have resulted in a drastic reduction in processing times and compliance costs.

International payments are now faster because of payment systems that use blockchain technology. Transactions that used to take several days now only take minutes, providing a more satisfying user experience.

Enhanced Compliance: It provided excellent compliance with anti-money laundering regulations in multiple geographies.

Higher Security: Tightening up bio-metric verification and making the assets movement stored on immutable blockchain would prevent financial crimes.

Collaboration: By joining blockchain consortiums, they worked with other industry members to commingle their brainpower and standardize trade finance processes for the rest of the financial ecosystem.

Banco Santander deployed AI, ML and Blockchain technologies to improve its AML capabilities significantly; this is a broad, successful approach. By utilizing state-of-the-art technologies, the bank can improve risk detection, streamline operations, enhance service delivery, and ensure compliance with global regulatory requirements.

5. Deutsche Bank

Overview

Deutsche Bank, one of the top global financial service providers, more recently emphasized bringing in AI, ML and Blockchain techs to built-up its AML frameworks. The stage is the bank's next steps in achieving efficiencies in its compliance, risk detection and transparency across its operations.

Challenges Addressed: Complicated Organizational Structure — Various business lines and global presence provided challenges for consistent AML compliance.

Regulatory audit: There were previous issues with compliance with money laundering, so we took special measures to ensure that it did not happen again.

Data silo: different systems, different data sources led to weak monitoring and analysis.

Processes which placed an enormous burden on compliance departments and came with high manual overheads were particularly labour intensive (this was inefficient and, therefore, expensive).

Designed advanced ML algorithms for multi-dimensional data to identify intricate money laundering transactions.

Integrated data (across transactional, customer and market data) for holistic risk analysis

Anomaly detection: Uses unsupervised learning to pinpoint anomalies and atypical behaviors.

Third-party integrations: Partnered with technology companies, such as Google Cloud, for scalable infrastructure and advanced analytics capabilities.

Advanced (IDP): Intelligent Document Processing:

AppContext: applies AI and NLP to automate the extraction and validation of data from compliance-related customer onboarding documents

Advantages: Decrease in the processing time and errors related to KYC and CDD procedures.

Realizing that determining if we were interacting with an AI system involves exploring complex relationships and hidden connections, some of which may be unlawful, is troubling to us.

Blockchain Platform took part in Marco Polo — a trade finance network implemented on R3 Corda blockchain technology.

Trade Transactions: Provides a foundation for complete end-to-end digitization of the trade processes, resulting in secure and transparent trade transaction management.

AML Advantages:

Immutable Records enhance auditability and compliance by providing records of trade transactions that cannot be changed.

Real-Time Monitoring — Real-time monitoring provides real-time trade activities tracking and validation of such trades to avert the occurrence of trade-based money laundering.

Investigated the viability of using blockchain for digital identity to increase customer verification speed and security.

Self-Sovereign Identity: The first working implementation of the concept whereby customers can control and share their identity information, reducing fraud and easing KYC processes.

It stores and shares sensitive customer information with only the allowed parties in a secured way (Data Security & Privacy).

Unified repository of aggregated data from multiple internal and external sources for comprehensive analysis. → Centralized Data Lake

AI/ML Processing:

Advanced Analytics: The ML models will then process the merged data to detect risks, anomalies, and suspicious networks.

Alerting: Certain high-risk activities can sometimes result in auto alerts; these are weighted using severity and time-to-impact.

Transactions and Verification in Blockchain:

Trade Finance Management: The Marco Polo network ensures secure and transparent exchanges by conducting and recording trade transactions.

Digital Identity Usage: Improving the onboarding experience for customers by using blockchain-based digital identities.

Compliance Review and Action:

Centralized Dashboards- Compliance officers can take advantage of centralized dashboards that merge AI insights and blockchain ledgers, providing the edge necessary for quality decision making.

Investigations and Reporting–Efficient processes allow for thorough investigations and report to regulators.

Ongoing Feedback and Improvement:

Repressor modeling (Data backed outcomes from investigations funnel into AI models for better detection in the future)

Process optimization: Frequent reviews promote continual process improvements in both compliance workflows and technology utilization.

Outcomes and Benefits

More Accurate Risk Detection: AI and ML systems helped the bank identify more complex money laundering, including previously undetected cases.

Operational Efficiency—Automation and use of advanced analytics reduced manual processing times by as much as 35%, freeing up resources for more strategic workloads.

Greater Transparency and Trust: Blockchain implementations enabled shared, incorruptible record upholding trust among the wider network of peers and stakeholders, including regulators.

Enhanced Regulatory Compliance: The integrated model resolved earlier compliance issues, improving regulatory relations, and lowering penalty risks.

Customer Convenience and Security: blockchain-based digital identities streamlined customer interactions, providing faster access to services besides increased data security and privacy.

Contributory benefits: Being part of a blockchain consortium has helped in fostering collaboration with other banks to bring about industry-driven improvements in AML practices.

Conclusion: Deutsche Bank has infused its AI, ML, and Blockchain tech strategy into the AML framework to enhance it with rigorous compliance validation checks while addressing its historical challenges. These results showed the ability of advanced technologies on a transformational scale to fight financial crimes, reducing detection risk, improving operational efficiency and ensuring adherence to regulation.

The top banks, such as HSBC, JPMorgan Chase, Standard Chartered, Banco Santander, and Deutsche Bank, are utilizing AI, ML, and Blockchain technologies in their integration, which are significant indicators of AML strategies. These advanced technologies provide powerful answers to address money laundering, increase operational efficiency, compliance with regulations and improve customer experience. As financial crimes grow in sophistication, the banking industry is under growing pressure to use and advance technology that can help secure the global financial system.

The adoption of AI, ML and Blockchain technologies by major global poker houses has been a milestone in the fight against financial crimes—money laundering. These technologies have allowed banks to further their Anti-Money Laundering (AML) capabilities through better risk identification, operational efficiencies, and the compliance with strengthening regulation. Integration with AI/ML enables processing enormous numbers of records in real-time and detecting intricate patterns or outliers.

As illustrated by the success stories of HSBC, JPMorgan Chase, Standard Chartered Banco Santander and Deutsche Bank — to name just a few — the potential for transformation with these technologies is real. These banks have not only improved their ability to detect money laundering and better prevent fraud, but they have also increased operational efficiency, customer experience and industry size. These institutions are leveraging AI, ML, and Blockchain to enhance compliance and risk management, enabling them to better protect themselves against sophisticated financial crime.

While financial crimes become increasingly sophisticated, deployment of this technology is not only about the adoption of new tech, but its adaptation is imperative. The banking sector must adopt and enhance AI, ML, and Blockchain solutions to protect customers, the integrity of the global financial system, and ensure regulatory compliance.

Five of the top small banks have experimented with, or implemented, machine learning (ML) for credit risk evaluation or management. Each case has a detailed coverage of ML models involved, external solutions or vendors that are applied and internal banks-made deliveries.

1. Credit Risk Management at Starling Bank (UK)

For instance, Starling Bank has created an artificial intelligence-based system "Starling Risk Analyzer" to optimize credit risk management in its digital banking. Starling Bank developed a system called "Starling Risk Analyzer" to assess the solvency of clients seeking loans and credit cards. They designed it specifically for issuing credits to small businesses and freelancers.

Technology Used: Starling Risk Analyzer used GBM for risk scoring and RNN to model time series like day of the week spending and income variation. It also featured the use of Explainable AI (XAI) methods for implementation transparency in decision-making.

Third-Party Solutions: Starling Bank built their own Digital First Bank using external providers like Finicity (a financial data aggregator) for real-time income verification and cash flow analysis. The bank also implemented Amazon Web Services (AWS) for elastic cloud computing and storage of data.

Starling Risk Analyzer saw 20% increase in loan approvals with negligible risk without changing the behavior of bank, but still better ability to assess credit risk for non-traditional customers. The deployment of XAI also improved customer confidence as it led to making the credit decision more visible.

2. Tandem Bank (UK): Credit Scoring using Machine Learning

Tandem Bank used a machine learning-powered credit scoring system called Tandem Score to analyze credit risk for its retail banking customers. It offered real-time credit scoring to underserved customers with little of a track record in borrowing or those with non-standard income sources.

Technology deployed: Tandem Score used Support Vector Machines (SVM) for classification and K-Means Clustering to drive customer segmentation based on risk profiles. Its designers built the system to learn better continuously by adapting to new data.

External solutions: Tandem Bank worked with the FinTech company Plaid to aggregate and analyze the transaction data of customers, enabling greater predictive accuracy for its Tandem Score. Google Cloud AI also served as the infrastructure to deploy their machine learning models and data processing at scale.

Tandem Score made it possible for the bank to lend to customers with non-traditional financial backgrounds. As a result, the bank increased its reach within the market by acquiring 25% more customers without increasing risk; it kept default rates at very low levels.

3. Shinhan Bank Vietnam: Credit Risk Prediction

Shinhan Smart Credit is being used by Shinhan Bank Vietnam for credit risk prediction for small and medium-sized enterprises (SMEs) as a domestic business. The system creators can adjust and improve it to meet the unique needs of lending to small businesses with inconsistent cash flow and limited credit history, making it more user-friendly and efficient.

Methods deployed: Shinhan Smart Credit relied on Random Forest (RF), and Logistic Regression models to assess credit risk. The system also leveraged Natural Language Processing (NLP) to analyze unstructured data from business documents and social media.

Partnership and other options: The bank collaborated with FPT Corporation, a top technology firm in Vietnam, to build machine learning models and implement them. Second, they incorporated data from the country's credit reporting agency, the Vietnam Credit Information Centre (CIC), to improve the accuracy of their credit assessment.

The bank could better predict credit risk for small and medium enterprises, through Shinhan Smart Credit, which led to a 30% decrease in non-performing loans (NPLs) in this segment. This expanded the bank's SME lending portfolio and increased small business growth and inclusion.

4. Metro Bank (UK) — AI in Real-Time Credit Risk Monitoring

Use Case: To manage credit risk across its retail and business banking operations, Metro Bank implemented a real-time credit risk monitoring system called 'MetroAlert'. As part of the system design, developers included continuous monitoring functionality. This feature alerts for high-risk consumer transactions and detects any transformation of benign financial activities into illicit behavior.

Technology used: MetroAlert used Convolutional Neural Networks (CNNs) for feature extraction and auto encoders for abnormality detection on the client transaction data. The system further employed Time-Series Analysis to recognize trends or patterns can form the basis for credit risk.

Solution developed with an external company: Metro Bank worked with Experian to enrich their credit scoring data and incorporate it into MetroAlert. The bank also employed Azure Machine Learning to distribute their AI models, as well as handling the system's real-time data streaming requirements.

Benefits:

The MetroAlert solution empowered Metro Bank to identify early indications of financial difficulty in its customer base, enabling the banking business to take early interventions, including loan restructurings and heightened monitoring. A proactive initiative that resulted in a **25% decrease** in the volume of loan defaults and drastically improved the bank's general risk governance.

5. Capitec Bank (South Africa): Hybrid ML for Credit Risk Assessment

Capitec Bank: Capitalizing on "The new incumbents" by developing a hybrid machine learning model to assess credit risk at scale within their rapidly expanding client base — Capitec Rick Guard By integrating long-accepted credit scoring techniques with sophisticated machine learning, the model could increase its predictive precision.

Capitec Rick Gaurd used a hybrid approach for technology implementation. They first employed XGBoost to short-list features in the initial stage, and then built a deep learning model using TensorFlow's Deep Neural Networks (DNNs) to capture non-linear relationships within the data.

Enterprise Solutions: Capitec Bank incorporated data from TransUnion to improve its credit scoring models. The bank also has a partnership with H2O.ai for automatic machine learning with hyperparameter tuning, which it used to optimize its Capitec Rick Guard.

What happened: Implementing Capitec Rick Guard resulted in a 15% increase in loan approval rates for low-risk customers, and we discovered that the default rate decreased by 10%. Benefits include a higher loan approval rate and a lower default rate.

Here are a few cases that show how machine learning and AI have had an impact on credit risk management for small banks. Incorporating internal solutions and leveraging external technologies improved these banks' financial position and enabled better credit risk assessment, allowing them to provide loans to a broader customer base.

A brief introduction on how machine learning has reformatted the bank's credit risk management, including its use-cases and more. Financial institutions have long favoured traditional credit risk models, such as logistic regression and decision trees. However, such models often cannot capture the complexity of modern financial data, which is non-linear and high-dimensional.

The paper introduces a new hybrid model that combines Convolutional Neural Networks (CNNs) with traditional machine learning algorithms, such as Support Vector Machines (SVM), Random Forest (RF), and Decision Trees (DT). This hybrid method makes the best use of CNNs for feature extraction and traditional models for classification, hence enhancing both the prediction accuracy and model robustness in credit risk predictions.

JP Morgan Chase and Starling Bank are two of banks around the world that have been able to show the benefits of using ML in credit risk management. This is because they have homegrown solutions that are tailormade for the requirements, besides opening to leverage external technologies and partnerships to fill their gaps.

In short, implementing ML and AI into credit risk management are entirely reshaping how banks observe and unwanted risks. Results show that integrating models and actual examples provides a more accurate prediction of outcomes, besides rooted insights for proactive risk management strategies. Adopting the notions and developing these technologies will help financial institutions navigate volatile economies, hedge portfolios and play their role in an ever-increasing speedy economic environment.

Reference – Further reading - Chapter 5

An end-to-end solution suite designed to meet your specific compliance and business requirements
https://www.oracle.com/financial-services/aml-financial-crime-compliance/
FICO - tonbeller-suite
https://fico.gcs-web.com/news-releases/news-release-details/idc-marketscape-names-fico-tonbeller-leader-aml-kyc
Address complex financial crimes with our end-to-end anti-money laundering (AML) compliance solution that monitors the entire customer life cycle
https://www.sas.com/en_us/software/anti-money-laundering.html
Dow Jones Risk & Compliance: Data and Risk Management
https://www.dowjones.com/professional/risk/
The leader in AI-driven fraud and AML risk detection
https://complyadvantage.com/
Pega KYC Solutions
https://www.pega.com/industries/financial-services/know-your-customer
Contextual Decision Intelligence for AML
https://www.quantexa.com/assets/x/670c53045c/solution-brief-contextual-monitoring_fincrime-final.pdf
Anti-money Laundering (AML) in Cryptocurrency
https://www.elliptic.co/anti-money-laundering-aml-in-cryptocurrency
Top 10 AML software for banks
https://complyadvantage.com/insights/top-aml-software-for-banks/
Navigate complex AML compliance challenges at any point in the customer lifecycle
https://risk.lexisnexis.com/anti-money-laundering

SIX

Using AI in Wealth Management

Introduction

Wealth management Banking includes a complete service that will provide private financial planning and drive investment for the high-net-worth people (HNWIs). This specific includes a headache free range associated with tailored financial solutions to help our clients to grow, manage and protect your prosperity. These services may cover:

Investment Management Providing clients with customized strategies, including equities, fixed income (bonds), global mutual funds and alternatives designed to meet our client's overall portfolio objective relative to risk tolerance and financial objectives.

1. **Financial Planning:**

A detailed plan that captures all our clients' financial goals, as well retirement planning, tax efficiency, estate planning and cash flow management.

Trust and estate services include help with estate planning, Trusts & Inheritance strategies for Wealth Transfer for future generation.

Tax Advisory Providing tactics to LinkedIn trying to reduce tax liabilities in a client's wider financial plan

Insurance Solutions: This would include life insurance, long-term care insurances and other products to transfer financial risks.

Philanthropic Advisory: Assisting clients with how they give their money away to achieve strategic initiatives (such as setting up a foundation for organized giving) or if it is tax planning sensitive.

Banks provide wealth management services through a private client services department or a platform for affluent clients with the expectation of investible assets over a certain threshold. The offering brings together financial, investment, legal and tax advice to provide comprehensive wealth preservation and promotion strategies according to individual requirements.

2. AI tools for Wealth Managers

Thanks to AI, wealth managers are now using the advanced technology as an indispensable aid in improving their capacity to deliver personalized financial advice, optimize investment portfolios and boost operational aspects within the firm. Wealth managers use AI-powered tools like Robo-advisors, predictive analytics & natural language processing in market analysis to big data for providing timely and accurate result-oriented investment suggestions. For example, through processing and synthesizing unstructured data combined with an understanding of the client's individuality, AI allows wealth managers to provide personalized advice that is best suited for each specific client's unique needs and wants.

Risk management and compliance also represent functions to which AI has multiple applications in wealth management. This is where wealth managers can use AI to identify risks, monitor market volatility, and adherence to compliance with regulations. This reduces the danger of costly mistakes and made available a much better economical motion.

Artificial Intelligence (AI) is no longer merely a technological fad in wealth management but an atomic force that has been reconfiguring the industry in multiple ways. This offers IT automation implementation from client's engagement enhancement to the automation of complex investment strategies with manifold AI influences. In this article, we look at how AI is increasingly being employed to automate and enhance wealth management processes — in terms of operational efficiency, client personalization, regulatory compliance and more — from both a financial technology perspective (FinTech) and financial services horizon.

1. AI in Wealth Management

The financial services and wealth management have seen decades of humanness and relationships. Yet, the way AI has transformed operations into existing wealth management firms is rewriting expectations on what data-driven insights and automation can do up to this point. Ninety-eight percent

(98%) of financial advisors say artificial intelligence (AI) is changing the way they give, and clients receive advice, according to Accenture.

2. Improving Client Engagement and Personalization

Personalized Client Experience on Scale:

Perhaps the most transformative impact that AI has had on wealth management is its capacity to generate personalized client experiences… at scale. Wealth management has historically been relationship-driven, requiring personalized advice and client engagement. Wealth managers can leverage AI to further this connection by offering personalized services crafted around granular client profiles.

2.1 AI-Driven Client Insights

Machine learning, natural language processing or other AI technologies are used to analyze volumes of client data such as transaction histories, behavioral patterns and financial goals, to name the least. These insights enable wealth managers to understand client needs better and provide individualized investment recommendations that are in line with their financial goals. Morgan Stanley offers the Next Best Action (NBA) tool that uses AI to deliver individualized recommendations to advisors about clients. → Option 1 It interprets a wide variety of datasets and makes use of market trends and customer information.

2.2 AI Communication Tools

AI-based communication tools — chatbots or virtual assistants have become the norm in wealth management. This functionality includes dealing with standard customer communications, answering routine questions, and giving basic financial advice. For instance, Erica is Bank of America's AI-powered virtual assistant that assists clients in managing their finances by giving individualized advice, answering questions and tips based on user behavior.

AI helps wealth managers provide personalized, consistent service to their clients over time and across channels, which increases both client satisfaction and client loyalty. Artificial intelligence is currently freeing up human advisors from repetitive tasks, allowing them to spend more time on advanced services such as developing personalized financial strategies and building stronger client relationships.

3. Investment Strategies and Portfolio Management

The scope of AI in investment strategy and well as portfolio management is also absolutely transformative. Conventional investment management uses historical data, human evaluation, and manual analysis. Unlike these more traditional tools, AI-driven tools significantly enhance portfolio management by allowing wealth managers to alter strategies on the fly and optimize investments through actual data.

Artificial intelligence is also reshaping portfolio management by its ability to process and analyze enormous data sets at speeds that humans simply cannot compete with. The combination of predictive analytics and AI makes for an even more powerful tool for the wealth manager. Predictive Analytics Technologies Let Wealth Managers Who Use It Forecast Market Movements, Help Identify Opportunities for Investment and Allocations while optimizing assets. J.P. Morgan, for a more concrete example, J.P. Morgan uses AI and machine learning based algorithms to analyze market data, economic indicators, and even client behavior patterns to offer much more accurate and up-to-date investment recommendations.

Wealth Tech Generative AI is another technology that is causing quite a few ripples in the wealth management world. Generative AI merges information from many sources, including financial news, market reports, and social media, to create new insights or investment ideas. It helps the wealth managers to track market trends and make better investment decisions.

4. Digital Wealth Management

Robo-advisors: The most famous application of Artificial Intelligence in investment management. Automated investment advice, powered by AI, these platforms deliver automated advice based on algorithms that consider your risk level, goals and market conditions. Consumer banking platform Marcus, part of Goldman Sachs, has leveraged AI to bring automation into wealth management aspects; delivering automated investment management and providing access to advanced investment strategies for all.

AI in portfolio management has its own obvious perks. For wealth managers, AI-driven tools also allow them to adjust their investment strategies in real-time, drive positive alpha at the portfolio level, and mitigate the risk of errors through human intervention. AI efficiently automates routine investment tasks, which allows wealth managers to concentrate on strategic activities, such as creating long-term investment plans and discovering new market opportunities.

Another change to the investment landscape has been Robo-advisors, which provide automated portfolio management and personalized investing advice. Rebalancing tools that periodically rely on AI to adjust the composition of portfolios based on market conditions to keep them in line with the goals and risk appetite of investors.

Read Chapter: Robo-Advisor 4.0

5. Automating Risk Management and Compliance

Importance of risk management and compliance in Wealth Management: How AI is solving it? AI can monitor and analyze huge flows of data in real-time continuously, taking human action where necessary, and is thus a central tool for monitoring risk and compliance.

AI-Driven Risk Monitoring

Artificial intelligence (AI) algorithms can passively monitor the sentiment of markets, economic indicators and financial news in real-time; they detect potential risks long before they materialize. This helps wealth managers reduce the risks and protect the investments of their clients. UBS, for instance, is using AI to improve its risk management by analyzing market data and identifying early warning signals of market volatility.

AI-based risk management tools can help wealth managers optimize their portfolios by making the right adjustments to investment strategies in line with shifting market conditions. This active risk management serves to not only enhance portfolio performance but also reduces the chance of large losses in volatile market conditions.

Compliance Automation

Next one is about compliance; AI Regulations in the financial services industry have grown ever more complex and will continue to do so over time; firms wanting to adhere to requirements to ensure they operate within the letter of the law. AI automates the monitoring of new regulatory changes but can also ensure investment strategies comply with the latest set of rules.

For example, AI applications can read through vast numbers of laws and regulations, identify material changes and flag compliance issues for humans to review in more detail. Regulatory breaches and enabling wealth management firms to operate more confidently and transparently.

This offers immense advantages to AI in risk management and compliance. Automating these processes aids not only in better efficiency and accuracy of risk management but can also reduce costs otherwise associated with compliance. Artificial intelligence (AI) by nature will entail greater precision and enable wealth managers to identify risks more effectively, which supports them to take informed decisions that protect the assets of their clients in a better way.

5. Addressing Ethical Considerations and Challenges

Though AI in wealth management provides enormous advantages but it also triggers several ethical challenges: These challenges are the "black box" nature of AI, data privacy issues and the demand for transparency and accountability in algorithms.

The Black Box Problem

One of the biggest ethical issues regarding machine learning comes from the black box, and it is that we do not really know how they get into their decisions. The AI recommendations' "black box" nature could leave wealth managers and clients in the dark about the reason behind a particular piece of advice. The lack of transparency in building these systems will cause issues with trust and adoption.

This means wealth management firms need to continue deploying machine learning but must choose machine learning models that are explainable and offer transparent explanations for why a decision it is making. Doing this will bring forth a heightened state of comfort to AI-driven tools, alleviating consumers' uncertainty regarding the validity of recommendations by these imaging systems.

Data Privacy and Security

Another major issue is data privacy, notably when it comes to the confidentiality of financial details. Data governance is a critical control wealth management firms are required to put in place to protect their client data and comply with privacy regulations. This includes responsibility for the curation of AI systems, control of data, and securing against unwanted access or breaches.

While data privacy adheres to GDPR rules, designing AI systems biased towards ethical aspects is necessary. We need to ensure that the algorithms used to power AI are not biased and work fairly, transparently, and accountably to address this. Addressing these ethical challenges will guarantee that any AI-based functionality built or integrated into the provision of financial advice becomes an enabler and a tool, rather than being another obstacle in its way through regulation.

REAL-WORLD IMPLEMENTATION AND FUTURE PERSPECTIVE

1- J.P. Morgan

Case Study–Portfolio Management: KNOW YOUR CLIENT (KYC)

Tech Deployed: J.P. Morgan uses AI and machine learning algorithms to assess data from a wide range of sources — market data, economic indicators, and client behavior. The bank's AI platform, COiN (Contract Intelligence), helps in the interpretation and processing of financial agreements.

Benefits: J.P. Morgan has used AI-driven portfolio management to better tailor its investment ideas, according to the bank, while Lex says clients have seen improved outcomes. The technology also enables advisors to deliver more personalized recommendations, leading to better client relationships and overall satisfaction.

2- Morgan Stanley

Case Study: Next Best Action (NBA) Tool for Financial Advisors

Tech Used: deliver personalized recommendations to clients by leveraging machine learning algorithms that crunch data inside Morgan Stanley's NBA tool. Using this data and a variety of additional information from client portfolios, market trends, and economic forecasts, the technology provides helpful advice.

Benefits: Financial advisors have achieved better client retention and higher client satisfaction scores by offering more personalized, timely advice thanks to the NBA tool. This has also improved efficiency by reducing the research and analysis time spent by advisors.

3- Goldman Sachs

Use case: Marcus by Goldman Sachs offers automated investment management

Tech Used: Goldman Sachs has leveraged AI and machine learning within its consumer banking arm, Marcus, to deliver a Robo-advising service. The AI platform tailors investment strategies to meet individual client needs and risk tolerance.

Benefits: This has levelled the investment playing field by bringing affordable sophisticated investment strategies (previously available only to high-net-worth individuals) to all. It has even simplified the investment side, making it cheaper and more scale able.

4- UBS

Case Study 1: AI Risk Management and Compliance

Tech Used: UBS uses AI & machine learning algorithms to watch its exposure and risk in various sector concentrations within its wealth management portfolios. The bank employs AI and machine learning to assess market information and identify earlier signs of risk, and to meet regulatory requirements.

Benefit: The AI-driven risk management system has improved the bank's ability to mitigate risks, reducing the potential for financial losses. It has also enhanced compliance by automating monitoring regulatory changes, ensuring that the bank's operations remain within legal frameworks.

5- Bank of America (Merrill Lynch)

Use Case Erica- AI based Financial Advisory

Tech Used: Bank of America's virtual assistant, Erica, leverages AI, machine learning and natural language processing to give clients financial advice. With Erica, labs explore users' financial patterns on an account-by-account basis and suggest potential opportunities from a financial action perspective based on their sway.

Benefits: Erica increased Client Engagement by delivering instant and personalized financial advice to clients. This means that human advisors have a lighter load, as they spend less time on easier client requests and more time on complex ones. This results in overall practice efficiency, better results, and happier clients.

6- Investec

Use Case: Improved Client Services and Portfolio Management

Tech Used: Investec uses AI and Machine Learning to analyze client data and market trends, providing individual investment insights. AI tools at the bank predict market movements and help adjust portfolios.

Benefits: By integrating AI, Investec has offered a more tailored investment advice, increasing client satisfaction and engagement. It has also been a boon for portfolio performance in volatile markets as the strategy appears to have a wonderful ability to react to market changes.

7- BBVA

Personalized Wealth Management Solutions Use Case

Tech Used: To offer personalized wealth management services to its clients, BBVA uses AI platform. Its AI tools analyze customer data, market conditions and economic indicators in seconds to create custom financial plans.

Benefits: By embedding AI, it has become possible to scale their wealth management offering and deliver more bespoke advice to a wider group of clients. Which has led to higher client retention rates and AUM growth.

8- CIBC FirstCaribbean

Case Study: AI-Powered Client Advisory & Risk Management

Tech Used: CIBC FirstCaribbean Applies AI For Better Investment Advice

By Analyzing Customer Behavior & AI also overseen Financial Targets To Offer Tailored Investment Suggestions The activities of monitoring the performance of the portfolio and optimizing strategy (with a view to risk management).

Benefits: The AI tools have significantly increased the accuracy of financial advice, subsequently enhancing client outcomes. It has reduced the bank's market volatility exposer and hence it is also a risk management machine for the bank, which as a safer investment, returns more stable profits on behalf of clients.

David Solomon, CEO of Goldman Sachs, highlighted the growing demand for AI in wealth management stating:

> *"As this technology develops, there will be a significant demand for AI-related infrastructure, helping firms deliver more personalized and efficient wealth management services."* He emphasized how AI enhances client insights and investment strategies, allowing firms to stay competitive in a developing market (Financial Planning).

Andrew Beatty, Head of Wealth at FIS, spoke about the potential of AI in portfolio development and client management, explaining,

> *"AI tools like robo-advisors have emerged as invaluable assets for tailoring investment strategies and optimizing risk management."* He also stressed the importance of maintaining transparency in AI-driven decisions to build client trust (FinTech circle).

Kimberly Richards, Managing Director at Accenture, discussed the role of AI in enhancing operational efficiency, noting that

> *"AI-driven automation can improve workflows by automating tasks such as portfolio rebalancing and compliance reporting, allowing wealth managers to focus more on personalized client engagement." Richards also emphasized the need for organizations to maintain client relevance by updating their AI strategies to ensure long-term value (Accenture Capital Markets Blog).*

In conclusion, the use of AI in wealth management is reshaping the industry by driving operational efficiency, enhancing client engagement, and offering personalized investment strategies. Financial leaders from Goldman Sachs and FIS highlight the importance of AI tools like robo-advisors and predictive analytics. These tools are invaluable for personalizing investment portfolios, automating tasks, and optimizing risk management (FinTech Circle, Financial Planning). Integrating AI enables wealth managers to provide more accurate and data-driven advice, democratizing access to personalized services reserved for high-net-worth clients (Citi).

However, the adoption of AI also brings challenges regarding transparency, regulatory compliance, and addressing biases within AI models. Ensuring that AI systems are explainable and fair is crucial for maintaining trust with clients (Oliver Wyman). The success of AI relies on balancing human expertise with AI-driven insights, enabling wealth managers to improve performance and comply with ethical and regulatory standards (Citi, FinTech Circle).

The future of AI in wealth management is promising, offering the potential for transformative growth, but it requires a careful approach that prioritizes both innovation and responsibility.

Reference – Further reading - Chapter 6

AI in wealth management: All systems go
https://www.accenture.com/us-en/insights/capital-markets/wealth-management-artificial-intelligence-all-systems-go

Can Generative AI Spark Innovation in Asset and Wealth Management – KPMG
https://kpmg.com/kpmg-us/content/dam/kpmg/pdf/2023/generative-ai-asset-management.pdf

Client experience – the new differentiator driving performance in wealth management
https://www.thewealthmosaic.com/vendors/corfinancial/news/client-experience-the-new-differentiator-driving-p/

2023 EY Global Wealth Research Report
https://www.ey.com/en_gl/wealth-management-research

AI is transforming asset and wealth management
https://www.pwc.com/gx/en/issues/c-suite-insights/the-leadership-agenda/ai-and-wealth-management-a-new-era.html

The AI Assembly at Wealth Management EDGE: The Future of AI
https://www.wealthmanagement.com/wealthstack/ai-assembly-wealth-management-edge-future-ai

Client experience tool kit in wealth management
https://issuu.com/thewealthmosaic.com/docs/twm_client_experience_toolkit_2024_edition_1_sing?fr=sNGUyMzY1ODY3NjM

BCG - AI and the Next Wave of Transformation
https://web-assets.bcg.com/78/f0/82b96e174fffb219f9f73177a3f0/2024-gam-report-may-2024.pdf

McKinsey - Digital and AI-enabled wealth management: The big potential in Asia
https://www.mckinsey.com/industries/financial-services/our-insights/digital-and-ai-enabled-wealth-management-the-big-potential-in-asia

The evolution of wealth management through AI
https://blogs.deloitte.ch/banking/2024/04/the-evolution-of-wealth-management-through-ai.html

JPMorgan is developing a ChatGPT-like A.I. service that gives investment advice
https://www.cnbc.com/2023/05/25/jpmorgan-develops-ai-investment-advisor.html

Inside Morgan Stanley's Big AI Test for Advisors
https://www.thinkadvisor.com/2023/07/24/inside-morgan-stanleys-big-ai-test/

Goldman Sachs AI on the Future
https://am.gs.com/en-us/institutions/insights/article/2023/an-ai-on-the-future

Sizing and seizing the AI investment opportunity
https://www.ubs.com/global/en/wealth-management/insights/chief-investment-office/house-view/daily/2024/latest-11062024.html
Embracing the real-world AI revolution - transforming financial services
https://www.investec.com/en_gb/focus/innovation/embracing-the-real-world-ai-revolution-transforming-financial-services.html
The Pursuit of AI-Driven Wealth Management
https://sloanreview.mit.edu/article/the-pursuit-of-ai-driven-wealth-management/

SEVEN

AI in loan origination

Introduction

The Artificial Intelligence (AI) revolution is one of the most progressive shifts in an array of industries, including banking. Perhaps one of the most significant examples of how AI is being applied in meaningful ways is through loan origination, used by banks to assess and approve or decline loan applications. In the past, loan origination was a slow and manual process that required copious documentation, very strict credit assessment and multiple layers of review that were largely done by people. Now, though, thanks to AI, banks can streamline these processes — improving efficiency, accuracy and ensuring customer satisfaction.

Ready to transform lending? Experience the revolution of AI in loan origination, improving speed, enhancing accuracy, boosting efficiency. Click below to learn more or get in touch with us soon to check our latest insights on how AI-driven tools will help fast-track your operations and make better lending decisions.

In the loan application, property dealers or agents must prepare, which will require them to follow a systematic process to make sure they are properly gathering all important documents and information. The property dealers need to prepare an application in the below steps, and fill out a Uniform Residential Loan Application (Form 1003) along with the loan borrower:

Here is the process that property dealers need to follow while making a loan application: -

1. Initial Interview with the Borrower

Collecting Basic Information: Talk about the financial status, requirements, and plans of your borrower.

Describe the Loan Process: summarize what to expect when applying for a loan, as well as what information and how long this process will take.

2. Pre-Qualification:

Step 2. Collect financial information: Read the borrower's problems about income, debt and credit score.

Estimate Borrowing Capacity — Estimate the amount the borrower might borrow given what you know about them.

3. Documentation Collection:

Verification of income: Gather pay stubs, tax returns and employment verification.

Gather bank statements, investment accounts and other asset documentation.

Debt and Liability Documentation: records of the current debt, such as credit card statements, loan statements, etc.

Filling Out Form 1003 (Uniform Residential Loan Application)

Enter the borrower's bio data, including their social security number, name, and marital status.

Employment Details: Include all current and past jobs with employer names, addresses and dates.

Income & Housing: Capture the borrower's income, housing-expense and other income sources.

List all assets and liabilities, such should as bank accounts and real estate owned, outstanding loans.

Loan and Property Information -Details of the loan that is being applied for and the property which are being purchased or refinance also needed.

4. Supporting Documentation:

Credit Report—the borrower's credit history & score.

Appraisal: Set An Appraisal to Find Out How Much The Home Is Worth

Title Report — Take a Title report to verify the legal history of the property.

5. Review and Submission:

Double-check your application: Verify the information to ensure accuracy and check restrictions accurately.

Borrower's Signature: The borrower should sign the completed Form 1003, as well as any other necessary forms.

Here, in this process, you submit the completed loan application and support documents to the Lender for processing.

6. Follow-Up:

Stay in touch with the Lender: Keep contacting the lender to follow up on your loan status and provide any information they ask you for.

Inform Borrower: let the borrower know if any additional steps will be necessary in order to expedite the home loan process.

This section has outlined the simple steps a property dealer should take to prepare their loan application rigorously, improving the probability of an efficient approval process.

Top 5 Banks in Asia (Use Cases)

1. Industrial and Commercial Bank of China (ICBC): AI-Based Credit Risk Assessment

For example, the largest bank in China, ICBC uses AI to transform its credit risk assessment process. Endowed with AI, ICBC is now better assessing the credibility of loan applicants while speeding up loan application processing time and delivering better risk assessments.

AI Integration in Credit Risk Assessment: ICBC incorporates FICO Score, and Trans Union's Credit Vision for AI based credit risk assessment. They analyze a wide range of data points that extend to traditional credit, behavioral, and alternative data sources. This then makes a more exact determination of credit risk by using the AI models to gauge the probability of default.

Results: The AI-driven credit risk assessment led to a 35% decrease in loan processing time at ICBC. The bank has also experienced a reduction in non-performing loans, as the AI models allow for much more accurate risk assessment. This has enabled ICBC to grow its loan business while keeping it safe.

2. Streamlining Document Processing Using AI — China Construction Bank (CCB)

China Construction Bank (CCB) enhanced its loan origination document processing workflow with AI to minimize human error and expedite processing time. It has helped CCB to work faster and offer a CCB service for its clients.

Document Processing with AI CCB leverages AI-driven platforms such as Ocrolus, HyperScience etc., to automate data classification, extraction and validation from loan documents. CCB utilizes these tools to enable the accurate and complete capture of all required information, helping to minimize the need for manual reviews and reducing potential errors.

CCB has brought in AI for document processing, which has resulted in time savings of 45 per cent. In addition, the bank has realized better compliance in terms of rules and regulations standards after using AI since the tools are equipped to handle documents with accurate consistency. This has increased customer service levels and operational efficiencies overall.

3. Mitsubishi UFJ Financial Group (MUFG) – Augmenting Property Valuation with AI

By implementing AI in the property valuation process, MUFG – one of Japan's largest financial institutions – can both improve accuracy and significantly decrease the time it takes to evaluate properties. By utilizing AI-powered tools, MUFG enhanced loan origination efficiency at its disposal.

Where AI Enters: MUFG uses AI software such as HouseCanary and Reggora to automate its property appraisal workflow. It has tools that offer data-driven valuations, can automate the order process, and deliver appraisal reports quickly. Appraisal review - AI models ensuring the appraisal data are compliant with market standards and loan requirements

Outcome: The utilization of AI in conducting property appraisal has helped MUFG to cut the time required for appraisals by 40%, as a result which allows the bank to reduce loan turnaround times. Additionally, better property valuation accuracy results in improved loan portfolio quality and ultimately less risk associated with over- or under-valuing assets.

4. State Bank of India (SBI) — AI Powered Income and Employment Verification

Using AI to verify income and employment for improved approval rates — State Bank of India (SBI has begun replacing people with machine learning processes in the origination of loans, resulting in better and faster credit decisions. Automating this important step has allowed SBI to better evaluate borrower eligibility as well protect itself from the risk of fraud.

Machine Learning for Income and Employment Verification: SBI has deployed several platforms, including Truework and Equifax Verification Services, that leverage machine learning to automate the verification of income and employment. Real-time verification by collecting and analyzing data from different sources such as payroll providers and financial institutions. AI models assess the credit risk of employment in the applicant pool, along with how reliable their job is.

Outcome: With AI driven Income and employment verification SBI has been able to cut down the time taken for verification by 30%, which eventually helped increase accuracy while assessing a borrower by up to 20%. It has allowed the bank to approve loans faster as well as helped in cutting down fraudulent loan applications, thereby improving its operational efficiency.

5. DBS Bank – AI-Based Automation for Debt-To-Income Ratio Calculation

Singapore-based DBS Bank, the largest bank in Southeast Asia had employed AI to automate computing the debt-to-income (DTI) ratio in loan origination. An addition of an AI feature to its solution led DBS to surpass traditional methods for calculation DTi, thereby boosting accuracy and increasing risk interpretation on borrowers.

AI tools, such as Plaid and Mint by Intuit, allow DBS Bank to consolidate debt data on a borrower and compare it against the income levels of that borrower to compute the debt-to-income ratio. The AI-powered platforms keep a tab on all the debts by segregating them, which in turn allows lenders to have complete details of how much the borrower owes. The DTI ratio is then worked out by the AI models, making sure it complies with bank lending criteria.

Conclusions An AI powered DTI ratio calculation improved the accuracy of risk prediction during DBS surgery by a 25%. The bank has also decreased loan processing time by 20%, allowing for quicker approval and improved customer service. This has firmly established DBS as one of the early movers in using AI for accurate loan origination process.

Across the banking industry, loan origination processes have largely been transformed thanks to the integration of Artificial Intelligence (AI). AI-driven solutions also help banks to automate repetitive tasks, optimize workflows, improve compliance with business rules and internal policies, achieve near-optimal accuracy levels and refined risk management technique—all aimed at simplifying the transactional process and customer experience. Examples from the leading banks in Asia — ICBC, CCB, MUFG, SBI or DBS show how AI brings optimization into multiple parts of loan origination process. These consist of aspects such as credit risk appraisal, document hunting, funds evaluation of assets, property valuation and income proof accompanied by DTI calculation.

The move to automated AI functionality is another stride in FinTech, as banks are increasingly integrating it into the finance space. A move that means a substitution of classical means, for modern tools such as machine learning, data analytics and automation. AI-Based Credit Risk Assessment: Banks are now able to make more financially independent lending decisions, all in spite of use of AI far ahead in recent time. This has led to lower default rates and higher loan portfolio quality.

The AI-powered income and employment verification has helped accelerate the process and lowered fraud risk of loan applications — a necessity to maintain lending integrity. This has allowed banks to more accurately assess the risk involved in providing credit to a broad spectrum of customers —

meaning lower risk without having to forego credit granting.

The combined experiences of these leading Asian banks underscores how AI is central to the banking sector as a key driver of innovation. Growing AI technologies are likely to make banks an increasingly bigger player in loan origination, providing new avenues for outperformance on efficiency, accuracy and customer satisfaction. For financial institutions, adopting AI and incorporating it into routine process, will offer them a unique selling proposition in the new age of global finance.

To sum up, the implementation of AI with loan origination is more than just a technological uplift but a change in bank logic. With this, it leads to a more efficient and accurate etc. loan practices which help the bank as well as their customers. AI is going to be a key driver in the future of banking as the financial sector evolves and further innovations are made in service delivery.

Top 5 Banks in Asia Use Cases

1. Industrial and Commercial Bank of China (ICBC): AI-Based Credit Risk Assessment

For example, the largest bank in China, ICBC uses AI to transform its credit risk assessment process. Endowed with AI, ICBC is now better assessing the credibility of loan applicants while speeding up loan application processing time and delivering better risk assessments.

AI Integration in Credit Risk Assessment: ICBC incorporates FICO Score, and Trans Union's Credit Vision for AI based credit risk assessment. They analyze a wide range of data points that extend to traditional credit, behavioural, and alternative data sources. This then makes a more exact determination of credit risk by using the AI models to gauge the probability of default.

Results: The AI-driven credit risk assessment led to a 35% decrease in loan processing time at ICBC. The bank has also experienced a reduction in non-performing loans, as the AI models allow for much more accurate risk assessment. This has enabled ICBC to grow its loan business while keeping it safe.

2. Streamlining Document Processing Using AI — China Construction Bank (CCB)

China Construction Bank (CCB) enhanced its loan origination document processing workflow with AI in order to minimize human error and expedite processing time. It has helped CCB to work faster and offer a CCB service for its clients.

Document Processing with AI CCB leverages AI-driven platforms such as Ocrolus, HyperScience etc., to automate data classification, extraction and validation from loan documents. CCB utilizes these tools to enable the accurate and complete capture of all required information, helping to minimize the need for manual reviews and reducing potential errors.

CCB has brought in AI for document processing, which has resulted in time savings of 45 per cent. In addition, the bank has realized better compliance in terms of rules and regulations standards after using AI since the tools are equipped to handle documents with accurate consistency. This has increased customer service levels and operational efficiencies overall.

3. These Will Be Mitsubishi UFJ Financial Group (MUFG) – Augmenting Property Valuation with AI

By implementing AI in the property valuation process, MUFG – one of Japan's largest financial institutions – can both improve accuracy and significantly decrease the time it takes to evaluate properties. On utilizing AI-powered tools, MUFG enhanced loan origination efficiency at its disposal.

Where AI Enters: MUFG uses AI software such as HouseCanary and Reggora to automate its property appraisal workflow. It has tools that offer data-driven valuations, can automate the order process, and deliver appraisal reports quickly. Appraisal review - AI models ensuring the appraisal data are compliant with market standards and loan requirements.

Outcome: The utilization of AI in conducting property appraisal has helped MUFG to cut the time required for appraisals by 40%, as a result which allows the bank to reduce loan turnaround times. Additionally, better property valuation accuracy results in improved loan portfolio quality and ultimately less risk associated with over- or under-valuing assets.

4. State Bank of India (SBI) — AI Powered Income and Employment

Verification

Using AI to verify income and employment for improved approval rates — State Bank of India (SBI has begun replacing people with machine learning processes in the origination of loans, resulting in better and faster credit decisions. Automating this important step has allowed SBI to better evaluate borrower eligibility as well protect itself from the risk of fraud.

Machine Learning for Income and Employment Verification: SBI has deployed several platforms, including Truework and Equifax Verification Services, that leverage machine learning to automate the verification of income and employment. Real-time verification by collecting and analyzing data from different sources such as payroll providers, financial institutions. AI models assess the credit risk of employment in the applicant pool, along with how reliable their job is.

Outcome: With AI driven Income and employment verification SBI has been able to cut down the time taken for verification by 30% which eventually helped increase accuracy while assessing a borrower by up to 20%. It has allowed the bank to approve loans faster as well helped in cutting down fraudulent loan applications, thereby improving its operational efficiency.

5. DBS Bank – AI-Based Automation for Debt-To-Income Ratio Calculation

Singapore-based DBS Bank, the largest bank in Southeast Asia had employed AI to automate computing the debt-to-income (DTI) ratio in loan origination. An addition of an AI feature to its solution led DBS to surpass traditional methods for calculation DTi, thereby boosting accuracy and increasing risk interpretation on borrowers.

AI tools, such as Plaid and Mint by Intuit, allow DBS Bank to consolidate debt data on a borrower and compare it against the income levels of that borrower to compute the debt-to-income ratio. The AI-powered platforms keep a tab on all the debts by segregating them, which in turn allows lenders to have complete details of how much the borrower owes. The DTI ratio is then worked out by the AI models, making sure it complies with bank lending criteria.

Conclusions An AI powered DTI ratio calculation improved the accuracy of risk prediction during DBS surgery by a 25%. The bank has also decreased loan processing time by 20%, allowing for quicker approval and improved customer service. This has firmly established DBS as one of the early movers in using AI for accurate loan origination process.

Across the banking industry, loan origination processes have largely been transformed thanks to the integration of Artificial Intelligence (AI). AI-driven solutions also help banks to automate repetitive tasks, optimize workflows, improve compliance with business rules and internal policies, achieve near-optimal accuracy levels and refined risk management technique—all aimed at simplifying the transactional process and customer experience. Examples from the leading banks in Asia — ICBC, CCB, MUFG, SBI or DBS show how AI brings optimization into multiple parts of loan origination process. These consist of aspects such as credit risk appraisal, document hunting, funds evaluation of assets, property valuation and income proof accompanied by DTI calculation.

The move to automated AI functionality is another stride in FinTech, as banks are increasingly integrating it into the finance space. A move that means a substitution of classical means, for modern tools such as machine learning, data analytics and automation. AI-Based Credit Risk Assessment: Banks are now able to make more financially independent lending decisions, all in spite of use of AI far ahead in recent time. This has led to lower default rates and higher loan portfolio quality.

The AI-powered income and employment verification has helped accelerate the process and lowered fraud risk of loan applications — a necessity to maintain lending integrity. This has allowed banks to more accurately assess the risk involved in providing credit to a broad spectrum of customers — meaning lower risk without having to forego credit granting.

The combined experiences of these leading Asian banks underscores how AI is central to the banking sector as a key driver of innovation. Growing AI technologies are likely to make banks an increasingly bigger player in loan origination, providing new avenues for outperformance on efficiency, accuracy and customer satisfaction. For financial institutions, adopting AI and incorporating it into routine process, will offer them a unique selling proposition in the new age of global finance.

To sum up, the implementation of AI with loan origination is more than just a technological uplift but a change in bank logic. With this, it leads to a more efficient and accurate etc. loan practices which help the bank as well as their customers. AI is going to be a key driver in the future of banking as the financial sector evolves and further innovations are made in service delivery.

Through AI virtual assistants or chatbots

A convey Chatbot Series: AI-virtual assistant capable of answering client questions, capturing application information and support borrowers during the loan application process (Amelia by IPsoft)

IBM Watson Assistant: Use AI chatbots to automate customer service, application status updates and document requests.

During the adoption phase, the legacy lenders will encounter numerous challenges. One of the key issues is their outdated lending systems, which cannot meet the needs of modern borrowers and make timely and accurate unit decisions. Financial institutions and property dealers must plan and oversee the integration of innovative technologies to overcome challenges and benefit from AI-driven loan origination.

On average, applying AI to the loan origination process saves time and improves accuracy as well as efficiency. AI-driven tools and solutions automate tasks that previously required significant human effort, leading to potential time savings of up to 60% in preparing loan applications, credit evaluation, and concluding documentation. This increased productivity allows financial institutions to process more applications in less time, enhancing their service delivery and improving customer satisfaction.

AI-driven applications lead to more accurate documentation and underwriting decisions. Automated systems analyze large volumes of data accurately and quickly, minimizing human error common in manual processes that must comply with regulations. It enables better underwriting outcomes and increases bank confidence in credit decisions, as AI allows for more complete and less biased risk assessment of customers. In return, this helps financial institutions to be more prudent in lending decisions, which will lessen the potential of defaults and eventually boost profit margins by their loan portfolios.

So, implementing AI in loan origination significantly reduces the manual work for property dealers and banking companies, as well increase the quality of credit assessment. Experts predict that AI technologies will revolutionize loan origination and management practices in the coming years, bolstering banks' belief in their lending operations.

Use cases of top banks

1. Wells Fargo Uses AI to Augment Credit Evaluation

To improve the accuracy and speed of decision-making, Wells Fargo is using AI in its credit evaluation process. The bank has reduced the loan origination time considerably by tapping into AI-driven tools, improving productivity and consistency.

AI in credit evaluation: Wells Fargo uses artificial intelligence tools such as Zest AI and FICO Score to evaluate the creditworthiness of loan applicants. These tools use machine learning techniques that learn from or analyze a plethora of data points and encompass traditional credit data, alternative data and behavioral patterns. With the help of AI models, Wells Fargo can predict credit risk with more accuracy and make better decisions when lending.

The reduction in loan processing time: Training credit checks using AI has resulted in a 40% decrease. Wells Fargo has also enjoyed reduced loan default rates because the AI models provide it with a more holistic picture of a credit applicant's credit health. The bank has lent to a wider set of customers and manages risk accordingly.

2. JPMorgan Chase–Automating Document Processing with AI

In loan origination, JPMorgan Chase is using AI solutions to help automate the document processing portion. It has significantly helped the bank to avoid manual errors and increased the processing speed, thus being regulatory compliant.

Loan document processing: JPMorgan Chase employs AI tools such as Ocrolus and HyperScience to prove the completeness and accuracy of loan documents much better than any human. The AI's platforms classify, extract and validate the data in all the document types, hence ensuring 100% capture of information essential for analysis. The AI solutions detect any inconsistencies or absences of data, which allows the system to get a logical answer faster.

Results: Implementing AI for document processing has reduced the number of errors in processing by 50%, and decreased time reviewing and approving loan applications by 30%. AI algorithms are also responsible for the improvements in adherence to regulatory standards we see in JPMorgan Chase and input similar data.

3. CitiBank–AI in Property Appraisal Rationalization

Citi has deployed AI in its property evaluation cycle to raise the perfection and speed of storing sales. Citi now uses AI-powered appraisal tools to streamline loan origination.

This leads Citi to make use of AI-powered HouseCanary and Reggora tools are integrated into the property appraisal workflow. Delivering accurate property estimates is the AI powered tool that also automates the order process, ensuring fast Appraisal Delivery for each loan. The AI models then analyze appraisal data and ensure that the appraised value is within market standards and loan requirements.

Outcome: Fasters processing of loan applications by enabling Citi to reduce the time spent on appraisals by 40%, using AI for property appraisal. In return, the bank has seen more precise property valuations and improved loan portfolio quality.

4. HSBC uses AI-driven income and employment verification

To offer greater ease of loan origination, the Bureau has supplemented its income and employment verification process with AI, merged within the HSBC. HSBC has shown the power of automating this very key step in determining whether a borrower is eligible and reducing incidence of fraud.

Income and Employment Verification with AI Integration: This is where HSBC uses solutions like Traweek & Equifax Verification Services, which are powered with Artificial Intelligence to perform the verification part for income and employment automatically. These monitor and source data from third parties, such as payroll providers and financial institutions, to enable real-time validation. They can even check the regularity of the employment of a borrower, and this only adds more credibility to their risk assessment.

HSBC has seen a 35% decrease in verification time and a 20% increase in borrower accuracy thanks to its AI-driven income & employment verification. This means that the time taken has reduced and HSBC has also minimized fraud applications.

5. Capital One: Using AI to Automate Debt-to-Income Ratios

Capital One used AI to automate an essential metric in loan origination-calculating the debt-to-income (DTI) ratio. The bank has also increased the precision of DTI calculations and its measuring of borrower risk with AI-driven tools.

For example, Capital One is using AI with Plaid & Mint by Intuit to digitize debt-to-income. Such tools compile all data regarding a borrower's existing debts and check whether this figure matches their level of income. Credit reports to be sure they have money available — AI-driven platforms to track and sub-categorize debts, telling the entire story of the borrower's financial obligations. The AI models then computed the DTI ratio to verify that it is within the lending limits of the bank.

Outcome: Introducing AI in DTI ratio calculation has resulted in an increase of 30% in the precision of risk assessment. The reduction has allowed CapitalOne to speed up the time-to-process for all loan applications by 25%, ensuring quick approval and faster value provision to their clients.

Top 5 Banks in Asia Use Cases

1. Industrial and Commercial Bank of China (ICBC): AI-Based Credit Risk Assessment

For example, the largest bank in China, ICBC, uses AI to transform its credit risk assessment process. Endowed with AI, ICBC is now better assessing the credibility of loan applicants while speeding up loan application processing time and delivering better risk assessments.

AI Integration in Credit Risk Assessment: ICBC incorporates FICO Score, and Trans Union's Credit Vision for AI based credit risk assessment. They analyze a wide range of data points that extend to traditional credit, behavioral, and alternative data sources. This then makes a more exact determination of credit risk by using the AI models to gauge the probability of default.

Results: The AI-driven credit risk assessment led to a 35% decrease in loan processing time at ICBC. The bank has also experienced a reduction in non-performing loans, as the AI models allow for much more accurate risk assessment. This has enabled ICBC to grow its loan business while keeping it safe.

2. Streamlining Document Processing Using AI — China Construction Bank (CCB)

China Construction Bank (CCB) enhanced its loan origination document processing workflow with AI to minimize human error and expedite processing time. It has helped CCB to work faster and offer a CCB service for its clients.

Document Processing with AI CCB leverages AI-driven platforms such as Ocrolus, HyperScience etc., to automate data classification, extraction and validation from loan documents. CCB uses these tools to enable the accurate and complete capture of all required information, helping to minimize the need for manual reviews and reducing potential errors.

CCB has brought in AI for document processing, which has resulted in time savings of 45 per cent. In addition, the bank has realized better compliance in terms of rules and regulations standards after using AI, as the tools handle documents with accurate consistency. This has increased customer service levels and operational efficiencies overall.

3. Mitsubishi UFJ Financial Group (MUFG)–Augmenting Property Valuation with AI

By implementing AI in the property valuation process, MUFG–one of Japan's largest financial institutions–can both improve accuracy and significantly decrease the time required to evaluate properties. On utilizing AI-powered tools, MUFG enhanced loan origination efficiency at its disposal.

Where AI Enters: MUFG uses AI software, such as HouseCanary and Reggora to automate its property appraisal workflow. It has tools that offer data-driven valuations, can automate the order process, and deliver appraisal reports quickly. Appraisal review - AI models ensuring the appraisal data comply with market standards and loan requirements.

Outcome: The utilization of AI in conducting property appraisal has helped MUFG to cut the time required for appraisals by 40%, as a result, which allows the bank to reduce loan turnaround times. Better property valuation accuracy results in improved loan portfolio quality and ultimately less risk associated with over- or under-valuing assets.

4. State Bank of India (SBI) — AI Powered Income and Employment Verification

Using AI to verify income and employment has improved approval rates at State Bank of India (SBI). The bank has replaced people with machine learning processes in the loan origination process, leading to faster and more accurate credit decisions.

Machine Learning for Income and Employment Verification: SBI has deployed several platforms, including Truework and Equifax Verification Services, that leverage machine learning to automate the verification of income and employment. Real-time verification by collecting and analyzing data from different sources, such as payroll providers and financial institutions. AI models assess the credit risk of employment in the applicant pool, along with how reliable their job is.

Outcome: With AI driven income and employment, verification SBI has cut down the time taken for verification by 30%, which eventually helped in increase of accuracy while assessing a borrower by up to 20%. It has allowed the bank to approve loans faster than well helped in cutting down fraudulent loan applications, improving its operational efficiency.

5. DBS Bank–AI-Based Automation for Debt-To-Income Ratio Calculation

Singapore-based DBS Bank, the largest bank in Southeast Asia, had employed AI to automate computing the debt-to-income (DTI) ratio of loan origination. The addition of an AI feature to its solution led DBS to surpass traditional methods for calculation DTi, boosting accurately and increasing risk interpretation on borrowers.

AI tools, such as Plaid and Mint by Intuit, allow DBS Bank to merge debt data on a borrower and compare it against the income levels of that borrower to compute the debt-to-income ratio. The AI-powered platforms keep a tab on all the debts by segregating them, which allows lenders to have complete details of how much the borrower owes. The AI models then worked the DTI ratio out, making sure it complies with bank lending criteria.

Conclusions An AI powered DTI ratio calculation improved the accuracy of risk prediction during DBS surgery by a 25%. The bank has also decreased loan processing time by 20%, allowing for quicker approval and improved customer service. This has firmly established DBS as one of the early movers in using AI for an accurate loan origination process.

Integrating Artificial Intelligence (AI) has transformed loan origination processes across the banking industry. AI-driven solutions also help banks to automate repetitive tasks, optimize workflows, improve compliance with business rules and internal policies, achieve near-optimal accuracy levels and refined risk management technique—all aimed at simplifying the transactional process and customer experience. Examples from the leading banks in Asia — ICBC, CCB, MUFG, SBI or DBS show how AI brings optimization into multiple parts of the loan origination process. These comprise aspects such as credit risk appraisal, document hunting, funds evaluation of assets, property valuation and income proof accompanied by DTI calculation.

The move to automated AI functionality is another stride in FinTech, as banks are increasingly integrating it into the finance space. A move that means a substitution of classical means for modern tools such as machine learning, data analytics, and automation. AI-Based Credit Risk Assessment, banks can now make more financially independent lending decisions, all despite the use of AI far ahead in recent time. This has led to lower default rates and higher loan portfolio quality.

The AI-powered income and employment verification has helped speed up the process and lowered fraud risk of loan applications — a necessity in order to maintain lending integrity. This has allowed banks to more accurately assess the risk involved in providing credit to a broad spectrum of customers — meaning lower risk without having to forego credit granting.

The combined experiences of these leading Asian banks underscores how AI is central to the banking sector as a key driver of innovation. Growing AI technologies are likely to make banks an increasingly bigger player in loan origination, providing new avenues for our performance on efficiency, accuracy, and customer satisfaction. For financial institutions, adopting AI and incorporating it into a routine process will offer them a unique selling proposition in the new age of global finance.

Implementing AI with loan origination is more than just a technological uplift, but a change in bank logic. With this, it leads to more efficient and accurate etc. loan practices which help the bank and their customers. As the financial sector evolves and more advancements are made in service delivery, AI will propel the future of banking.

Reference – Further reading - Chapter 7

FICO® Score 10 Suite, Predictive Power, Explainability, Transparency
https://www.fico.com/en/products/fico-score

Regulation Z's Mortgage Loan Originator Rules Review Pursuant to the Regulatory Flexibility Act
https://www.federalregister.gov/documents/2023/03/16/2023-05295/regulation-zs-mortgage-loan-originator-rules-review-pursuant-to-the-regulatory-flexibility-act

TILA-RESPA integrated disclosures (TRID)
https://www.consumerfinance.gov/compliance/compliance-resources/mortgage-resources/tila-respa-integrated-disclosures/

7 AI-Powered Loan Origination Software for Lenders
https://jisort.com/blog/ai-powered-loan-origination-software-for-lenders/

Put AI on the frontlines against fraud
https://www.zest.ai/learn/blog/put-ai-on-the-frontlines-against-fraud/

4 Key Ways AI is Powering the Lending Industry
https://www.ocrolus.com/blog/ai-affecting-lending-industry/

Hyperautomation for Mortgage Processing
https://www.hyperscience.com/solutions/mortgage-processing/

Turn real estate data into opportunities with a solution designed to fit your needs.
https://www.housecanary.com/

Reggora Launches AI-Powered Appraisal Review Solution for Lenders
https://www.reggora.com/press/reggora-launches-ai-powered-appraisal-review-solution-for-lenders

The Importance of Mortgage Employment Verification and Benefits of Using Truework's Automated VOE
https://www.truework.com/resource-center/blog/Lenders-Guide

The most trusted digital finance platform
https://plaid.com/why-plaid/

Loan origination systems (LOS): A thorough guide for financial institutions
https://www.ranosys.com/blog/insights/how-can-financial-institutions-optimize-their-loan-origination-systems/

Fiserv offers a full range of loan origination systems
https://www.fiserv.com/en/solutions/processing-services/lending-solutions/loan-origination.html

EIGHT

AI in Investment Banking

Introduction

By integrating Artificial Intelligence (AI) and Machine Learning (ML), the investment banking is facing a substantial change in supporting the financial services sector. These emerging technologies are changing the field by allowing organizations of all sizes to use enormous heaps of information for bettering as soon as, improving customer experiences and streamlining workflows. This shift in technology breaks from the status quo and offers entrepreneurs an unprecedented opportunity for innovation and productivity.

1. **Market Demand and Industry Adoption**

The rate of adoption of AI and ML in investment banking is increasing at an unimaginable rate. AI-powered banking in 2021, this AI in banking, is worth USD 14. Thought leaders have forecast a CAGR of 32.6% from 2022 to 2030. There are many contributing factors to facilitate this growth, such as bigger necessity of automation, increasing interest in data-driven insights and the wider digitalization of banking.

AI can do a lot for investment banks; from strategy positioning to risk management and making customer experience more personalized. Implementing AI technologies is less about the competition and more about changing the way investment banks do business.

2. **AI means it is everywhere — Predictive Analytics in Market Forecasting**

In financial services, one of the highly transformative uses for AI in investment banking has been predictive analytics. It uses historical and real-time data to analyze market trends, look for investment opportunities, and measure potential risks based on huge datasets in a way that has never been achievable before.

1. **Deployment in Investment Banks**: Investment banks are using supervised (train and test) and unsupervised learning algorithms to predict market movement. Banks use linear regression and support vector machines models to learn from their transactional data (supervised learning) to infer patterns that can predict future outcomes. Contrarily unsupervised learning models, i.e. clustering algorithms unveils concealed patterns in the data which from left of center provides the unobtained understanding of market dynamics.

2. **Natural Language Processing (NLP)** has used unstructured data sources such as news articles, postings on social media, and financial reports. One piece included sentiment analysis, which is a subset of NLP and offers an insight into market mood and investor sentiment. This helps banks make smarter decisions based on reviewed content that reveals the tone and context surrounding market conversations.

3. **Big Data & Real-Time Analytics:** Investment banks can now leverage huge datasets from different sources for processing with big data technologies, such as Apache Hadoop and Apache Spark. These include transaction records, social media activity and news feeds. Banks can react real-time to market changes, which represents a tremendous advantage in fast moving environments.

4. **Data visualization tools** like Tableau, Power BI, and Google Data Studio are essential for visualizing complex datasets. These tools enable analysts and decision-makers to observe data with greater clarity. They can transform raw data into meaningful insights, presented through interactive dashboards and visualizations.

3. Algorithmic Trading & Market Making with AI

Algorithmic trading, powered by AI (Artificial Intelligence), has changed the way we conduct trading operations and made high-frequency trading (HFT) and smart order execution at speeds and frequencies unattainable to humans. These types of deals catalyzed by technology are now a foundational part of investment banking today.

In High-Frequency Trading (HFT) and AI, high-frequency trading platforms, designed for low-latency performance, carry out many trades in milliseconds. Native investment banks such as Goldman Sachs and J.P. Morgan use HFT to take advantage of small price discrepancies from disrespectful trades, which humans cannot operate. Today, competitiveness lives on these platforms.

Smart Order Routing (SOR) Algorithms: SOR algorithms provide trade execution optimization by intelligently routing orders across many exchanges to get the best price available. These are algorithms considering price, volume and a host of other factors, designed to deliver trade executions on the cheap for banks — and that return to their clients.

How AI powers risk management systems AI-driven risk-management systems monitor trading activities in real time, and evaluate risks such as market exposure, liquidity or position sizes. Predictive modeling within these systems detects anomalies, manages risk limits, and helps prevent losses with regulatory adherence.

Regulatory Compliance and AI: Given the complexity of regulatory environments, compliance will only be achievable using AI. Technical compliance: The tools like monitoring trading activity and providing audit trails will be necessary for transparency and legal requirements. Applying AI to enforce compliance for investment banks, reducing the risk of regulatory breaches and penalties.

4. Issues in implementing AI and ML

Certainly, these advantages are sound on paper, however, the path to capitalizing on the full potential of AI and ML in investment banking is fraught with headwinds that banks must overcome.

1. Data Quality and Integration: Need for higher quality, contextually relevant data to enable AI / ML models Unfortunately, most banks suffer from data silos and different data caps, which results in not an objective predictions and poor decision-making processes. Incorporating AI with older technologies also exacerbates data management issues, creating a need for greater resources to ensure strong data infrastructure and governance.

2. Regulatory and Ethical Implications: In banking, regulatory oversight around AI is in a nascent phase and the standards can differ across geographies. This can be difficult when some of the AI algorithms, known as "black box" models, are opaque. Challenges with ethical concerns, including bias in AI decision-making and transparency of AI-driven processes. These issues need to be addressed by the banks, causing pressure on their trust among customers with a strong governance framework.

3. Special talents are required to implement AI. For example, in investment banking, there is a high demand for specialist resources to carry out AI implementation successfully. Banks need to require massive talent investment externally and internally. They should work towards ai-skilling their existing workforce to realize the potential of their investments in AI. The fast-moving nature of technology makes this problem even more difficult, which demands learning and pivoting in real-time.

Investment and Resources: Operationally AI & ML implementations are expensive. This is a significant amount of capital involved in setting up the technology, data sourcing and talent. Smaller banks could find it difficult to keep up with those larger institutions which have far bigger pockets to assign towards AI pursuits, further widening the gulf between industry front-runners and their smaller counterpoints.

5. Trends and Opportunities Going Forward

Investment banking experts predict that as AI grows and matures, its impact will rise even further, leveraging the technology for novel solutions. Key trends include:

1. **AI-Driven Customer Experiences**: Investment banks are transforming customer experience through AI-based processes Chatbots powered by AI, and virtual assistants are answering simple queries, recommending investment solutions as per customer profile and needs.

2. **Sustainability and Ethical AI:** The increasing prevalence of AI has led people to be more concerned about ensuring the proper, sustainable use of said technologies. Designers and implementers are using AI in investment banks with these goals in mind, enabling them to focus on transparency, fairness, and ethical implications when making AI-based decisions related to

both the world's economy and its environment.

3. **Market expansion:** As AI can process a huge amount of data, it becomes an excellent tool for cohorts to spot opportunities in new markets. AI robot is a tool that some investment banks used to navigate into new markets, assessing risks and balancing their global investments accordingly.

Use Cases Global Banks

1. J.P. Morgan Chase: COiN (Contract Intelligence)

Use Case: Document Review and Contract Management

Coin, the AI-powered tool to review and manage legal docs built by J.P. Morgan It accomplishes this by using machine learning to extract the most important data from thousands of subclauses included within a legal contract where prior, it needed a team to read each document.

J.P. Morgan's technology team developed COiN in-house and integrated it with IBM Watson capabilities as part of their proof of concept. The solution processes and analyzes documents by using natural language processing (NLP) and machine learning algorithms.

The system allows users to train it to mark and parse data accurately using reinforced learning models from a large dataset of legal documents. This system can accurately segment and categorize the key clauses and terms by understanding and interpreting the language in contracts (features of NLP).

COiN saved thousands of working hours by reviewing documents in seconds and improved the operational efficiency. The bank improved the efficiency of its paper inspection process by implementing more accurate document review, reducing human errors, and enhancing regulatory compliance. This enhancement allowed legal teams to be more strategic in their time and minimized repetitive operational work.

2.Goldman Sachs: Marquee Platform

Use Case: Client Data Analytics / Market Insights

Marquee, a sophisticated analytic tool Goldman Sachs developed to share its own data and market insights with clients. It provides a myriad of services, such as portfolio management tools, risk analytics, and AI based market trend analysis.

Marquee fits in with several major AI data analytics platforms. Tableau for visualizing data and Python-based machine learning libraries (TensorFlow and Scikit-learn) for developing a model. It also uses APIs to integrate real-time data.

Through machine learning algorithms, the platform makes analyses of market data and generates predictive insights. The platform trains these models over past data to predict the performance of stocks in the market and determine safer investment options. Function: Marquee uses AI to offer clients customized, data-driven insights based on each client's portfolio and investment approach.

By taking advantage of Marquee, Goldman Sachs has provided a differentiated service to its customers when the market is highly competitive. This makes real-time, AI-driven insights accessible to clients so they can make better investment decisions. It has led to better satisfaction among clients while boosting the banks' revenues from advice. It has also reduced the time and effort needed to analyze market data by better integrating the bank's internal processes on an improved platform.

3. Bank of America: Erica Virtual Assistance

Use Case: Customer Interaction and Investment Advisory

Bank of America introduced an AI-powered virtual advisor Erica to its retail banking customers and has now extended the virtual assistant to support investment banking clients. Erica answers question and provides tailored market insights, tracks investment portfolios of clients and predicts next stock movements using AI tech.

Erica was developed on technology from multiple vendors — IBM Watson for NLP, cognitive computing and various tools in Machine learning, to name a few. The assistant was incorporated into its existing digital avenues of the bank to enable users to find their way conveniently.

AI and ML Technologies: Erica uses NLP to know about the customer's questions in natural language, so it can reply accordingly. Powered by machine learning models that analyze client portfolios and market data, the assistant provides personalized investment advice and predictions. By taking advantage of deep learning algorithms, the assistant learns from user interactions and becomes better at responding.

A major use case of Erica at Bank of America is its improved customer service capabilities, as it allows the bank to offer personalized 24/7 support to their clients. AI-powered insights through Erica have boosted client engagement and satisfaction, resulting in higher customer retention. Human advisors carry less workload today and can attend to more complex client needs.

4. Citi: AI-Powered Trading Desk

Use Case: Algorithmic Trading and Risk Management

Citi is using AI-driven models on its trading desk to improve the accuracy and efficiency of its trading strategies. The bank uses artificial intelligence to predict market movements, optimize trading algorithms, and manage risks.

Note: Citi achieves dynamic rerouting using cognitive and autonomous techniques, which entails using an in-house proprietary algorithm and third-party IBM Watson or TensorFlow. The bank has also integrated Bloomberg and Reuters real-time data feeds that flow through the AI models.

Citi: Citi is setting up a trading desk for digital assets, using supervised learning models to predict future prices from historical price data. Tesla and the bank to optimize trading strategies by learning from outcomes use reinforcement learning. AI-powered risk management systems monitor market changes and re-adjust trading strategies to prevent high-risk trades.

Using AI on Citi's trading desk Emerging technologies such as AI and machine learning have enabled Citi to improve the efficiency and accuracy of its trading. The bank has been able to complete trades faster and with a higher accuracy, leading to higher profits. AI-scored risk management has likewise minimized the bank's vulnerability to market volatility, further improving its embedded risk profile. By utilizing AI, Citi has gotten ahead in algorithmic trading, which provides a leg up.

5. UBS: SmartWealth Platform

Use case: Wealth Management and Automated Advisory

SmartWealth is UBS's own AI-based Robo-adviser, which offers tailor-made investment advice for customers. The service leverages AI to analyze the financial goals and risk profile of a client, which results in customized investment strategies.

Several technologies partners have been engaged to develop SmartWealth, including the BlackRock Aladdin platform for portfolio management and IBM Watson for its AI-powered analytics. The platform integrates with UBS's internal data systems to provide a single view of the client portfolio.

The platform analyzes client data using machine learning algorithms and predicts the most suitable investment strategies based on individual profiles. It employs natural language processing (NLP) to interface with customers, so that the circumstances allow recommendations to be explained. The portfolio optimization tools, powered by AI, tailor the investment strategies according to market conditions and client specifications.

SmartWealth for UBS has allowed the bank to deliver a customized and efficient wealth management service. Clients benefitted from advice that catered to their investment objectives, which maximized the chances of successful investing. The platform has also enabled UBS to offer their advisory services to a wider group of clients, including those with smaller investment portfolios, without degrading the quality of service. As a result, UBS built on its leading market position in this segment and both the assets under management and customer satisfaction grew.

Banks Use cases from Asia

1. AI-based Trading Analytics by ICICI Bank (India)

Use Case: Algorithmic Trading and Market Analysis

AI-driven analytics to boost its algorithmic trading operations at ICICI Bank. The bank has AI models which process vast amounts of data and predict market movements to design more effective trading strategies.

In order to build and implement their AI trading analytics, ICICI Bank partnered with top AI tech providers such as IBM and Infosys. The bank uses

Tensorflow and some Python packages, such as Scikit-learn for model development.

The AI system of ICICI uses sophisticated supervised learning models to predict market movements based on historical data. The bank uses deep learning models that can recognize subtle financial patterns in vast amounts of data, helping to identify trading opportunities that conventional methods can sometimes overlook.

AI usage has resulted in higher accuracy of trades and increased efficiency for ICICI Bank. Artificial intelligence-based analytics have allowed the bank to make trades faster and more accurately, thus improving its profitability. Because of the AI models, the bank's trading operations have become more stable due to minimized trading errors.

2. **DBS Bank (Singapore) Limited:**

Use Case: Wealth Management, Personalized Investment Advice

New NAV Planner: A new digital investment platform at DBS Bank, enabled by artificial intelligence (AI), which our customers can access for personalized financial planning and investment advice. In the platform, AI analyzes the financial situation of a client and recommends investment strategies tailored to their needs.

DBS worked with technology partners such as IBM Watson for AI and Salesforce for CRM integration. DBS uses proprietary advanced data analytics tools for visualization and relies on other vendors, such as Tableau or Alteryx for data processing.

Machine learning algorithms are used to evaluate clients' financial data, such as income, expenses, assets & liabilities in the NAV Planner. This AI learns specific investment strategies to recommend based on the financial goals and risk appetite of the client. The platform also provides AI-powered recommendations that learned over time, increasing in accuracy and relevance as you engage.

DBS goes big on personal investment advice for all: with the launch of NAV Planner, could DBS have revolutionized the way it interacts with its retail clients? As the result, the AI-driven platform has increased customer satisfaction through tailor-made financial approaches that match individual objectives. The network has already allowed DBS to push the boundaries to expand its reach to service more customers with a digital-first yuan. Since its launch, the bank has recorded satisfactory gains in customer engagement and assets under management (AUM).

3. Mitsubishi UFJ Financial Group (MUFG) (Japan): AI-driven Risk Management

Use Case: Risk Management and Regulatory Compliance Area

For example, MUFG has rolled out AI solutions for its risk management activities. The bank makes use of AI/ML for leading edge real-time market risk, credit risk and operational risk monitoring, ensuring compliant operations across its investment banking.

MUFG, a Japanese financial services giant and bank holding company, partnered with IBM Japan and Hitachi Systems to create an AI-enabled risk management platform, according to local news outlet the Nikkei on April 21st. Cognitive computing, Natural Language Processing: The bank relies on IBM Watson along with Custom ML models built on TensorFlow and Keras.

MUFG uses machine learning models to analyze large volumes of data from various sources, including market feeds, transaction records, and financial reports. They undertake this to enhance their risk management system. It uses anomaly detection algorithms and recognizes suspicious behavior which may risk the bank, alerting them to take action. Performance check: We use NLP to read regulatory texts.

Since then, the AI-enhanced risk management system has further increased MUFG's visibility in monitoring and managing risks in its investment banking business. By improving risk assessment, the bank significantly reduced their potential exposure, better predicting instances when they were more likely to incur losses because of unforeseen market events. The system has achieved this by simplifying the bank's compliance procedures, making it more efficient to regulate while consuming fewer resources. The bank has long been a leader in risk management in the Asia-Pacific region, and this innovation has only enhanced this reputation.

4. Ping An Bank: AI for Investment Consulting (China)

Use Case: Customer Service, Investment Advisory

A virtual financial advisor deployed by Ping An Bank used the AI in customer-facing and investment advising. Using a machine-learning advisor has helped NatWest deliver tailored investment propositions and financial planning guidance to clients, with including best-of-breed technology improving their overall wealth management services.

Pin An Technology, a technology arm under the group, collaborated with Ping An Bank to co-develop the AI products. Under the hood, it uses AI tools as a service like Alibaba Clouds AI suite and Baidu NLP, Baidu Machine Learning services.

Through advanced natural language processing (NLP) technology, the AI advisor talks to the client in a human-like fashion to interpret their investment goals and investment preferences. Based on the financial history of the client and data of the market, machine learning models provide investment strategies. It also uses reinforcement learning to improve its advice, based on the feedback from the clients.

By giving timely, personalized advice to clients, the AI-powered investment advisor has boosted customer satisfaction at Ping An Bank. The clients gain more interactive and appealing advisory experience, ensuring trust and loyalty levels shoot up. In addition, using the AI advisor has allowed Ping An Bank to extend its wealth management services, providing high-grade products and services for more clients. This has led to greater client retention and AUM growth for the bank because of this intonational innovation.

5. OCBC Bank (Singapore): Trading Optimization by AI

Use Case: Trading Strategy Optimization and Execution

This is one example of how OCBC Bank applies AI with its trading strategies and execution. Using machine learning, the bank has developed a trading model that looks at trade data and specific fields of market data to improve trade execution and profit.

OCBC reduced share trade completion time to less than 10 minutes using an AI-powered equity trading optimization platform, in partnership with

Refinitiv and Amazon Web Services. Its machine learning tools are AWS SageMaker, while it relies on Refinitiv for data analysis.

The trading optimization platform uses supervised learning models to predict future market movements and optimally design a set of trading strategies. Deep learning algorithms analyze more involved market data to enable the bank to spot patterns that traditional approaches would miss. This means that the system can change trading strategies to suit the prevailing market conditions in real-time.

OCBC Bank's trading performance has shown significant breakthroughs with the recent integration of AI-trading optimization. The bank has also reduced trading costs and improved profitability, with higher execution speeds. The models have also helped the bank hedge risk from market volatility better, resulting in more stable trading results. This innovation allows OCBC to lead in AI-based trading in the region and gives OCBC an advantage over global markets.

The above use cases show how top Asian banks have leveraged the power of AI and ML in investment banking to bring innovation, efficacy, and enriched customer experiences. In an increasingly digital world of finance, these banks have leveraged sophisticated solutions and partnered with the providers of technology to rise as pioneers in the financial industry.

Use Cases–smaller or investment-centric banks

1. Cowen Inc (USA) AI-Powered Equity Research

Use Case: Equity Research and Market Analysis

Cowen Inc., a smaller investment bank historically known for equity research and sales, has been successful in using AI-driven tools to enhance its research product. The bank uses AI to process large datasets and makes its equity research reports more targeted and timelier.

Cowen teamed up with Alphasense for AI-enabled market intelligence and Sentieo for data analytics. These platforms help Cowen analyze large datasets like financial reports, market news, and earnings transcripts.

At Cowen, the AI systems use natural language processing (NLP) to sift through reams of text data from sources such as earnings calls and financial filings. By providing improved datasets to analysts, machine learning algorithms help them identify trends and patterns that ultimately allow for more accurate recommendations and insights.

AI has helped Cowen improve the efficiency and value of its equity research. Previously, this research was only available as an exclusive product, but now AI provides customers with targeted input faster and more flexibly. That technological advantage has enabled Cowen to stand out in the crowded field of equity research and stimulated further client engagement and growth in revenue from research.

2. Jefferies Group LLC (USA): AI-Driven Customer Experience Platform

Use Case: CRM & Personalized Advisory

Innovation: Jefferies, a global investment banking company, is using AI to improve its client relationship management (CRM). The bank has deployed tailor-made AI tools to deliver personalized investment advice for pre-emptive client servicing.

Vendor and Tools: leveraged Salesforce Einstein, an AI-enabled CRM system for organizing, processing, and leveraging client data. Tableau-Data Visualization and Predictive Analytics.

At Jefferies, the CRM system uses machine learning models to analyze client data and predict their needs. This allows investment advisors to provide highly targeted investment recommendations through AI. For example, the AI layer of Jefferies' CRM system runs on top of the ML models that analyze clients' data to predict needs and recommend personalized investment products.

This has helped Jefferies to maintain closer, one-to-one relationships with its clients using the AI-enabled CRM. They have enhanced client satisfaction and retention rates by predicting the client needs and preferences. Integration of CRM in AI has also automated the client handling process, which decreased the time, agility, and efforts required by a human advisor.

3. Stifel Financial Corp. (United States) — AI-based M&A Analysis

Use Case: Mergers and Acquisitions (M&A) Advisory

A mid-sized investment bank, Stifel, has used AI to beef up deal analysis and valuation in its M&A advisory services. The bank uses AI to process a broad range of market conditions, company financials, and industry trends, which gives more precise M&A advice based on data.

Vendors and Tools: Deal management platforms (Stifel using Intralinks), Cognitive analytics built upon AI tools developed by companies such as IBM Watson. The bank also uses DealCloud — a CRM and deal management platform with AI capabilities to organize its M&A operations.

Stifel trains their AI using machine learning algorithms to understand the financial statements, market data and historical deal outcomes in order to evaluate ideal M&A targets. This involves processing and interpreting a large amount of textual data, such as press releases and analyst reports, which are known as Natural Language Processing.

By including AI in M&A analysis, Stifel has generated more accurate valuations and strategic recommendations for its clients. The bank has benefited from better deal assessments, translating into better outcomes for its clients. The AI-driven analysis has also brought down the time needed to examine potential deals, permitting Stifel to oversee a greater volume of transactions.

4. Raymond James Financial (US): Artificial Intelligence for Risk Assessment and Compliance

Use Case: Risk Management and Regulatory Compliance

Raymond James Financial, a small investment-centric bank, has implemented A.I. tools to better integrate its risk management and regulatory compliance processes. The bank uses AI to track trades, risks, and to verify that operations are in line with regulatory standards.

Raymond James uses programs to detect and combat risk, like SAS Risk Management and NICE Actimize regulatory technology. Featuring risk and compliance tools using AI and machine learning.

Within Raymond James, the AI-driven risk management system uses machine-learning models to analyze trading patterns in order to spot any risks or irregularities. The bank stays abreast of changing regulations by monitoring and interpreting regulatory updates with NLP.

AI-enhanced Risk Management and compliance tools have made Raymond James an industry leader in detecting and preventing risk in real-time. This makes the bank compliance process achievable while decreasing the chances of regulatory failures and their attend in fines. It facilitates an increase in the operational efficiency and helps build a better stature of the bank in terms of reliability and integrity among the Investment banks.

5. Greenhill & Co., Inc. (US) — AI-Powered Deal Sourcing

Use Case: Deal Sourcing and Market Intelligence Area

Greenhill is a boutique investment bank focused upon M&A advisory, restructuring and capital raising that has adopted AI for deal sourcing and market intelligence. AI identifies M&A targets and industry trends for the bank.

Partners: Greenhill is working with AI-focused FinTechcos like Dealogic and Pitchbook, platforms that leverage Artificial Intelligence (AI) on deal sourcing and market intelligence. These algorithms are in-house tech relying on proprietary machine learning for certain deal-sourcing tasks the bank needs.

Greenhill's AI system uses machine learning algorithms to examine vast amounts of market information, which helps it identify potential takeover targets and trends. Predictive analytics, which uses historical and current market data to give insights on the probability of deal closure, also powered this.

Click here to know how an AI-driven deal has helped Greenhill Human Nature in identifying and pursuing high-potential M&A opportunities for sourcing. The bank is seeing an increased hit rate on M&A deals, while also becoming more efficient and effective in deal sourcing. Greenhill is using AI tools to gain an edge in the market by finding opportunities that its competitors are not noticing.

Smaller banks are using artificial intelligence and machine learning to drive innovation and gain a competitive edge. Leveraging cutting-edge solutions and working closely with technology partners, they have been able to boost operational efficiency, upgrade client services and enhance their footing in the investment banking domain.

Reference – Further reading - Chapter 8

Artificial Intelligence Market Size & Trends
https://www.grandviewresearch.com/industry-analysis/artificial-intelligence-ai-market
Unleashing a new era of productivity in investment banking through the power of generative AI
https://www2.deloitte.com/us/en/insights/industry/financial-services/financial-services-industry-predictions/2023/generative-ai-in-investment-banking.html
How to search
16 Tips on How to Search Better with Sentieo's award-winning AI-Powered Search!
The quickest way from a billion points of data to a point of view
https://www.sas.com/en_us/software/viya.html
Datasite For financial institutions
https://www.datasite.com/en/solutions/industry/financial-institutions
J.P Morgan – COiN – a Case Study of AI in Finance
https://superiordatascience.com/jp-morgan-coin-a-case-study-of-ai-in-finance/
Goldman Sachs Announces the Launch of Marquee® MarketView
https://www.goldmansachs.com/pressroom/press-releases/2023/goldman-sachs-launches-marquee-marketview
BofA's Erica Gets Live Chat as Gen-AI Virtual Assistants Catch Up
https://corporateinsight.com/bofas-erica-gets-live-chat-as-gen-ai-virtual-assistants-catch-up/
Account Online with ICICIDIRECT
https://www.icicidirect.com/ilearn/stocks/articles/ai-stocks-in-india
DBS Rolls Out AI-Powered Digital Investment Advisory Feature
https://fintechnews.sg/50286/wealthtech/dbs-rolls-out-ai-powered-digital-investment-advisory-feature/
Ping An Asset Management
https://group.pingan.com/media/perspectives/Ping-An-AMC-Launches-Intelligent-Investment-Risk-Advisor-KYZ-Risk.html
OCBC Securities launches Singapore's first AI stock-picker
https://asianbankingandfinance.net/news/ocbc-securities-launches-singapores-first-ai-stock-picker

NINE

The Rise of Robo Advisor 4.0

1. Introduction

Technological improvements are reshaping the financial field. Robo Advisor 4.0 and Robo-Safe of Deloitte are path breaking innovations surrounding Investment Banking and Transaction Monitoring, respectively. These solutions have helped establish a new age of financial security and customer service by incorporating some of the most advanced machine learning algorithms and AI.

True Robo Advisor 4.0 stands for automated financial advisors powered by the most advanced Artificial Intelligence, including Machine Learning, Natural Language Processing and super custom investment strategies. Robo-advisors offer a smooth and systematic IP experience, which through this plug and play mechanism allows us to serve the customers at large scale with higher grade asset management advice. Key features include:

Advanced Machine Learning: Using sophisticated algorithms to analyze unlimited data and discover hidden patterns or tendencies which will enable you to make better investment choices.

2. Robo Advisor 4.0.

Customized investment strategies based on the individual profiles, goals, risk tolerances, and financial situations of our clients.

Integration: Tying into wider financial planning systems, offering a complete solution to personal finance management.

Better UI an UX: Intuitive interfaces that make investing easy by clients.

Deloitte is transforming transaction monitoring with its Robo-Safe approach, which employs supervised machine learning to improve fraud detection and prevention.

Collect data and prepare: Gathering preprocessing massive transactional data is important for validation.

Feature Engineering: Deriving new features from data to model transaction behavior.

Training and validation of the model: Detecting anomalies by an ensemble of supervised machine learning models

Engage: Machine learning to adapt to changing fraud patterns.

In doing so, The Robo Advisor 4.0 devises a fully comprehensive solution to investment banking by providing an uplift to both professional portfolio management and transaction security.

3. Enhanced Portfolio Management

Using data analysis and to personalize investment tips and plan, a Robo advisor 4.0 can give you customized advice along with your portfolio optimization. Robo-advisors automate such mundane tasks which help in lowering cost and scaling up their business model, making it possible for financial institutions to serve a much wider spectrum of customers efficiently.

Robust Transaction Monitoring

The Robo-Safe approach provided by Deloitte aligns with the portfolio management to enable real-time transaction monitoring for instant detection and prevention of ongoing fraudulent practices. In this way, combining personalized financial advice with strong fraud prevention keeps US Financial a safer and more effective environment for your money.

Intuitive Investor is a robo-advisor solution created by Wells Fargo, and it comes with several features that assist clients in the management of their investments. The following are the key areas and features of Wells Fargo's Intuitive Investor Robo-advisor you need to know.

Passive Portfolio Management

Key Features: Automated portfolio management, including ongoing monitoring and rebalancing of investments with Intuitive Investor. It keeps the asset allocation consistent with the client's individual risk tolerance and investment objectives.

Tailored investment strategies

It generates tailor-made investment strategies through several complex algorithms after evaluating the personal profile of each client. Based on your financial goals, the risk you can take, investment horizon and current financial situation, it creates the best possible investment plan for you.

Diverse Investment Options

Intuitive Investor has a multitude of different investment/streaming choices, including diversified portfolios made up of exchange-traded funds (ETFs). These diversified portfolios comprise equities, fixed-income, and alternative investments.

Low Fees

The most significant benefit of robo-advisors is their cost-effectiveness. Intuitive Investor prices attract IM clients because of low management fees, which can open the door of professional investment management for more customers who may not be used to dealing with it.

Financial Planning Tools Integration

Wells Fargo can integrate it with their other wealth planning solutions to give advisors a complete picture of a client's financial status. By taking a holistic view, clients can align necessary strategies to help manage their investments while keeping other financial priorities in mind, such as retirement planning, saving for education, and managing debt

User-Friendly Interface

The platform available in the Intuitive Investor app offers a user-friendly experience that simplifies investing. The intuitive dashboard lets clients look at their portfolio performance, measure progress against financial goals, and cater to changes as they happen.

Risk Assessment and Control

The platform features powerful risk assessment tools that enable clients to learn their own risk tolerance so they can make investment choices. This automated system monitors and adjusts the portfolio throughout the trading day to stay within defined exposure parameters with the client.

Resources for Learning and Help

Wells Fargo: Wells Fargo offers an extensive library of educational resources to help clients make more informed investment decisions. Clients receive personalized advice and support from a team of financial advisors, combining the best in automated management with human expertise.

Security and Reliability

Those benefits also extend to Intuitive Investor, which is part of Wells Fargo and likely enjoys the bank's robust security measures, reliability and so on. Investors rely on the secure, steady handed environment that Intuitive Investor creates for their investments.

Automatic Rebalancing

With a Robo-advised platform, it will also rebalance portfolios for the desired asset allocation. The above feature helps to control the risk and keep the portfolio in line with his investment strategy.

Tax-Loss Harvesting

The Intuitive Investor offering includes tax-loss harvesting (selling securities at a loss to offset taxable gains) on ETF investments. This can be a way to help clients reduce taxes and increase after-tax returns.

Vanguard clients receive personalized advice from human advisors.

1. Personalized Financial Plan

Construct a personalized financial plan crafted with the Customer's investment objectives, risk acceptances and length of time.

Advisors frequently review the plan and update it to match the clients' aims.

2. Portfolio Automation

Enables investment portfolios to be monitored and rebalanced continuously.

Employs a broad array of Vanguard's low-cost ETSs and mutual funds.

3. Low Fees

Provides competitive access fees — costing less compared to traditional advisory services.

Vanguard has even slowed expense rations, which helps even more with the cost of investing.

4. Detailed Financial Planning

Long-term financial goals, including retirement planning and saving for education.

Provides Resources and tools for clients to stick with Their Financial Plans

6. Vanguard Account Integration

Works with clients' pre-existing Vanguard accounts to give them a more complete portrait of their finances.

Gives clients a simple way to manage and track investments inside the Vanguard platform.

7. User-Friendly Interface

Offers an intuitive online platform and mobile app to view account holdings and plan finances.

Clients can check in on their portfolio, see how they are faring toward their goals and have a chat with their advisor.

8. Tax Efficiency

Uses tax-efficient investment strategies, such as tax-loss harvesting and tax managed asset allocation

Assists clients in reducing their tax toll and increasing after-tax returns.

9. Security and Trust

Valuable protections of Vanguard's well-known security and fiduciary oversight.

They can trust that their investments are being managed in a way that is beneficial to them.

The best Robo-advisor offerings are the Wells Fargo Intuitive Investor, Vanguard Personal Advisor Services, and Charles Schwab Intelligent Portfolios. These platforms provide users with comprehensive financial planning services, automated portfolio management, tax-efficient investing, and low-cost, high-trust security. This allows us to help our clients more easily and confidently reach their financial aspirations.

1. Source: Wells Fargo - Intuitive Investor

Use Case: Wells Fargo wanted to make it for their customers to access and manage their investments. Our vision was to provide a wealth management service that linked automated investment management with financial planning customized to clients' individual financial goals and risk profiles.

Technology:

Intuitive Investor from Wells Fargo uses state-of-the-art algorithms and machine learning for a fully automated, personalized portfolio management. The artificially intelligent platform keeps a pulse on market dynamics. Besides client portfolios automatically mitigation investments into.

Functionality:

Automated Portfolio Management — The platform does all the work and maintains your investment strategy by automatically rebalancing portfolios to keep asset allocation in line with your strategy.

Customized Investing Solutions: Intuitive Investor creates unique investment portfolios based on the client's profile, including financial goals, risk tolerance, and time horizon.

This also includes tax-loss harvesting, where the platform will sell securities for you at a loss to help offset other gains.

Clients can easily track their portfolio health, progress towards financial goals, and make necessary adjustments through a user-friendly design.

Educational resources: Clients can read through an extensive library of educational materials and even talk to financial advisors, combining Robo-management with human advice.

Benefit Achieved: Intuitive Investor already democratized professional investment management by delivering it at scale, offering low fees and making it easy to use. Which has expanded Wells Fargo's target market and allows them to cater to more of the public seamlessly. Due to the platform's customization and automation of investment strategies and portfolio management, the bank has seen high client satisfaction levels. As a result, there has been a rapid increase in clients seeking their wealth management services.

2. Vanguard: Personal Advisor Services

Use Case: Vanguard sought to bridge the gap by combining the best qualities of human financial advisors with automated investment management. The main idea was to provide personalized financial planning with low fees and tax efficiency through a platform.

Technology:

Vanguard Personal Advisors Services use high-quality algorithms for portfolio management, together with the expertise of human advisors. Vanguard Personal Advisors Services notifies clients if their share portfolio has rebounded and adjusts its size to align with their investment strategy and risk profile.

Functionality:

Hybrid Model: Clients receive custom advice from Vanguard's human advisors besides automated portfolio management.

Bespoke Financial Plan: Advisors liaise with clients to create a proper financial plan and update client objectives as needed.

Ability to Invest with Tax Efficiency: Costs related tax (tax loss harvesting/tax efficient asset allocation)

Comprehensive Financial Planning: This service offers retirement planning, education savings, and any long-term financial goals.

Simple to Use Interface: The platform has an intuitive online interface and a mobile app that makes account information and financial planning easy.

Security and Trust — Vanguard has a well-deserved reputation for security, so you can feel secure your investments will be safe with Vanguard.

Benefit Achieved: Vanguard Personal Advisor Services landed on the right mix that balances clients who want at least some human handholding while also wanting the automation efficiency online management provides. By keeping fees low, and focusing on tax efficiency, Vanguard attracted a diverse range of clients, which improved customer stickiness and growth in assets under management.

3. Charles Schwab — Intelligent Portfolios

Use Case: Charles Schwab aimed to provide clients with an automated investment solution, free of advisory fees, that catered to price-sensitive investors in need of a low-cost, efficient product.

Technology:

It implements advanced algorithms to create a diversified portfolio, Charles Schwab Intelligent Portfolios. The platform monitors the conditions of the market and client portfolios ongoing, doing automatic rebalances when needed to stay in line with the targeted asset allocation.

Functionality:

Algorithm-Based Portfolio Management: A cost-effective option for individuals who want to opt for algorithmic trading with zero advisory fees at all.

Bespoke Investment Strategies: Clients can integrate their investment strategies in line with their financial objectives, risk appetite, and time frame.

Automated Rebalancing: The system rebalances portfolios automatically to help control risk and maintain the client's investment strategy.

Tax-loss Harvesting: Tax-loss harvesting to minimize tax liabilities for clients.

User-friendly interface: The platform keeps flexibility by combining an intuitive online interface and mobile app for clients to monitor and manage their portfolios.

Customer Support Around the Clock: We offer 24/7 phone support with the added benefit of financial professionals aiding.

Benefit Achieved: The choices that it could provide and accessibility in being an investment management solution made a competitive appeal for Schwab customers looking for cost-effective services. Schwab discovered a large group of potential investors, including those who couldn't afford the more expensive advisory services, by providing a free, automated solution. Schwab FinTech, a platform known for its cost effectiveness and ease of use, has gained significant market share at Schwab direct. It has achieved a large AUM and faces minimal competition, reducing fees.

The case studies highlight how all three banks use Robo-advisor technology to meet client needs, integrate with existing financial systems, achieve high customer satisfaction, and drive business growth.

Reference – Further reading - Chapter 9

Intuitive Investor® from Wells Fargo
https://www.wellsfargoadvisors.com/services/intuitive-investor.htm
Wells Fargo Intuitive Investor Review 2024
https://www.investopedia.com/wells-fargo-intuitive-investor-review-4769349
Investopedia's 2023 Robo-Advisor Consumer Survey
https://www.investopedia.com/investopedias-2023-robo-advisor-consumer-survey-8303191
Vanguard Personal Advisor Review 2024: Pros, Cons and How It Compares
https://www.nerdwallet.com/reviews/investing/advisors/vanguard-personal-advisor-services

What is a robo-advisor?
https://www.schwab.com/automated-investing/what-is-a-robo-advisor?src=XKZ&ef_id=Cj0KCQjwgL-3BhDnARIsAL6KZ69jjpnSUcde4prsSJEgMyLaEnyKJ32h7jeeyvRF8YarwYWQKS3Rq8kaArMuEALw_wcB:G:s&s_kwcid=AL!5158!3!563641296915!e!!g!!intelligent%20portfolio%20schwab!657672170!33393815276&keywordid=kwd-383847944601&gad_source=1&gclid=Cj0KCQjwgL-3BhDnARIsAL6KZ69jjpnSUcde4prsSJEgMyLaEnyKJ32h7jeeyvRF8YarwYWQKS3Rq8kaArMuEALw_wcB
Schwab Intelligent Portfolios®
https://www.schwab.com/intelligent-portfolios?src=XLS&ef_id=Cj0KCQjwgL-3BhDnARIsAL6KZ69z9iZ-jr2XTZ6Ck6F3EX3T71vMQhBG-8wi_7WKdA9S4cvNE_2mub4aAtGrEALw_wcB%3AG%3As&s_kwcid=AL%215158%213%21563641296915%21e%21!21g%21!21intelligent%20portfolio%20schwab%21657672170%2133393815276&keywordid=kwd-383847944601&gad_source=1
Deloitte Robo safe approch
Deloitte's Robo-Safe Approach
https://www2.deloitte.com/content/dam/Deloitte/de/Documents/financial-services/Robo_No_2.pdf
Implementation of Robo Advice 4,0 from Deloitte.
implementations of Robo Advice 4.0 in Banks:

TEN

Deep Machine Learning Based Hybrid Model for Credit-Risk Prediction in Banking

1. Introduction

In banks, credit risk management is a key practice used to manage uncertainties regarding borrower returns. It is crucial in the banking system to prevent potential losses and ensure the safety of investments. Banks use logistic regression and decision trees for credit risk assessment to evaluate the likelihood of clients incurring losses for financial institutions. These frameworks often cannot handle vast and complicated data types of finance at present — non-linear connection with high numbers of dimensions. This has created a demand to take far more sophisticated methods that can get integrated with these massive challenges.

In recent years, researchers have combined classical machine learning with deep learning techniques to improve the generalization and interpretability of predictive models. To create a credit-rick prediction system based on Hybrid Deep Machine Learning with Convolutional Neural Networks (CNN) integrated with algorithms classifiers SVM, RF, and DT. The model is based on extending the data image features using CNNs and combining the classification abilities of traditional models to predict credit risk.

2. Background and Related Work

Credit risk, also known as default risk, is a loss that a lender incurs by lending to someone who becomes unable to meet required terms. Financial institutions must quantify their default risk because profitability and sustainability are significant to them. Credit risk is of utmost importance to financial institutions which have historically modelled using statistical methods such as Logistic Regression (LR) and Linear Discriminant Analysis (LDA). These models assume a priori cost distribution and may not account for factors like vaccine implementation rates in complex scenarios.

Thanks to machine learning, more flexible and powerful credit risk assessment methods are available. Neural networks, particularly CNNs, have largely contributed to the rise of deep learning by being able to learn and extract features from raw data. This capability can be helpful for managing unstructured data, such as text or images that are often present in a financial dataset. Ensemble methods like Random Forests and SVM provide robustness (Random forests) and capability of fitting complex, non-linear relationship between X and y in case of complex classification.

In the literature, there are many works that already use deep learning and machine learning to predict credit risk. Indeed, research in image recognition and natural language processing has shown that hybrid models like this deliver better accuracy than either end-to-end model. Using models and machine learning techniques, both classical (random forests, for example) and deep learning, to predict credit risk is still new. The aim of this study is to address such a gap by developing and accessing a hybrid model.

3. Methodology

Camadev Credit Prediction used CNN with other classifiers, such as SVM, RF and DT, in Table. It uses the strengths of deep learning and classical machine learning algorithm combined to make a more accurate prediction.

Data Preprocessing This study used the dataset of a local bank in Ethiopia. The dataset contains attributes of the borrower, including age, income, credit history and loan amount. Preprocessing of data took several stages:

Handling missing values is crucial for data cleaning because in any predictive or classification model, missing values can lead to biased or incorrect prediction. Remove incomplete records or impute data by distributing the missing values.

Normalization: To avoid one feature dominating our model, we normalized the data from 0 to 1. The sensitivity of CNNs again proved the importance of this step in the scale of input data.

Feature Extraction with Convolutional Neural Networks (CNN): CNNs mainly process images but can also extract features from structural data. This model uses a CNN composed of a few convolutional layers, followed by pooling layers.

Convolutional Layers: The convolutional layers use filters on input data to determine the shape and features. The filters slide across the input data and perform convolution operations, which capture spatial hierarchies in the data.

After Convolutional layers, pooling layers are used to reduce the dimensionality of the feature maps, which helps with reducing the computational complexity of the model. Max pooling: In max pooling, the algorithm takes the highest value for each feature map region.

4. Machine Learning Algorithm for Classification:

SVM- Support Vector Machine: SVM is a very efficient and effective classifier when working with high dimension, complicated data. It creates a hyperplane in multi-dimensional space to classify the different classes of data points. SVM uses an RBF kernel to identify the non-linear relationship between data points in this model.

Random Forest (RF) is a type of ensemble model which builds various decision trees in training. Random Forest (RF) can predict either the class mode or the average prediction, making it a versatile method for classification and regression tasks. RF also helps control overfitting and handles unbalanced datasets effectively, which makes it an excellent choice for predicting credit risk.

Decision Tree (DT): DT is the powerful yet simple algorithm which predicts on base of feature values by splitting data. Yes, DT is likely to overfit but its only in the hybrid architecture to check how better models can also handle these OOV cases.

5. Hybrid Model Practical Aspects: Implement the hybrid model in two phases.

Feature Extraction: Initially, CNN is trained to extract the features from the input data. Finally, SVM, RF and DT use the features to predict.

Model Training & Evaluation: We use 80% of the dataset for model training and testing. We perform hyperparameter tuning for each classifier to achieve better performance. The SVM optimization involved tuning parameters C and gamma based on cross-validation results. For RF, we adjusted the number of trees (n_estimators) and maximum depth of tree. Last, we optimized DT by using different criteria, such as Gini or entropy.

Technical Aspects

Dealing with Imbalanced data; in credit risk prediction, the challenge is often that the number of defaulters is less than the non–defaulters. We will end up with models favoring the majority class, and this is an imbalance. The proposed model used techniques like SMOTE (Synthetic Minority Oversampling Technique) to balance the classes of the training dataset. To solve this problem, we used the RF classifier, which is robust to imbalanced datasets.

Hyperparameter Tuning: Building machine learning models hinges on the selection of the hyperparameters. In this study hyperparameters tunning for SVM, RF, and DT classifiers using grid search and random search techniques. We conducted a grid search for alpha and the regularization parameter (C) for the SVM with RBF kernel. For RF, we used a random search to determine the hyperparameters such as the number of trees and maximum depth available.

Despite the deep learning model's reputation as a "black box", researchers attempted to interpret the model's predictions. The RF and DT classifiers calculated feature importance scores, allowing us to understand which features were important for predicting credit risk. We use SHAP (SHapley Additive exPlanations) values to explain individual predictions and gain an intuition of how a unique feature contributed to the model's decision.

6. Case Studies:

Use Case 1: Identifying High-Risk Borrowers

How Our Approach Could Help Lenders in Practice when traditional credit history does not predict the risk in certain loan applications (as intermediate by Zidisha), the purpose study was to assess whether our CNN-SVM hybrid model is suitable for lending industry.

Introduction: Most financial institutions suffer from the problem of identifying borrowers with a high risk of defaulting on their loans. Logistic regression or simple decision trees are examples of traditional credit scoring models, and they rely on linear relationships between variables and predefined thresholds for predictions. But modern financial data comes with the added complexity of non-linear relationships, interaction effects, and noise that these models may struggle to deal with.

Results: (1) We implemented the CNN-SVM hybrid model on the high-risk and low-risk borrower subset. We added features like credit history, debt-to-income ratio, recent employment status changes and transactions. The data passed through an input layer, which then fed into CNN. CNN's high-level capability to extract highly complex features enables it to easily identify patterns that traditional algorithms may go unnoticed. By utilizing the output of the CNN as input data, the SVM, renowned for its ability to classify higher dimensional spaces, was employed.

Results: The CNN-SVM model significantly outperformed the traditional models in identifying high-risk borrowers. It had a recall of 99.6%, which shows that whenever a borrower really was a high risk, the model correctly identified them. It also had a strong precision percentage at 97.5%, meaning the model rarely predicted high (bad) risk for a low-risk borrower.

Interpretation: In this case study, the CNN-SVM model can capture variability from a combination of many variables using the feature extraction procedure of CNN. In a traditional model, a borrower with an unchanging income who has taken large withdrawals and increased credit utilization in the very recent past may not classify as high risk. Nor the traditional ways can detect these nuanced risk indicators, but a hybrid model can. Such a capability can be especially useful in finance because risk profiles are both complex and constantly moving.

Conclusion: The outcomes from this case study show that the CNN-SVM hybrid model may provide a useful solution for raising the level of risk assessment of financial institutions. This would help the bank understand how the potential risk can be mitigated by changing the loan terms, credit counseling, or even account monitoring. Ultimately, this lowers defaults and default-related financial losses.

Use Case Study 2: Loan Defaults Early Warning System

Objective: The purpose of the second case study was to construct an early warning system with the CNN-SVM hybrid model. This model allows lenders to predict defaulters before loan defaults and take actions preventing the same.

Context: To effectively manage credit risk, it is important to have an early warning system (EWS) in place for loan defaults. This is because many credit monitoring systems only detect broad changes in borrower behavior over an extended time horizon and may lack the capability to identify sudden shifts in risk factors that can lead to default. There are service recognition systems that cannot value some variables over the others, eventually missing signals.

We used a CNN-SVM hybrid model to conduct this case study on a data set of active loans. The model used characteristics such as repayment history, transaction data, income volatility and macroeconomic variables, such as unemployment rates and inflation. CNN computed and extracted characteristics that could serve as a precursor to the stress of finances, e.g. delay in payments, sudden decrease in income. An SVM then classified these features to determine if a borrower was likely to default on the loan.

Results: The CNN-SVM model generated a very early warning system being able to predict default of borrower's minutes in advance before the true default happened. The system had a precision rate of greater than 95%, suggesting that well over 90% of the borrowers flagged by the system truly were in danger and deserved further attention. As a result, the recall rate was nearly perfect, unearthing most defaults.

Interpretation and implications analyses showed that the CNN-SVM model in the present study provides many data-processing capabilities to assess an extensive array of risk signals. For example, the model could learn to find a pattern where it saw that people with a drop in income over the last time period and increased credit card spend and increased delay of payments are more likely to default. Traditional models might miss such subtle changes — but the hybrid model could take them as harbingers.

Implication: If integrated, this early warning system could be a key insurance for financial institutions in better managing credit risk. Such efforts allow banks to act when a default is only imminent and offer relief like loan restructuring, financial advice or increased account monitoring, all before the default. Though this seems like an aggressive play, it not only saves the financial institution from potential losses but also allows borrowers to keep their credit in good standing.

Results and Discussion

The evaluation of the hybrid model was based on a series of performance metrics, i.e., accuracy, precision, recall, F1-score, and Area Under the Curve (AUC). The applied results reveal that the proposed CNN-SVM hybrid model performed significantly better by leveraging the advantages of both types, compared to single type of CNN and other potential hybrid combinations.

Experimental results show that the CNN-SVM model outperforms the standalone CNN approach (86.7% accuracy) and a hybrid version with either an RF (95.5% ROI) or DT (96.9%) classification engine). The most accurate model that can predict both classes like, who will be the defaulter and who will not be.

That is why calculating precision and recall in credit risk prediction is important. Both false positives and false negatives can be extremely costly in financial terms, via the incorrect marking of a borrower as defaulting or failing to identify him. The CNN-SVM model achieved the highest precision of 97.5% for each one, along with a recall of 99.6%, to reduce both types of errors significantly.

F1-Score and AUC: The F1-score is the harmonic mean of precision and recall. The higher the F value, the better the recovery and prediction rate.

Classification Error: The classification error, which measures the fraction of incorrect decisions, was the least for CNN-SVM, showing it did a better job compared to other comparison models

We further compared the hybrid models with baseline models, comprising logistic regression and individual decision trees. Also, these hybrid models outperformed the baselines, which gives us a rough idea that classical machine learning, combined with deep learning, is also an efficient technique.

Literature has shown a hybrid model of SVM and CNN, RF, DT with CNNs for credit risk prediction. By incorporating deep learning while taking advantage of the strengths of both traditional machine learning and deep learning algorithms, the proposed model yields a better tradeoff between accuracy and robustness. In fact, the CNN-SVM Hybrid model showed excellent performance in most of the metrics, which may suggest that it is an interesting tool for financial institutions to improve their credit risk management.

Further research of incorporating other machine learning algorithms like Gradient Boosting Machines (GBM) or Extreme Gradient Boosting (XGBoost) with the ensemble model could be novel. Researchers could validate the generalizability of the model by applying it to a wider range of datasets from different regions or industries. Integrating interpretable AI methods, like SHAP values, for example, can improve the interpretability of our model, providing action-able insights for financial decision makers as well.

7. Banks with credit risk prediction ML models

The top five banks undertook credit risk using machine learning (ML). Some solutions that are enabled using this may be (a) customizing ML models developed elsewhere, (b) Introducing external vendor solution into their landscape or even (c) develop their in-house.

1. JP Morgan Chase, ML for Credit Risk analysis.

Example: JP Morgan Chase built "AI-Driven Risk Assessment System (ADRAS)", for a solution that can reduce the time taken by its credit risk evaluation application. The system can analyze borrower data and predict the chances of defaults by also integrating structured as well as unstructured data sources.

Technology Used: ADRAS (with GBM for ranking feature importance and neural networks to detect more complex patterns. The system also incorporated such insights as reading through social media, news articles and financial reports using Natural Language Processing (NLP) approaches to identify topics that were not captured in structured risk model scales.

Outside Solutions: JP Morgan Chase partnered with OpenAI and leveraged their language models for its NLP capabilities to analyze textual data. To improve real-time decision-making, the bank deployed FICO's Falcon Platform for fraud detection as part of an overall implementation with ADRAS.

We could increase the accuracy of our risk predictions by 20% for JP Morgan Chase after we integrated advanced ML models and external NLP solutions to better evaluating credit risk. That truly worked well in cutting the quantity of non-performing loans, making credit standing portfolios additional efficient and delivering enhanced financial overall health into the bank.

2. Wells Fargo: Modelling the Predictive Power of Risk

The Use Case Example: Wells Fargo implemented an in-house ML tool "Predictive Credit Risk Analytics (PCRA)" to improve its credit risk management techniques. Its content analyzed those customer credit histories and real-time transactional data to predict which ones were most likely to default — by this point probably several levels of indirection from anything a human would recognize.

Technology Used: PCRA used the Random Forest (RF) for accurate classification of high-dimensional data, owing to its robustness and Support Vector Machines (SVM) because of their ability to account for nonlinear relationships. We used the Synthetic Minority Over-sampling Technique (SMOTE) to handle imbalanced data so that the model can recognize defaulters and non-defaulters as well.

External Solutions: Also, partnered with IBM Watson of Wells Fargo to better understand customer behavior using cognitive analytics over massive data sets. The bank also leveraged SAS Advanced Analytics for data management and predictive analytics, which were incorporated into PCRA to speed up the analysis.

Benefits: Tentam has seen recall rates improved to over 95% with the predictive models in PCRA, enabling the bank to better predict which customers are likely not going to pay. As a result, Wells Fargo could get out in front of things with loan restructuring and saw an overall default reduction of 15%, resulting in more lending practices.

3. HSBC: Instant Credit Risk Estimation

HSBC has launched a real-time credit risk scoring system called "Dynamic Credit Evaluation System (DCES)." This system continuously monitors and adjusts credit limits based on the financial behavior of potential borrowers.

This system could provide real time credit risk faced by the company based on ongoing transaction level data.

Technology Used- DCES used Convolutional Neural Networks (CNN) for feature extraction from complex financial datasets, and SVM for classifying risk levels using the extracted features. We developed this as a system based on real-time data processing, using Apache Kafka for streaming data and Apache Flink for processing those in real time.

External Solutions: HSBC partnered with Amazon Web Services (AWS) to leverage cloud computing infrastructure to process and store a plethora of data. HSBC began using Palantir Foundry to unify diverse data sets and extract intelligence which would enable them to take meaningful action in the aftermath.

It improved the bank's ability to test credit risk, reprice and limit the credit of loans had a 30% PRICES in risk management efficiency in this division. The bank could improve portfolio health and lower its risk of bad debt through this proactive approach.

4. Asset securitization, Short-Term Money Markets and Bank of America: An Early Warning System for Loan Defaults

Bank of America has implemented an early warning system called Proactive Risk Management (PRM) to predict and prevent loan defaults before they happen. PRM analyses multiple risk indicators and sends out real time alerts for potential defaults.

Technology: Here PRM used the various combinations of traditional method such that CNNs for feature extractions and SVM for classification tasks. To train and deploy the model, we integrated it with Microsoft Azure Machine Learning service, a cloud-based AI platform that provides a precise scalable solution to our efficiency problem.

EXTERNAL EXPLORATION: working with Equifax, Bank of America improved its benchmark prediction power by incorporating expanded credit data from partners to PRM. The bank also used H2O. ai AutoML Studio with its automation hyperparameter tuning and model optimization capabilities at a glance.

Pros: Bank of America leveraged the PRM system to spot its high likeliness defaults weigh in advance with an accuracy rate of >95%. This would let in the bank to take you remain, for example, reprogramming of debt, minimize of non-performance and reduction in financial losses.

5. Citibank — Hybrid ML models to predict Loan Credit Risk

Case Study: Citibank created a credit risk scoring model, called CitiRisk Insights, applying a blend of machine learning techniques to enhance the performance and improve accurate assessments of borrowers. Using a similar model, Citibank applied it to borrower default probabilities. They did it by analyzing a mix of financial data streams, each with comprises unique information about the borrowers.

Technology used: CitiRisk Insights leveraged CNNs for capturing high-level features from complex data with RF and DT classifiers, leading to precise prediction. Citibank used its own data and a Google Cloud AI Platform to build the model, which Citibank then trained.

Externally Developed Solutions, such as consortium partnerships, offer benefits by utilizing shared data. For instance, Citibank collaborated with Experian to incorporate advanced credit scoring data, enhancing the reliability of predictive models. Most importantly, the success of CitiRisk Insights leveraged TensorFlow for developing and deploying deep learning models.

Actions Take-aways for peers and other banks: The accuracy of the CitiRisk Insights model was 98.6%, a significant improvement over origin score-based models. The CitiRisk Insights model's increased accuracy improved credit risk evaluation reduced false positives and negatives, and enhanced loan application approval decisions, resulting in improved credit portfolio quality for the bank.

These use cases demonstrate how top banks have used machine learning-based credit risk management solutions, combining their internal innovations with external technologies and services. The resulting systems have driven substantial advances in credit risk assessment, predictive accuracy, and overall risk management performance.

The top five banks in Asia already provide machine learning (ML) to evaluate or manage credit risk. Every use case gives the details of the ML models used (external or internal developed) and, if the banks were

partnering with another vendor.

1. Industrial and Commercial Bank of China (ICBC): Artificial Intelligence in Credit Risks Management

Use Case: ICBC replaces "manual" credit assessments to improve accuracy. Obviously, a real-life use case is fitting. So many of these AI accelerators with a banking as well insurance company across the backyard... say no way! The point of the system was to analyze big data on customer behavior, credit history, and regional economic trends to determine credit risk.

Technology Used: SmartRisk has used XGBoost (Extreme Gradient Boosting) for feature selection and classification, as it is efficient in handling large datasets with high dimensionality. With such sequential data–like a time-series credit transactions, they used Long and Short-Term Memory (LSTM) networks, which helped improve the accuracy of predictions for credit risk.

External Solutions: We provide auto parts lifecycle and shopping application; Partner with Alibaba Cloud to use the cloud computers for processing data in large cases at reasonable cost. The TIHON team adopted Credit tech solutions from Ant Financial to embed various types of alternative credit scoring data, including payment histories on e-commerce platforms.

China Pro-Holly SmartRisk process in professional classes, High-risk loan bargaining, then default rate fell 25%! Its advanced analytics capabilities enabled ICBC to make more insightful credit decisions, leading to enhanced credit portfolio management and lower financial risk.

2. Nanyang Technological University (NTU): SBI Machine learning for retail credit risk

Case in Point: Bank of Later came up with an internal machine learning model, "Bank of Later Insight", to predict retail credit risk better. The model would evaluate loan applications based on a variety of borrower data, such as income, spending habits and credit history.

Technology Used: SBI Insight uses the combination of RF (Random Forest) and SVM (Support Vector Machines) to classify the Borrowers into different categories of risk. All these factors boosted the resilience of the model because it used ensemble learning in combination with predictions from multiple algorithms.

Externally Tool: SBI combined Credit Risk Score of Experian into their model to improve the predictive power. One way they achieved this was by using IBM Watson, a form of cognitive computing, to integrate unstructured data into their risk assessment. This included transcripts from customer contacts and their social media footprint.

Benefit: SBI Insight 18% More Accurate Credit Risk Prediction, Enhancing Loan Approvals This led to a 15% reduction in non-performing loans (NPLs) and increased financial stability of the bank's retail loan portfolio.

3. DBS Bank (Singapore): Early Warning System with AI for Corporate Lending

Case in Use: DBS Bank developed a corporate lending, AI-based credit risk management system, named "DBS ForeSight." The system monitored financial and operational data to recognize early signs of financial distress in corporate clients.

Technology Used: DBS ForeSight deployed RNNs and Auto-encoders to understand time-series data providing anomaly detection in financial performance. The system combines Natural Language Processing (NLP) technologies to glean insights from news articles, financial reports, and industry publications.

Integration with other solutions: For DBS, they used MS Azure to deploy their AI models and deployed them through Azure Machine Learning services. They leveraged Palantir Foundry for data integration and analytics, enabling them to unify structured and structured data sources in a platform tailored for risk analysis.

Benefits: Using DBS ForeSight, the bank could spot warning signs of potential defaults up to a few months in advance, enabling them to take preventive actions such as restructuring or higher monitoring. This allowed DBS to improve its credit risk management in the corporate lending portfolio by almost 90% of accuracy accorded with predicting corporate defaults.

4. MUFG (Mitsubishi UFJ Financial Group): AI-based Credit Scoring System

MUFG has developed an AI-driven credit scoring system, "MiraCredit", to improve the accuracy of credit risk assessments for individual and small business loans. Example: Use Case It worked with a multitude of different sources of data, from traditional financial data to alternative types (including even things like social media activity and online reviews).

Usage of Technology: MiraCredit deployed Gradient Boosting Decision Trees (GBDT) for predictive modelling and unleashed Deep Neural Networks (DNNs) to accommodate highly complex, non-linear data relationships. To increase interpretability of their decisions, they LIME- and SHAP-like features by adopting Explainable AI (XAI) techniques.

Secondary Data: MUFG shared it had collaborated with Nikkei Research to get external datasets they could use to improve the predictive power of MiraCredit. They also used Google Cloud AI services for continued real-time processing of credit applications and machine learning model deployment at scale.

Advantages: MiraCredit increased audit accuracy in evaluating credit risk by 22%, thus making more reliable credit decisions and, respectively, reduce loan default cases. The explain ability features of the system also played a role in gaining regulatory approval, increasing trust from customers and making the lending process more transparent.

5. Predicting Credit Default: CCB Case (Hybrid AI Models)

Case: CCB Guardian, a hybrid AI model for credit risk prediction to improve both retail and corporate lending risk management. The system was going to marry the old school credit scoring methods with newer and highly sophisticated AI-powered analytics.

Method Applied: CCB Guardian used a hybrid feature extraction — Convolutional Neural Networks (CNNs) and ensemble classifiers, including Random Forest (RF) and Decision Tree (DT). The platform could operate high-volume data, such as historical customer transaction types, credit scores, and macroeconomic stats.

Out-of-the-box Solutions: CCB used Tencent Cloud's AI Platform to power the system for data processing and machine learning. In addition, the bank applies Baidu's AI capabilities to analyze unstructured data as customer feedback and news reports by using NLP methods.

Benefits: The CCB Guardian system has an accuracy rating of 98% for predicting credit risk, which is better than previous models. A better segmentation of risk assessment and a sharp drop in the default rate, which contributed towards strengthening risk management activities within the bank.

The above use cases illustrate how some of the leading banks in Asia have adopted machine learning and AI technologies to improve their credit risk management processes. With internal developments and the use of external technologies and services, these banks have generated major advancements in predictive accuracy, risk management efficiency, and financial robustness.

Five of the top small banks have experimented with, or implemented, machine learning (ML) for credit risk evaluation or management. Each case has a detailed coverage of particular ML models involved, external solutions or vendors that are applied and internal banks-made deliveries.

1. Credit Risk Management at Starling Bank (UK)

For instance, Starling Bank has created an artificial intelligence-based system "Starling Risk Analyzer" to optimize credit risk management in its digital banking. Starling Bank developed a system called "Starling Risk Analyzer" to assess the solvency of clients seeking loans and credit cards. They designed it specifically for issuing credits to small businesses and freelancers.

Technology Used: Starling Risk Analyzer used GBM for risk scoring and RNN to model time series like day of the week spending and income variation. It also featured the use of Explainable AI (XAI) methods for implementation transparency in decision-making.

Third-Party Solutions: Starling Bank built their own Digital First Bank using external providers like Finicity (a financial data aggregator) for real-time income verification and cash flow analysis. The bank also implemented Amazon Web Services (AWS) for elastic cloud computing and storage of data.

Starling Risk Analyzer saw a 20% increase in loan approvals with negligible risk without changing the behavior of bank, but still better ability to assess credit risk for non-traditional customers. The deployment of XAI also improved customer confidence as it led to making the credit decision more visible.

2. Tandem Bank (UK): Credit Scoring using Machine Learning

Tandem Bank used a machine learning-powered credit scoring system called Tandem Score to analyze credit risk for its retail banking customers. It offered real-time credit scoring to underserved customers with little of a track record in borrowing or those with non-standard income sources.

Technology deployed: Tandem Score used Support Vector Machines (SVM) for classification and K-Means Clustering to drive customer segmentation based on risk profiles. Its designers built the system to learn better continuously by adapting to new data.

External solutions: Tandem Bank worked with the FinTech company Plaid to aggregate and analyze the transaction data of customers, enabling greater predictive accuracy for its Tandem Score. Google Cloud AI also served as the infrastructure to deploy their machine learning models and data processing at scale.

Tandem Score made it possible for the bank to lend to customers with non-traditional financial backgrounds. As a result, the bank increased its reach within the market by acquiring 25% more customers without increasing risk; it kept default rates at very low levels.

3. Shinhan Bank Vietnam: Credit Risk Prediction

Shinhan Smart Credit is being used by Shinhan Bank Vietnam for credit risk prediction for small and medium-sized enterprises (SMEs) as a domestic business. The system creators can adjust and improve it to meet the unique needs of lending to small businesses with inconsistent cash flow and limited credit history, making it more user-friendly and efficient.

Methods deployed: Shinhan Smart Credit relied on Random Forest (RF), and Logistic Regression models to assess credit risk. The system also leveraged Natural Language Processing (NLP) to analyze unstructured data from business documents and social media.

Partnership and other options: The bank collaborated with FPT Corporation, a top technology firm in Vietnam, to build machine learning models and implement them. Second, they incorporated data from the country's credit reporting agency, the Vietnam Credit Information Center (CIC), to improve the accuracy of their credit assessment.

The bank could better predict credit risk for small and medium enterprises, through Shinhan Smart Credit, which led to a 30% decrease in non-performing loans (NPLs) in this segment. This expanded the bank's SME lending portfolio and increased small business growth and inclusion.

4. Metro Bank (UK) — AI in Real-Time Credit Risk Monitoring

Use Case: To manage credit risk across its retail and business banking operations, Metro Bank implemented a real-time credit risk monitoring system called 'MetroAlert'. As part of the system design, developers included continuous monitoring functionality. This feature alerts for high-risk consumer transactions and detects any transformation of benign financial activities into illicit behavior.

Technology used: MetroAlert used Convolutional Neural Networks (CNNs) for feature extraction and auto encoders for abnormality detection on the client transaction data. The system further employed Time-Series Analysis to recognize trends or patterns can form the basis for credit risk.

Solution developed with an external company: Metro Bank worked with Experian to enrich their credit scoring data and incorporate it into MetroAlert. The bank also employed Azure Machine Learning to distribute their AI models, as well as handling the system's real-time data streaming requirements.

Benefits: The MetroAlert solution empowered Metro Bank to identify early indications of financial difficulty in its customer base, enabling the banking business to take early interventions, including loan restructurings and heightened monitoring. A proactive initiative that resulted in a 25% decrease in the volume of loan defaults and drastically improved the bank's general risk governance.

5. Capitec Bank (South Africa): Hybrid ML for Credit Risk Assessment

Capitec Bank: Capitalizing on "The new incumbents" by developing a hybrid machine learning model to assess credit risk at scale within their rapidly expanding client base — Capitec Rick Guard By integrating long-accepted credit scoring techniques with sophisticated machine learning, the model could increase its predictive precision.

Capitec Rick Guard used a hybrid approach for technology implementation.

They first employed XGBoost to short-list features in the initial stage, and then built a deep learning model using TensorFlow's Deep Neural Networks (DNNs) to capture non-linear relationships within the data.

Enterprise Solutions: Capitec Bank incorporated data from TransUnion to improve its credit scoring models. The bank also has a partnership with H2O.ai for automatic machine learning with hyperparameter tuning, which it used to optimize its Capitec Rick Guard.

What happened: Implementing Capitec Rick Guard resulted in a 15% increase in loan approval rates for low-risk customers, and we discovered that the default rate decreased by 10%. Benefits include a higher loan approval rate and a lower default rate.

Here are a few cases that show how machine learning and AI have had an impact on credit risk management for small banks. Incorporating internal solutions and leveraging external technologies improved these banks' financial position and enabled better credit risk assessment, allowing them to provide loans to a broader customer base.

A brief introduction on how machine learning has reformatted the bank's credit risk management, including its use-cases and more. Financial institutions have long favored traditional credit risk models, such as logistic regression and decision trees. However, such models often cannot capture the complexity of modern financial data, which is non-linear and high-dimensional.

The paper introduces a new hybrid model that combines Convolutional Neural Networks (CNNs) with traditional machine learning algorithms, such as Support Vector Machines (SVM), Random Forest (RF), and Decision Trees (DT). This hybrid method makes the best use of CNNs for feature extraction and traditional models for classification, hence enhancing both the prediction accuracy and model robustness in credit risk predictions.

JP Morgan Chase and Starling Bank are two banks around the world that have been able to show the benefits of using ML in credit risk management. This is because they have homegrown solutions that are tailormade for the requirements, besides opening to leverage external technologies and partnerships to fill their gaps.

In short, implementing ML and AI into credit risk management are entirely reshaping how banks observe and unwanted risks. Results show that integrating models and actual examples provides a more accurate prediction of outcomes, besides rooted insights for proactive risk management strategies. Adopting the notions and developing these technologies will help financial institutions navigate volatile economies, hedge portfolios and play their role in an ever-increasing speedy economic environment.

Reference – Further reading - Chapter 10

Melese, T., Berhane, T., Mohammed, A., & Walelgn, A. (2023). Credit-Risk Prediction Model Using Hybrid Deep Machine-Learning Based Algorithms. **Scientific Programming, 2023**. Article ID 6675425.
https://doi.org/10.1155/2023/6675425
Towards Data Science. The Role of Machine Learning in Credit Risk Assessment.
https://towardsdatascience.com/credit-risk-modeling-with-machine-learning-8c8a2657b4c4
Credit Risk Management platform
https://www.verifiedmarketresearch.com/product/credit-risk-management-platform-market/
Here are relevant reports on : credit-risk-management-market
https://www.marketsandmarkets.com/report-search-page.asp?rpt=credit-risk-management-market
Artificial Intelligence and Machine Learning in Financial Services
https://crsreports.congress.gov/product/pdf/R/R47997
Artificial intelligence in banks
https://www2.deloitte.com/content/dam/Deloitte/ca/Documents/audit/ca-audit-abm-scotia-ai-in-banking.pdf
McKinsey- Risk Advanced Analytics
https://www.mckinsey.com/capabilities/risk-and-resilience/how-we-help-clients/risk-advanced-analytics
AI Credit Scoring: The Future of Credit Risk Assessment
https://www.datrics.ai/articles/the-essentials-of-ai-based-credit-scoring
New Age Lending /Credit Scoring Platform With AI/ML
https://www.ibm.com/blogs/digital-transformation/in-en/blog/new-age-lending-credit-scoring-platform-with-ai-ml/
AI and Model Risk Governance
https://www.jpmorgan.com/technology/news/ai-and-model-risk-governance
Navigating the Future of Credit Risk: The AI and Automation Advantage
https://bankautomationnews.com/allposts/ai/navigating-the-future-of-credit-risk-the-ai-and-automation-advantage/
HSBC: Embracing the cloud to lower risk exposure through rapid insight and analysis capabilities
https://cloud.google.com/customers/hsbc-risk-advisory-tool
Risk Management Strategies of Bank of America
https://studycorgi.com/risk-management-strategies-of-bank-of-america/

ELEVEN

Use of AI in Trade Finance

AI has been disrupting almost every industry possible; trade finance is one of the most rapidly modernized sectors in Favor of widespread AI adoption.

Introduction

Use of AI-powered automation in trade finance has drastically improved efficiency, accuracy, and compliance for a wide variety of critical functions. These AI and machine learning technologies have a wide range of use cases. For example, businesses can use them for vessel monitoring and tracking, as well as for examining documents under documentary credits. They offer significant time efficiency savings by automating operations and mitigating risks.

AI systems might cover various processing stages by retrieving information from different databases, grouping products, estimating risks, and guaranteeing regulatory conformity. The major banks have also used these technologies, such as Deutsche Bank, HSBC and Standard Chartered, that lead to better compliance and risk management.

Vessel Monitoring and Tracking: AI in vessel monitoring and tracking allows for real-time data collection, predictive analytics, and compliance monitoring. Standard Chartered and Deutsche Bank are among those fine-tuning ways to track vessels movements using AI powered tools, to optimize routes and watch for signs of potential violations.

OCR and NLP technologies help to automate data extraction, validation, and discrepancy identification in AI-powered examination of documents under documentary credit. This will reduce human errors and processing time. Banks are using AI to automate data extraction, validation, and discrepancy identification in the examination of documents under documentary credit, which has proven to be more efficient and accurate. Examples like HSBC and Standard Chartered show this.

Again, there is no better example of AI than in the matching of the wording for a discrepancy to post result back into refusal notice. With automated discrepancy detection, classification and wording generation, AI enhances clue letters are easy to understand, straight to the point and meet all regulatory requirements. Examples of this implementation are HSBC, Standard Chartered or sector-neighbor capture Deutsche Bank, which now benefit from better operational efficiency and compliance after leveraging AI.

Conclusively, AI and ML in trade finance operations facilitate a bank to perform complex functions with utmost accuracy and speed. The digital transformation combines multiple emerging technologies which not only automate workflows and minimize manual intervention in your organization but also improves regulatory compliance and reduces the enterprises' risk. Examples from the frontiers of trade finance at leading banks have shown just that — AI driven automation is a Gamechanger for an otherwise dated, disjointed and overly complex trade environment. Enabling tools. This technology not only simplifies the workflow and reduces manual intervention, but it also ensures better regulatory compliance and risk management. Several of the largest banks have showed that AI-powered automation is a genuine breakthrough in trade finance. Provides a solid answer in today's trade environment.

Trade Finance Automation with AI/ML

1. Scanning & OCR Capability

Using AI-powered Optical Character Recognition (OCR), you can make physical documents into digital text.

Extracts data from trade finance documents, including invoices, letters of credit and shipping documents.

With Advanced OCR, it is possible to detect multiple fonts with styles and handwriting, instead of just a single font.

2. Out of the Box% 98 Data Extraction

Authorization / AI/ML model for extracting data at high precision using trade finance documents

For pre-trained models, they have a score that is over 98% accurate in extracting relevant data points, such as transaction details, amounts and dates.

It can easily unite with the current system as well and does not require a type of extensive set up.

3. Multiple Language Support and Wished For Translations

With the support of languages across different AI-driven systems, global trade finance becomes more cohesive.

Multilingual Processing: Integration with a variety of Optical Character Recognition (OCR) and Natural Language Processing (NLP) libraries ensures accurate scanning, reading, and processing of your documents in multiple languages.

Global Reach: Customers from various regions can trade together with documents in their native languages.

4. Easy for Uptrain for Any New Document/Form Type

Note that we can enhance AI/ML systems to adapt with new document types and forms.

Adaptability — untrain the models with new samples of documents to achieve higher results when processing unknown formats.

Ongoing Education: The system grows with the business, enabling new paper types to be added as they appear.

5. Post using Many Document Formats and API

Document upload and processing via AI/ML Systems is very flexible.

Supports Multiple Formats — PDF, Image, Scanned copies

API Integration: Yobota powers their existing platforms for you to upload and enter documents into the system.

6. File ID and Dividing the Files

Trade Finance article classification model.

Classification–Applying Machine Learning (ML) algorithms to identify original documents such as invoices, bills of lading and letters of credit based on their content & structure. Within in set of documents, review each document to segregate.

Upon categorization, organization helps in the workflow of processing all kinds of documents with ease.

7. Documentary Credit document TCP and ISBP Level of Checking, etc.

Companies now readily find out compliance with industry standards and regulations in trade finance documents using AI, making it the most common use.

Screening for UCP and ISBP: Confirmatory Check of Documents against the Uniform Customs and Practice for Documentary Credits (UCP) and International Standard Banking Practice (ISBP).

In-depth Inspection: Covers the identification and authentication of various forms of documents on their conformity to the requirements associated with trade finance transactions.

8. Identifying the Checks with Compliance / Non-Compliance

AI-driven systems analyze trade finance documents to identify inconsistencies.

Password Complexities: discrepancies between current details and expected values show possible exposure, fraudulent use of accounts or services.

Automated Checks: Compare document details on how they should appear, alerting to compliance issue or discrepancies

It minimizes the risk of human error, meaning that the system can only process documents that fully comply with local laws and regulations. It flags those documents that are missing key specifics for review.

Identification of Complying and Discrepant Checks

AI-driven systems identify discrepancies in trade finance documents.

Automated Checks: Compare document details against expected values, identifying compliance issues or discrepancies.

Accuracy reduces the risk of human error, ensuring that the system processes only compliant documents, while flagging discrepant ones for review.

Workability Check for Incoming SWIFT Messages (MT700, 710, 720, 707)

Parsing of Messages: The AIML system will parse SWIFT messages, filtering incoming messages and extracting key data elements and transactional details.

Standard Chartered conducts a compliance check where they run the messages through AI algorithms to check them against SWIFT standards and format specifications (MT700, 710, 720, 707).

Rule-based Validation: AI-fueled rule engines validate the messages for adherence to internal and external compliance regulations catching any discrepancies or errors.

The automated workflow will push validated messages to processing queues while requiring manual review for non-compliant messages.

Clinical monitoring: AI continuously monitors new messages and would ideally alert in real time if it flags or suspects any message of a critical issue.

A workflow that automatically identifies data files as part of the process for regulatory review using AI-based algorithms

1, Data Review.

Data Aggregation: AI collects data from a variety of sources inside the organization (e.g., internal databases, customer transactions), and additional sources external to the org (e.g., regulatory reports).

Normalization of data — Machine learning models normalize the data formats so that there is consistency across different sources.

Real-time Data Integration: AI-powered platforms connect data in real-time so that regulatory reports are always based on the most current information.

2. Data Validation and QC

To automate validation testing, an AI algorithm tests the data against regulatory stipulations to ensure its completeness, accuracy, and compliance.

Machine learning models can flag the data to fix or notify anomalies, inconsistencies, or errors in the data for error detection and correction.

Continuous data quality monitoring through AI to guarantee that regulatory standards are always in place.

3. Regulatory Reporting

Automated Report Processing — When given all the data necessary, AI systems can produce regulatory reports using this information and moving it into required regulatory text/doc formats.

Compliance Check — AI-powered rule engines ensure all the reports are compliant to regulatory guidelines and standards prior to submission.

On the spot actualizations: Just as quickly provide actual-time updates and alerts on adjustments to regulatory requirement, assuring into fact is all the time in compliance.

4. Risk Management and Compliance Monitoring are 2 most important thing as far as the trading business goes.

Predictive Analytics: Machine learning models examine data patterns and forecast historical trends that may show potential compliance risks, enabling proactive management.

Regulatory Surveillance—to track trading-related transactions and activities efficiently, ensuring regulatory compliance and predicting issues before they become significant challenges.

AI identifies anomalous patterns or behaviors that could show noncompliance or potentially regulatory risk, too.

Automated Process for AI-Training (to screen for The Potential of dual-use goods)

1. Collecting and Semi-Supervised Joint Training of Data

Data Aggregation — AI systems combine data types spanning trade databases, product catalogues and regulatory lists from a range of different sources. Bank also added a B2B Documents Collection from Bank to other party.

Data normalization: Machine learning models normalize data to adhere to standardized formats. Because it's really challenging to do application standardization, all the companies are using different formats of LCs, guarantees and bills. Artificial Intelligence which converts all applications to a standard format.

Ai platforms offer real-time data integration, enabling the existing information to be assessed and updated continuously. Banks' application to generate, check and allow B2B documents functions online in real-time 7x24.

2. Product Classification

AI — powered NLP algorithms then began CORS analyses of product descriptions | spec data-points as well auto generating Classification Listings to identify dual-uses.

Machine learning models are employed to determine the classification of dual-use goods by comparing them to recognized standards and lists for distribution.

3. Monitoring and Reporting

Continuous Monitoring: AI systems are watching trade transactions and goods shipments for possibly dual-use items.

Automated Alerts: Using NLP, AI delivers real-time alerts for any subset of goods identified as potential dual used to facilitate rapid response and decision-making.

Regulatory Reporting is not only capable of generating compliance reports and documentation for regulators, it ensures a path for accurate and best hired reporting.

5. Decision Support

Recommendation Systems: AI recommends us with measures depending on the evaluation of dual-use features to facilitate decision-making.

Use Case: AI models build and simulate across various scenarios to measure the potential ramifications and risks of dual-use goods.

Bank Applications for AI/ML in Dual-Use Good Review

AI-infused systems are at work in banks evaluating how they might dual-purpose materials are in their trade finance operations. AI models review product data and extract dual-use classification of products.

Pros: Better adherence, lower regulatory enforcement risk and strengthened decision-making.

Vessel Monitoring and Tracking with an AI-Enabled Automated process

1. Data Collection and Unification

TERRASTAR Data Integration provides AIS data from vessels, which allows for real-time visibility of vessel location and movement.

Satellite Data: brings together data and satellite imagery for those times when it is near impossible to get AIS signals.

Weather and Environmental Data — Integration of the weather and environmental data to understand and even predict vessel movements.

Here are the types of data that we can store on your behalf: Historical Data includes the collection of historical movement and transaction data for pattern recognition and predictive analytics.

2. Real-Time Monitoring

Geofencing: AI systems establish virtual boundaries (geofences) to track if vessels have entered or exited designated areas.

Optimized Routing: ML models elaborate on the real-time data to deliver the routes that are timely and conserve fuel and delay.

Anomaly detection: AI implemented in this algorithm will find the abnormal behavior of a ship, if it deviates from its planned route or stops at some unexpected point, which would show that any unusual activity like smuggling or piracy.

3. Predictive Analytics

Estimate Vessel Arrival Time: AI algorithms calculate estimated time of arrival (ETA) for the vessels at the near real-time and historical level.

Risk Assessment–Predictive analytics evaluate risk for delays because of weather, geopolitical events or port congestion.

This is called supply chain optimization. AI expects potential disruptions on your way and prepares suggested routes or warns about delays.

4. Reporting and Alerts

Automated Reporting — AI systems provide stakeholders with reports on vessel movements, compliance status and risk assessments.

Real-Time Alerts- AI sends Alerts with real time to any anomalies found, potential risks, or breaches.

Interactive dashboards give a clear visual display of vessel movements, risks, and compliance status for easy monitoring

Artificial Intelligence-Powered Automation Mechanism for Creating the Discrepancy Wording ready for Uploading in Refusal Notice

1. Discrepancy Detection

The first component, Automated Document Analysis, employs AI-enabled OCR and NLP to scan trade documents, extract data, and match it with letter of credit terms and conditions.

Rule-Based Validation: It cross-checks the discrepancies as per the pre-defined rules of UCP 600, ISBP, etc.

Detecting Anomalies: This involves a machine learning model to catch inconsistencies in data and any potential outliers.

2. Discrepancy Classification

Now, the question is how to feature the AI part. Which functions are used to identify differences? Are some of those discrepancies categorized by level, description, or date? And how does the system deal with each of them?

NLP models understand the context behind discrepancies, enabling them to determine a class for it accurately and generate a response.

3. Suggestion: Generate Words of Discrepancy

Template-Based Creation: AI generates discrepancy wording by type and nature of the discrepancy, using predetermined templates and language patterns.

Background-NLP technologies parse the discrepancies and then generate clear & concise language to satisfy regulatory requirements.

Different Phrases: The AI provides diverse phrases and words that can cater to the specific requirements and demands of the bank.

4. Refusal Notice Made Automatically

Document Assembly: AI automatically assembles the refusal notice—intelligent enough to pull in discrepancy wording generated directly into sections of the notice.

Thanks to a little template integration and the wording being built in, that consistency is all but granted and you are on track with compliance.

Real-Time Updates—AI keeps pace with real-time updates and alerts user for the change in regulatory requirements so as not to violate wording and notices.

5. Workflow Review and Approval

Automated Routing: AI routs refusal notifications produced to the personnel for review and approval

Collaborative review: With AI driven platforms, the agencies can conduct a collaborative review involving multiple stakeholders, thus ensuring that it is accurate.

AI systems enable the final approval step, making it sure they have been through all needs and validation before notice sent.

Use cases of Top banks have implemented innovative technology, created Straight Through Processing (STP), and inducted AI and ML.

HSBC: The external tools used for implementing AI, ML, and other advanced technologies.

Use Case: To improve transparency, security, and compliance through seamless documentation processes in trade finance operations, HSBC, a leading global bank, is leveraging IBM's TradeLens blockchain platform.

Technology Used: TradeLens Blockchain Platform By IBM: TradeLens helps in secure and transparent management of trade finance documents with the use of blockchain technologies. This ensures that all recipients access the same data simultaneously.

AI-Powered Document Processing uses AI advances to verify trade documents automatically with minimal human oversight, resulting in a significant decrease in errors.

By employing ML models to analyze trade finance documents, HSBC can expect and address potential risks and inconsistencies for better risk management.

Benefits:

Transparency: Blockchain provided HSBC with an accessible and secure record of all trade transactions that could not be changed or altered, resulting in a lower risk of fraud and errors.

Improved Compliance: The AI-based document verification system ensured trade document compliance with international trade laws, reducing the risk of penalties for potential rule violations.

Operational Efficiency: HSBC has achieved a 60% increase in document processing speed by using AI and blockchain to automate document verification. This has resulted in a significantly higher transaction handling capacity for HSBC.

Predictive ML models can help HSBC identify and prevent risks, improving their Risk Management Strategy.

2. Citi Implements Bolero ePresentation for Trade Finance

Use Case: One of the biggest banks in the world, Citi, was looking to digitize its trade finance operations. They did it via Bolero's ePresentation platform. This is helping to digitalize the presentation of trade documents and automation of key processes.

Technology Used: Bolero ePresentation Platform: A secure electronic platform from Bolero for the presentation and exchange of trade finance documents to ensure a fully digital processing dedicated end-to-end.

AI-powered Document Validation: Bolero uses AI algorithms that validate trade finance documents against predefined criteria to guarantee their accuracy and compliance.

Bolero's platform is supported by RPA (Robotic Process Automation) to eliminate repetitive steps in document workflows, reducing manual work for staff.

Benefits: Efficient Operations: Using Bolero's ePresentation platform for transmitting trade documents helped digitize the processing of its trade finance documents, resulting in a 70% reduction in processing times.

Enhanced Compliance:

The introduction of AI-driven document validation ensured that each piece of documentation was in line with the rules and regulations set by federal authorities, reducing the risk of erroneous or non-compliant work.

Lowered Costs: Reduced the expenses of manual document handling by automating document workflows via RPA and AI.

Bolero's encrypted document exchanges also ensured that Citi trade finance operations remained safe from any data leaks, reducing security risks.

3. Implementation in Deutsche Bank-Traydstream AI-based Trade Finance Solution

Use Case: With an ambition to enhance efficiency in their trade finance operations, Deutsche Bank integrates Traydstream's AI-based trade document handling and compliance checking solution.

Technology Used: Traydstream AI-Powered OCR and NLP:

Traydstream platform performs the digitization of trade finance documents using OCR and this data is then further processed by NLP to verify its accuracy and compliance.

Traydstream Machine Learning models used to detect discrepancies in trade finance documents mitigating the risk of errors and delays in processing.

Compliance Management Tools: The platform includes compliance management tools to confirm that all trade finance documents comply with international standards, from UCP 600.

Benefits: Faster Processing: Traydstream reduced the "review" processing time using its AI driven solution by 65%, which allowed Deutsche Bank to manage more transactions.

The AI-enabled platform proactively identified discrepancies, resulting in improved accuracy and compliance-checked documents being processed only.

Cost Efficiency: Through automated trade finance document processing, Deutsche Bank could further streamline processes and decrease operational costs, enabling them to use resources more productively.

Streamlined Compliance: Traydstream's compliance verification tools ensured that documentation had the information for every material fact required to comply with the applicable international trade laws to avoid paying any penalties.

4. Standard Chartered Bank Incorporation with Fusion Trade Innovation Solution.

Use Case: Standard Chartered Bank wanted to strengthen its trade finance business by integrating Finastra's Fusion Trade Innovation platform for the automation of document processing and risk management.

Technology Used: Finastra Fusion Trade Innovation Platform–Including AI-powered document processing that has OCR for trade document digitization and NLP text analyses for validation.

Finastra's Machine Learning Models: Finastra machine learning models predict risks and catch discrepancies in trade finance documents giving time to manage prudently.

A blockchain for trade finance enables secure transactions, linking the platform to the benefits of blockchain technology to ensure transparency and minimize fraud risks.

Benefits: Improved operational efficiency: integrating Finastra's platform has reduced the time taken in document processing by 60% and allowed Standard Chartered to handle more transactions.

Improved Compliance: AI-based analysis ensured all trade finance documents adhere to global standards, eliminating potential risks for incorrect compliance.

Identifying Discrepancy at An Early Stage: ML model proved to be a savior for Standard Chartered as it early noticed the discrepancy and helped them avoid unwanted risk.

Cost reduction: Automating the trade finance operations with Finastra operational cost letting bank to allocate more resources strategically.

5. Trade Finance solution by the BNP Paribas on Komgo's Blockchain Platform

Use Case: Using Komgo's blockchain platform, BNP Paribas wanted to digitalize trade finance transactions and increase transparency in its operations.

Technology Used: Komgo — uses the blockchain to create a secure and transparent trade finance transaction management platform, giving transparency, which is currently lacking in the system of paper-based trade.

AI Document Management: AI algorithms in Komgo help automate the validation and processing of trade finance documents, minimizing human intervention.

Smart Contracts: Automates the execution of trade finance agreements with smart contracts which enforce compliance and reduces disputes.

Benefits: Improved Transparency: BNP Paribas invested in Kongo's blockchain platform to maintain transparent and immutable records of trade finance transactions, effectively preventing abuses or mistakes.

Greater efficiency: BNP Paribas cut the time that it takes for the bank to process trade finance documents using AI-based document management by 70%, helping the bank manage more transactions.

Risk Mitigation: Smart contracts facilitated the auto-execute of trade finance contracts as per terms preventing disputes and delays.
Cost savings: Implementation of blockchain and AI through Komgo reduced the operational costs of manual handling documents and risk management.

Top 5 leading Asian banks, including the external solutions used to implement AI, ML and other groundbreaking technologies.

1. Introduction of Fusion Trade Innovation on DBS Bank

Use Case: By further automating the verification of trade documents and improving compliance checks, DBS Bank intended to reduce documentary credit processing. To do that, the bank chose Finastra and its cutting-edge Fusion platform.

Technology Used: Finastra — A platform within Finastra's open innovation ecosystem. This tool includes an AI-led Optical Character Recognition (OCR) process to digitalise trade finance documents like LOC, BoL & invoice data extraction and processing capabilities.

NLP: The platform uses natural language processing algorithms to scan and validate the extracted text for compliance with international trade standards.

Machine Learning Models — Our ML models at Finastra can predict potential risks and automatically identify discrepancies in the results of documentation.

Blockchain Integration — The platform uses blockchain to protect trade finance transactions, limit fraud and ensure transparency

Benefits: Improved Efficiency: Finastra's platform enabled automation of over 70% of manual verifications, leading to trade transactions being processed in less time.

Compliance Made Easy: By analyzing data on an AI-powered platform, compliance was improved, which reduced errors and risks of non-compliant.

Risk Mitigation — By using predictive ML models, DBS Bank could root out any discrepancies early on and predict problematic areas.

Reduced cost: Enabled by AI and blockchain, Finastra could reduce the operational costs related to document verification and fraud prevention.

2. Trade finance risk management Moody's Analytics ICICI Bank

Use Case: Leveraging Moody's analytics to evaluate and monitor risks in trade deals, particularly in high-volatility markets, ICICI Bank aimed to improve its follow-on trade finance risk scenery.

Technology Used: These ML models, part of Moody's Analytics Risk

Management Solutions, analyze data from diverse sources like trade finance consummation and political information to assess transaction risks.

Predictive Analytics — Moodys predictive tools can forecast risks before they become realities, such as currency swings and supply chain interruptions.

Natural Language Processing (NLP) tools developed by Moody's extract anomalies from trade documents and external unstructured sources, suggesting risk and compliance issues.

Benefits: Proactive Risk Management:

ICICI Bank could identify transactions that may be at high-risk using ML models developed by Moody's, and hence, could take actions based on the rules set if required.

Better Decision Making: Predictive analytics offered ICICI a more reliable view and, as a result, decreased monetary risks caused by unanticipated hosts.

Improved Adherence:

By conducting NLP-based analysis on these trade documents, they could be double-checked against international best-practices, resulting in fewer instances of non-compliance with related-party loan standards float Value, thus reducing the likelihood of regulatory fines.

3. JAPANESE BANK INTRODUCES DOKA-NG Trade Finance Software Package Used by MUFG

Use Case: Mitsubishi UFJ Financial Group (MUFG) has automated the examination of letters of credit (LC) documents for compliance with international trade rules using Surecomp's DOKA-NG solution, seeking greater processing efficiency.

Technology Used: Surecomp DOKA-NG: A trade finance solution that utilizes AI and ML to examine and verify the authenticity of all related trade finance documentation automatically.

NLP (Natural Language Processing): Surecomp leverages NLP algorithms to validate trade documents for regulatory compliance, such as UCP 600.

Robotic Process Automation (RPA): The platform uses RPA to assist users in processing repetitive tasks, such as data input and document classification, improving overall efficiency.

Benefits: Faster Processing Time: With Surecomp's AI-driven automation for document underwriting cutting the time to analyze documents by 60%, transaction processing became expedited.

Better Accuracy: With AI and NLP, we could scrutinise the documents using international standards to reduce errors.

Operational Savings: The automation of import processing decreased the operational cost MUFG spent while document processing and gave them more space to allocate resources effectively.

Improved Compliance: All documents went through Surecomp's solution to verify compliance with international trade regulations, resulting in reduced regulatory risks

4. Windward Secures Deal with Bank of China to Integrate its AI-Powered Maritime Intelligence

Use Case: Bank of China (BOC) From Manual Efforts to Automated Transaction Monitoring: BOC aims at improved visibility and transparency on its trade finance operations; employs Windward AI-powered live vessel-input monitoring solution on particularly high-risk transactions.

Technology Used: Maritime Intelligence Platform (Windward): Windward's AI that combines AIS with satellite imagery and weather data to track vessels in real time.

Risk Management Predictive Analytics: Windward ML models evaluating vessel movements and risks, like delays or deviations from planned routes.

Secure Transactions with Blockchain: The BOC made use of Windward's blockchain solution to employ transparency and security in trade finance transactions.

Benefits: Enhanced Transparency: Windward's solution offers BOC information on where all vessels are in real time, allowing them to act before a delay occurs

Improved Security: Integration with blockchain technology provided transaction security, lessening the chances of fraud and increasing trust between trading partners.

Operational Efficiency This allowed the BOC to better manage trade finance transactions inside a system with greater automation and less manual intervention.

5. Trade Finance Document Processing using ICBC and Traydstream

Use Case: Solution — ICBC could enhance trade finance document processing using Traydstream's AI-powered solution. This solution can deal with extensive trade finance documents such as letters of credit and bills of lading.

Technology Used: Logistics with OCR and NLP by Traydstream:

The platform of Traydstream can be identified to be a potent solution for unstructured data categories or semi-structured documents like those in trade finance that levied OCR and NLP.

Discrepancy Detection through AI: Traydstream explores discrepancies in trade documents using its machine learning models, minimising processing delays.

Traydstream uses Robotic Process Automation (RPA) to enable an automated workflow, beginning from data extraction to final document validation and approval.

Benefits: Efficiency Gains: Traydstream's platform addressed a 65% standard processing time reduction of trade finance documents, meaning ICBC could now process more transactions.

The AI-driven platform improved accuracy by 100% by detecting discrepancies and processing only compliant documents.

Reducing Cost: Combining AI, ML, and RPA in Traydstream has eliminated the expensive manual processing of documents.

Improved Compliance:

Traydstream's update of all trade finance documents to international standards minimized the risk of punitive sanctions.

AI-based technologies are changing trade finance, which optimizes the efficiency, accuracy and compliance of many crucial functions in the industry. The application of AI and machine learning are now indispensable across the industry, from vessel monitoring/tracking to document examination under documentary credits to operate efficiencies and mitigate risks. Leading banks such as Deutsche Bank, HSBC, and Standard Chartered have already adopted these technologies. They help enhance compliance, reduce operational costs, and enable more strategic decision-making capabilities. AI-driven automation is a major leap forward for the trade finance industry, offering sound answers to some of the most pressing problems in the ever-develop world of global trade. Innovative efficiency will grow further than AI and ML mature in trade finance.

Reference – Further reading - Chapter 11

How AI optimises international trade finance
https://group.bnpparibas/en/news/how-ai-optimises-international-trade-finance
Syngenta and HSBC complete paperless trade finance transaction via TradeLens
https://container-news.com/syngenta-and-hsbc-complete-paperless-trade-finance-transaction-via-tradelens/
TradeLens: How IBM and Maersk Are Sharing Blockchain to Build a Global Trade Platform
https://www.ibm.com/blogs/think/2018/11/tradelens-how-ibm-and-maersk-are-sharing-blockchain-to-build-a-global-trade-platform/
The leading cloud-based platform driving the digitisation of global trade.
https://www.bolero.net/
Citi Trade Finance
https://www.citibank.com/tts/sa/latam/icg-innovation-expo/digitizing-trade-finance/assets/docs/Electronic_Trade_Loans_Best_Practices.pdf
Deutsche Bank taps Traydstream to automate document checking for trade finance products
https://www.finextra.com/pressarticle/93620/deutsche-bank-taps-traydstream-to-automate-document-checking-for-trade-finance-products
Real-world asset tokenisation: A game changer for global trade
https://av.sc.com/corp-en/nr/content/docs/Standard-Chartered-Real-World-Asset-Tokenisation.pdf
The Most Advanced Trade Check
https://traydstream.com/trade-finance-solutions-for-banks/
The Largest Multi-Bank Trade Finance Platform
https://www.komgo.io/
RIVO for financial institutions
https://surecomp.com/solutions/for-financial-institutions/rivo-for-financial-institutions/
vessel tracking and real-time monitoring solution
https://windward.ai/solutions/trading-and-shipping/?_gl=1*l28gvc*_up*MQ..&gclid=Cj0KCQjwxsm3BhDrARIsAMtVz6NOrTM-Y3gSmLYLbyanRJ69RYsdXRTOTT90iEPVH8dVa3sF59wWSFsaArPgEALw_wcB

TWELVE

Use of AI in Financial Market

Introduction

AI and ML will reshape the financial market, and the developing time will highly appreciate the future of AI technology. Ever-improving technology, the sudden abundance of data, and the insatiable hunger to reduce costs and improve outcomes define the financial industry and power of this evolution. AI and ML technologies are rapidly maturing and changing the way financial institutions are run. They provide new avenues for better decision-making, risk management, and customer engagement. These are process streamlining technologies, but they ultimately will get institutions to a level where they can compete in this data-driven environment.

In Commerce — Banks and Investment Firms–AI & ML are being heavily implemented to augment trading strategies, improve risk management, customer service or fraud detection! This is being spearheaded by firms such as JPMorgan Chase, Goldman Sachs and Morgan Stanley.

Hedge Funds and Asset Management: AI/ML is being used to trading, manage portfolios, and for market predictions by quantitative hedge funds and asset management companies. This trend is gaining momentum as the efficacy of these technologies in generating alpha and mitigating risk becomes clearer.

The Global Embedded Finance Market Report from Allied Market Research provides insights into the industry's growth and trends, without delving into every market detail. Analysis from Allied Market Research suggests that the global embedded finance market is projected to grow at a CAGR of 25.4% from 2023 to 2032. By 2032, it is estimated to reach $622.9 billion, compared to $66.8 billion in 2022.

Most experts believe that as AI/ML continues to evolve, financial institutions will make heavy investments in these technologies to keep their innovations ahead of the curve and remain competitive. This entails investments earmarked for technology infra, talent acquisition, R&D.

Prospects of AI/ML

1. Exclusory Predictive Analytics: In time, AI/ML models should get more powerful in mining enormous volumes of data emanating from disparate sources like social media, economic factors, market sentiments and predict the outcomes. This results in more accurate predictions and, therefore, better investment strategies.

2. Combining AI with Quantum Computing: At the edge of processing power, quantum computing offers a novel way to boost computational power and tackle complex financial models and data sets on a scale not seen before. Trading strategies, risk ratings, and portfolio optimizations will undergo a significant improvement thanks to quantum computing.

3. Decentralized Finance (DeFi) and Blockchain Integration — In the developing DeFi space, where decentralized applications (dApps) built on blockchain platforms are bootstrapping new financial ecosystems, AI/ML will be foundational. In DeFi markets, AI could bolster security, automate smart contracts and deliver real-time analytics.

4. Individualized Financial Services: AI/ML technologies will give birth to individual behaviors and make it possible to customize financial products and advice in the future, allowing for a personalized financial services pattern. This will improve customer retention and satisfaction.

5. Better Risk Management: Through real-time risk scoring and Predictive Analytics, AI/ML will further enhance the processes of Risk Management for organizations. In doing so, financial institutions will have better tools to navigate risk and adhere to local laws.

6. Ethical AI and Explainable: As AI/ML becomes further entangled into financial decision-making, the leading trend will be in ethical AI and explain ability. It will be important to create models that are visible to humans, allowing them to be vetted.

7. The future would signify increased collaborative systems blending human

and AI capabilities. Financial professionals will use AI systems where they are best suited to complement their decisions.

8. Robo-advisors and AI-driven financial advisory services will become more common, giving relatively simple ways to provide powerful investment to the masses of peoples in a cost-effective manner. It will also democratize financial planning and wealth management.

AI in Financial Market.

1. Algorithmic Trading

Algorithmic trading enables a system to trade automatically at unprecedented micro-second speeds and frequencies, freeing the trader from operating as manually. Some of the large data title processing that AI/ML models carry out is to find patterns in gigantic reams of info and predict when stocks will rise or fall. For instance:

High-Frequency Trading (HFT): Firms such as Renaissance Technologies use AI-based algorithms to place trades within milliseconds entering and exiting financial positions infraction some timeframes of seconds to minutes, allowing them to predict short-term market conditions by analyzing historical trend data using real-time market information.

Quantitative Trading: Quant hedge funds like Two Sigma and Citadel use machine learning models to analyze financial data, social media trends, economic indicators, and other relevant data points to forecast stock prices and execute trades.

2. Sentiment Analysis

Technological development: AI / ML model -based analysis to determine the mood of news articles, social media posts, and other text sources for predicting stock markets. Natural Language Processing (traders use NLP) methods to analyze the market sentiment on stock prices.

Thomson Reuters MarketPsych Indices — This product running analysis over sentiment data from financial news and social media to provide updates on market sentiment. Investors use this data to help with trading decisions.

RavenPack is an AI-driven technology company, providing real-time macroeconomic data from news and social media for financial professionals.

3. Time Series Analysis

Traders make stock price predictions using machine learning models, especially those suited for time series analysis, based on old data.

Researchers have proven that Long Short-Term Memory (LSTM) Networks, which belong to the category of Recurrent Neural Networks (RNNs), are highly effective in time series forecasting. By learning these sequences of past stock prices and other indicators, they can better predict stock prices.

Prophet is a forecasting time series tool, developed by Facebook and open source. Analysts used it to forecast stocks prices and trends where they would model the seasonality and add in external factors.

4. Risks and Portfolio Constraints

AI/ML models predict stock price volatility & returns with AI/ML Models to manage risks and optimize portfolios.

Aladdin, a platform created by BlackRock: an AI risk assessment and investment analysis tool. This has applications for such things as predicting stock price moves and in value weight portfolio optimization to get more return for much less risk.

Wealthfront Automated Investing: This is a robo-advisor that uses AI to handle investment portfolio. It harnesses the power of data to predict the direction of a stock, and its integration with the basket creator aids in balancing portfolios. By evaluating each individual risk profile it ensures that your investments are allocated to suitable assets.

5. Compliance — fraud detection, market surveillance

They help to identify abnormal trading patterns and by judging whether a variety of activities in the market are fraudulent or manipulated by AI/ML techniques.

Nasdaq SMARTS: a machine learning-based surveillance technology for detecting potentially abusive trading practices. It uses historical data and current trades in real time to identify suspicious behavior.

AI is in the game of finance: Goldman Sachs uses AI for anti-fraud and anti-market manipulation inputs. The system uses algorithms to scan trading data for irregular volumes, which could be a sign of insider trading or other manipulations.

6. Retail Warrant Prediction Model

Retail investors can use AI/ML tools to predict stock prices.

Kavout: This AI-powered platform uses machine learning in order to review financial data and provide stock ratings; Kai Score Investors can use the Kai Score to predict how a stock overpriced or oversold over time and market sentiment.

Trefis: that uses AI for disaggregating stock prices into individual components and forecasting future price movements. It offers retail investors a foothold on what moves stock prices and how various forces make them move.

7. Customized Financial Advice

Personalized financial recommendations based on investment goals and market conditions powered by AI/ML algorithms.

Betterment — Betterment is a robo-advisor that uses AI to deliver customized investment solutions. It makes predictions about performing stocks and invests in assets that balance with the client's financial goals and risk tolerance.

Schwab Intelligent Portfolios: A service that offers investors Robo-advised, AI-created and managed diversified portfolios. It does this by forecasting stock prices, as well as rebalancing investments for the highest returns.

1. HFT with AI Algorithms.

Application: High-Frequency Trading for Renaissance Technologies

Tech Used: AI driven Trading Algorithms, Real-time data processing, Recognition of Patterns

SOLUTION FOCUS: Renaissance Technologies use the most advanced AI algorithms to enable high-frequency trades. These are all algorithms, which go through past data and live market information to get patterns of stock prices within milliseconds. The AI models leverage the shorter-term market inefficiencies to trade even faster than any human trader. The idea behind this process involves refining trading strategies to optimize market positions for profitability and a competitive edge.

2. Using ML Models to Quant Trading

Two Sigma and Citadel apply several Quantitative Trading Strategies

Technology & Tools: Machine learning models, data analytics platforms, predictive modelling.

At Two Sigma, and Citadel Solutions, your focus will be on the development of ML models for quantitative trading strategies. These models specialize in sifting through massive datasets (financial data, social media trends, economic indicators, etc.) to predict forces of balance in stock prices and market trends. These organizations can use ML tools to extract the hidden patterns and correlations, which helps them to make more precise predictions for high returns from their financial trades in the market.

3. Sentiment Analysis Using NLP Tools for Market

Examples: Thomson Reuters MarketPsych Indices and RavenPack

Technology & Tools: Natural Language Processing (NLP) sentiment analysis engines, real-time analytics platforms.

Case in Point: Thomson Reuters' MarketPsych Indices and RavenPack are some of the current cutting-edge tools with sentiment analysis capabilities for financial markets. AI-based platforms operating on natural language processing to evaluate data from news articles, social media posts, and different text sources. Then they boil this data to useful insights. This sentiment analysis helps the financial market companies in predicting the movement of stock prices and market trends. This information is valuable for investors to implement in their trade strategies to be smarter and more logical about their decisions by following the real-time sentiment analysis.

4. Getting Stock Prices Forecasting Done with the use of Time Series Analysis

LSTM Networks & Facebook Prophet: A Use Case for Forecasting Stocks

AI:&ML Model Used: LSTM, Prophet (Open Source by Facebook), Time Series Forecasting Model

Solution Direction: Consider using LSTM networks (a type of RNNs) for time series forecasting in financial markets. Companies employ LSTMs to process sequences of historical stock prices and associated indicators, learning complex temporal dependencies that lead to better prediction of future price movements. Prophet — Facebook data scientists launched this one, which is very popular to forecast stock prices. It factors in seasonality and trends, accounts for external variables to predict correctly. It uses such tools for financial markets companies to calibrate their trading strategies by reliable and accurate stock price forecasts.

5. AI Platforms for Risk Management and Portfolio Optimisation

Example: BlackRock Aladdin, and Wealthfront Automated investing

Technology & Tools: BlackRock Aladdin, AI-driven risk management tools and portfolio optimization algorithms

A solution focus example: Aladdin, BlackRock's AI-powered platform for risk management and portfolio optimization for financial market companies The system uses Big Data science to estimate the volatility and returns of stock prices before they occur, thus offering invaluable advice in investments. Wealthfront Wealthfront extensively uses AI to manage investment portfolios through its Automated Investing platform, selecting risk-appropriate asset allocation for each individual. Such AI tools enable companies to reduce risk, drive returns, and increase their portfolio performance.

6. Machine Learning for Fraud Detection and Market Surveillance

Case Study: Nasdaq SMARTS and The Goldman Sachs AI Surveillance Systems

Tech & Tools: Machine learning algorithms, anomaly detection models, real time monitoring systems

Example: Nasdaq SMARTS, and Goldman Sachs work with advanced machine learning algorithms on their market surveillance systems that help to recognize fraudulent activities and market manipulations Historical analysis of data and observation of real-time trades by these systems help to point out any anomalous patterns which might represent fraud. The models continue to learn from new data and hence get more narrow eyes for the detection of fraudulent activities. By approaching the problem proactively, financial market companies can keep the market clean and ensure enforce-able safeguards against regulatory non-compliance.

7. AI PLATFORMS FOR PREDICTIVE ANALYTICS IN RETAIL INVESTING

Kavout: Use Case of Kai Score and Trefis AI Platforms for Trading Data

Technology & Tools: Kavout Kai Score, AI Predictive analytics, financial data analysis platforms.

Solution in Focus: Kai Score is a means of boiling down financial data into stock ratings by use of machine learning provided through the Kavout AI platform. The Kai Score provides a valuable metric for retail investors who wish to make more informed decisions about stocks by providing an index of previous price movements and the sentiment in the market. The company has machines that can eat nearly anything, which FactSet experts believe will help the firm normalize its margins over our forecast period. Retail investors can now gain access to predictive analytics in a way that only large institutions and hedge funds have been able to do so far.

8. AI-Driven Robo-Advisors for Personalized Financial Advice

Betterment and Schwab Intelligent Portfolios [Case Study]

Tech and Tools: AI-Fueled Robo-Advisers, Predictive Analysis, Auto-Investment Algorithms.

Source Focus: Betterment and Schwab Intelligent Portfolios are two over-the-top Robo-advisors, offering machine-learning-based Robo-advice personalization. These platforms create individual investment strategies that consider portfolio allocation, understanding the client and the market trends, as well as risk tolerance. With this information, the AI tools can predict stock trends and allocate assets in real-time to maximize returns while aligning with a client's financial goals. It provides lower cost customized investment solutions that improve customer satisfaction.

The largest hedge funds, including many of the world's biggest financial institutions, are using advanced AI and ML technologies to revolutionize their trading practices. While these companies are achieving much better results by deploying state-of-the-art tools such as AI-driven trading algorithms, NLP for Sentiment Analysis, LSTM Networks for Time Series Forecasting and Machine Learning models for Fraud Detection. They offer higher standards of trading accuracy, risk management and investment insight, which are the keys to differentiate themselves in a rapidly growing financial market environment.

Reference – Further reading - Chapter 12

Allied Market Research - "Embedded Finance Market by Component, Application, and Industry Vertical: Global Opportunity Analysis and Industry Forecast, 2023-2032."
https://www.alliedmarketresearch.com/embedded-finance-market-A110805#:~:text=Embedded%20Finance%20Market%20Research%2C%202032,25.4%25%20from%202023%20to%202032.

How AI Trading Technology Is Transforming the Stock Market
https://intellias.com/artificial-intelligence-predicts-financial-markets/

The Intersection of Finance and Artificial Intelligence: AI-Powered Investment Tools
https://site.financialmodelingprep.com/education/financial-analysis/The-Intersection-of-Finance-and-Artificial-Intelligence-AIPowered-Investment-Tools

How Two Sigma Uses Machine Learning to Make Trading Decisions
https://www.twosigma.com/articles/a-machine-learning-approach-to-regime-modeling/

THOMSON REUTERS MARKETPSYCH INDICES
https://www.matteomotterlini.com/site/wp-content/uploads/2019/12/ff0ec6207c707ae59141dfe784644d2e.pdf

RavenPack - "RavenPack: Transforming Unstructured Data into Actionable Insights."
https://www.ravenpack.com/products/edge/data/news-analytics

Facebook Prophet - "Prophet: Forecasting at Scale."
https://github.com/facebook/prophet?tab=readme-ov-file

BlackRock's Ala and Portfolio Optimization."
URL: https://www.blackrock.com/aladdin

Nasdaq SMARTS - "Nasdaq SMARTS: Surveillance Technology for Market Integrity."
URL: https://www.nasdaq.com/solutions/nasdaq-smarts-surveillance

Kavout's Kai Score - "Kavout's AI-Powered Kai Score: Helping Retail Investors Make Better Decisions."
URL: https://www.kavout.com/kai-score

Betterment - "Betterment: AI-Driven Personalized Investment Advice."
URL: https://www.betterment.com/investment-strategy

THIRTEEN

Use of AI in Transaction Monitoring

Introduction

Keeping track of billions of transactions has become more complex as people worldwide transition to digital payments. 1.2 trillion worldwide non-cash payments hit in 2023 and already banks have reported a suspicious-activity spike by the end of 2024. With regulations increasing, banks are required to have stronger systems for risk management and detection of features like frauds, money laundering and terrorist financing.

Rule-based systems, upon which traditional monitoring methods are based, inundate banks with false positives. These false alarms raise operating costs and increase the workforce, creating additional investments in workforce and technology. When meeting with regulators, banks must provide explanations for flagged transactions, further complicating matters.

AI giving a new twist. The solution leverages machine learning models to identify abnormal behaviors among large volumes of transaction data and adapt to new patterns from emerging threats. AI not only helps decrease inaccurate positives but increases the security posture. However, the key issue with AI is its decision-making mechanism that we often call a "black box" problem. That has regulators worried, as banks are failing to show how AI reaches conclusions on questionable financial data.

Types of Transaction Using AI

1. AI in ATM, ACH Transactions

Banking activities such as Automated Teller Machine (ATM) and Automated Clearing House (ACH) transactions, etc. ATMs are used by customers to withdraw cash, while ACH is used for activities like direct deposits or transfers. Vulnerability consumed them as they realized they were easy targets for scams and fraud. Criminals might attempt to phish for card information, account takeovers or unauthorized transfers.

ATM and ACH Transaction Monitoring

The bank must monitor ATM and ACH transactions. Those transactions occur in high volume, which is the attractiveness of criminals. If the businesses hosting ATMs have their machines compromised, victims can experience significant losses because of simple things like ATM skimming, which involves stealing your card information, or "unauthorized transfers."

Next is to detect suspicious activities for fraud prevention through monitoring. It is also the regulator to ensure compliance with regulations from banks and security of customers' assets.

Major Monitor Techniques of ATM Transactions

Banks monitor transactions as they occur (Real-Time Monitoring): Banks have systems in place that track ATM transactions when the transaction happens. So, they can flag actions — such as huge withdrawal or many transactions in a brief period. Banks can therefore provide fraud detection if they see something wrong.

Geolocation Tracking: Banks track ATM transactions by location. If someone uses a card at two different locations thousands of miles apart within 24 hours, that could show someone cloning or stealing your credit card. These are anomalies that banks can pick up on early with geolocation.

Behavioral Analytics:
Banks analyze the way a customer behaves, which includes what they do and if there has been any unusual activity going on, amplified data only can bolster corporate fraud protection. So, for instance, it will flag someone who makes

many small withdrawals but then moves a bigger sum. It serves to find fraud by identifying irregular activity for banks.

Through Card Usage Monitoring, banks track and capture the number of times a card is used, as well as monitoring its location. Repeated use of a card in rapid fire might show that someone is trying to push the limits or scamming the system. The bank opts to freeze the card or carry out further investigation.

However, skimming — where criminals install a device on an ATM to steal card details can uoy) read more about this here) — is one of the riskiest occurrences. Skimming is a type of fraud that banks can prevent using special tools to detect signs of persistent fraudulent behavior.

Mobile, Online Banking Fraud Monitoring Services

Risks of Using Mobile & Internet Banking

Mobile and internet banking has made it convenient for customers to have control of their money from wherever transactions they are performing. But this convenience also introduces new threats. Criminals breach into accounts, hack the platform at large and exploit any rivets in security or inject deceptive malware to harvest data.

Monitoring mobile and internet banking

Mobile and internet banking is more convenient with can lose your wallet or have it snatched, which supports delays in physical transactions. Bank holdup also fuller does not reduce anymore nowadays, but one thing that increases every day is a prospective bank effort where we get no warning till many days later when our checking account balance shows zero. Cybercriminals' penchant for remaining means behind computer screens, scouring victim activity like predatory cats built for natural hunting, plays into this situation. Thieves often attempt to commit fraud by gaining control of an account, stealing the identity, or making unauthorized transfers. To detect these threats in real-time, monitoring of such transactions is important.

Further Banks also must consider laws such as Anti-Money Laundering (AML) and Know Your Customer (KYC). Being aware of digital banking also helped banks to comply so that it will not back them into a legal issue.

Vitals ways in which to consider mobile web banking

Immediate Alerts: Banks follow mobile banking actions a fraction of the next. Any suspicious activities that involve trading large amounts or being logged in to Binance from another device comes for an alert. Banks can then halt the fraud in its tracks.

Location and Device Tracking: The bank will verify which devices, as well as location, the customers are using. Then, the system alerts if a device is used from a different location or shows similar characteristics that suggest the customer is far away from their regular zone. This can help in preventing credentials from being stolen by fraud or hacked accounts.

Behavioral Analytics: how customers transact and how often their login will be used by banks for analysis. When customers make large payments or log in at strange hours, the system is programmed to detect unusual activity.

Multi-Factor Authentication (MFA): At the time of signing in, banks add extra layers to ensure the customer is who they claim to be. For example, sending an OTP to the customer's phone or asking for a fingerprint scan. MFA ensures transactions are made by authorized users.

App Security Assessments–To secure the logic and integrity of bank mobile applications from any kind of manipulation. They are looking for fingerprints of malware / unauthorized hacks. Customer data will be inaccessible to hackers.

Credit Card & Debit Card Transaction Monitoring

Credit Card Fraud — cause for concern?

Every day, millions of people rely on credit and debit cards for payment transactions. This wide use puts them at high risk of fraud. Your card can be used for illegitimate actions, such as cloning or stealing your card number.

Banks use these logs to monitor transactions and secure customers, avert financial losses according to PCI-DSS (Payment Card Industry Data Security Standard) standards.

Strategies to Monitor Credit and Debit Card Transactions

Real-Time Monitoring: Banks monitor every card transaction using a real-time system. Whatever the amount spent, this system analyses it all. And if something looks suspicious, the bank can flag that transaction for further review.

Behavioral Analytics — The bank tracks the behavior of its customers, which includes how frequently they shop or their location. This transaction raises suspicions, as a customer who typically spends $20-100 CAD suddenly makes a purchase of $2000 CAD in an obscure market.

Using locating card or any transaction online is being a check with geolocation and IP monitoring followed by the banks. If someone uses a card in two distant places within an hour, it may be a fraud. When you use a card in New York, and then an hour later someone uses the same cards to make purchases in London, your bank could block that transaction.

A velocity check records the frequency and speed at which a card user may use their cards. Fraud Suggests fast Transactions or unexpected behavior That includes, for example, drawing on the red flags about multiple uses in different locations a short time a part of one card.

Multiple Levels of Authentication: Banks may require additional confirmation, such as sending a one-time password (OTP) to the cardholder's phone when they bill it for high-risk purchases. Only the authorized user can perform the transaction.

Merchants Category Monitoring allows banks to track where and how cards are being used by looking for merchant categories. For example, if a cardholder uses the association to shop in grocery stores but drops large amounts of money every month at luxury retailers, that transaction will raise an alert. The association uses it for fraud detection based on spending behavior.

Cross-Channel — Banks monitor all channels, which include the in-store POS purchases, online shopping and ATM withdrawals of users. Since sometimes attackers cannot exploit vulnerabilities in one channel, you may find fraudsters impersonating your users through multiple channels at the same time.

Integration with AI and Machine Learning: These tools can help banks identify fraud through past pattern learning. Systems learn and detect fraud. AI also lowers false positives, which translates to fewer blocked genuine transactions.

Trade Transactions in Banks

Trade finance keeps global commerce moving by enabling moving goods and services across borders. It is based on monetary tools such as the letter of credit, infrastructure and remittances. Archival image, video games and the trade-related laundering problem. However, international transactions can be an easy target for moving large quantities of money that eschew existing regulations. The bank is required to oversee trade transactions by law in order not to lose funds and secure the global financial system.

Why are Trade Transactions Tracked?

Since trade transactions are multilateral, involving various parties and countries along with several instruments used, they leave footprints everywhere, which can be hard to follow back. Criminals are abusing this complexity to hide illicit activities, such as trade-based money laundering (TBML). As with other forms of trade-based money laundering, criminals use TBML to move illicit proceeds across borders. Manipulating invoices, whether by inflating or deflating them, can result in significant financial losses for banks and other entities.

Banks track trade transactions to monitor these illegal activities and provide a healthy compliant secure-trade finance running through their banks. Banks adopt monitoring to comply with international standards set by FATF and other AML and CTF laws, not to avoid regulatory hurdles.

Key strategies for chain trade monitoring

1. Proof of Documentation and Validation Checks

Trade transactions have a lot of documents that accompany it like invoices, bills of lading and letters of credit. These documents must be scrutinized by banks for their genuineness and uniformity. The goods on the invoice may be signed at an incorrect value, potentially indicating fraud. Allowing banks to check information in documents among themselves with the help of automated tools reveals such discrepancies.

2. This includes KYC (Know Your Customer) and Due Diligence.

It may seem obvious, but successful monitoring of these topologies begins with knowing who you are dealing with. Banks rely on KYC and due diligence to paper the trade counterparties. They verify the company; owner and it is financial health. Higher risk countries/industries/clients need enhanced due diligence (EDD) from banks. Banks can better assess the risk of each transaction by knowing these parties.

3. Query Against Black/Master Sanction Lists

For banks, trade transactions cannot involve any person or company that figures on a sanctions list in one of the countries. Organizations such as the United Nations, European Union, and U.S. create lists to increase the effectiveness of sanctions. Office of Foreign Assets Control (OFAC) If a person associated with a transaction is on their watch list, banks are required to investigate and report the finding to authorities.

4. Anomalies in Price and Quantity

If goods spike or plummet in price, it can show TBML and put banks on alert. For example, over-invoicing allows criminals to move more money than they should be able to; under- invoicing that enables evading tax payments. Banks declare the value of goods based on prices and similar past data tools. There are large variations, which banks flag up for more detailed investigation.

5. Dual-Use Goods Monitoring

We refer to certain products as dual-use goods because they can be used for both civilian and military purposes. Authorities control these items and enforce tight export controls. Banks monitor these goods to ensure that dual-use items, which can create weapons, do not end up in the wrong hands.

6. Trade Corridor Monitoring

They move on trade routes, referred to as corridors. Banks often monitor these routes for changes like the use of unexpected circuitous paths, new parties entering transaction chains, or significant sudden increases in record trade amounts. As abnormal activities take place along such trade corridors, it can be an indicator of suspicious transactions.

7. End-Use Verification

Banks in high-risk or sensitive industries may sometimes need to investigate the ultimate purpose for which the goods are used. Banks can employ third-party agencies or technology to monitor the movement and utilization of goods post-transaction. This helps them ensure that items are used as intended and not diverted through illegal methods.

8. AI and Machine Learning

Trade transaction monitoring is going to be seen more and more with essential AI/ML tools. Such technologies identify patterns or potential risks by studying sample data amounts. For example, AI can detect strange trade flows or complex ownership structures and even TBML patterns. Machine learning also enables AI systems to improve over time by catching behavior that looks more and more suspicious.

Banks use Cross-border Transactions Monitoring

Cross-border transactions, a critical aspect of global finance, make it possible for capital, goods and services to move between countries. But they entail risks including fraud, money laundering and terrorist financing and tax evasion and regulatory breach. Complexity of cross-border transactions with various currencies, countries and laws makes this monitoring very crucial for the banks. They say effective monitoring will ensure the soundness of the banking system and enable banks to meet international regulations.

Cross-Border Transaction Monitoring

International transactions are difficult and risky to do than just domestic transactions because of regulatory distinction, exchange rate difference & governing authorities of different countries. By exploiting this complexity, criminals can subvert AML processes and use lifting to launder illicit proceeds for their funds and to fund terrorism or evade taxes. Since the sums of money that pass through these transactions are often so large, they can entice victims of con artists.

Monitoring cross-border transactions allows for the identification and halting of these illegal activities. It provides more depth to the banks for international regulatory processes like FATF recommendations and AML laws. Monitoring not only preserves the reputation of the bank but also minimizes their losses.

When monitoring cross-border transactions, there are several general types of key techniques one can use.

1. Thanks to Sanctions Lists Screening

Many WTO and tax regulations dictate banks should verify against cross-border transactions if sanctioned individuals, company or country is involved in a trade. This entails compare people and companies in a transaction again sanction lists from bodies like the UN, EU, or OFAC. The system then either flags the transaction for manual review or submits it to relevant law enforcement authorities.

2. Currency Exchange Monitoring

The exchange of currencies is a sizeable chunk of any cross-border transaction. Criminals can manipulate this exchange rate to launder money or avoid taxes. Banks also attempt to recognize an abnormal action by checking out how much and the amount of money. For example, if one were to convert enormous sums of money, it might show suspicious behavior.

3. Monitoring and Detecting Anomalies — in Real Time

Banks monitor cross-border transactions on a real-time basis using systems. Using machine learning to detect anomalies which do not fit normal patterns. For instance, high-risk countries sudden large transfers or new partners may invite an alert to carry out a deeper investigation.

4. Geographical Risk Assessment

Cross-border transactions are at varying levels of risk depending on the countries in question. For geographical risk, banks consider factors such as political stability, regulatory capability and links with financial crimes. For transactions with high-risk countries or regions, banks implement additional checks.

5. Customer & Counterparty Due Diligence (CDD)

In cross-border transactions, banks need to verify the identity of customers and transaction counterparties. They need to understand the customer's business and confirm that it is a genuine transaction. Such as Exposed Persons (PEPs), they need Enhanced Due Diligence (EDD) or those countries deemed higher risk deals. By doing this, the transaction becomes compliant.

6. TBML Detection -based the trade

TBML takes place with cross-border transactions associated with international trade. Criminals manipulate the value, number or quality of goods to transfer illegal funds overseas. Banks conduct TBML surveillance, using automated algorithms to search for anomalies like market price-to-declared values (for goods) or shipping routes.

7. Monitoring blockchain and cryptocurrencies

Transactions processed via blockchain, and cryptocurrency have become popular in cross-border operations, but because these methods operate in a decentralized and anonymous manner, tracing them can be more difficult. Banks require specific systems to oversee these transactions, detect illicit activity and adhere to an expanding series of regulations for digital assets.

8. Sharing and Collaboration

Cross-border transactions bring international financial crime related to money laundering as a dark side for banks that need to collaborate with other banks, regulators and law enforcement. This could be as collaboration pacts, such as FATF, and Egmont Group to combat financial crimes. Sharing information helps catch criminals and stop money laundering, fraud, terrorism financing.

Peer To Peer Transaction Monitoring

P2P cash exchange is necessary in the contemporary banking landscape. They enable people to send money to at one another and with the coming in of digital payment platforms and mobile apps including online banking; it has facilitated a variety of P2P transactions. However, this convenience has attracted attending malicious actors in various parts of frauds right up to serious crime and money laundering. Robust monitoring systems by banks are necessary to keep peer-to-peer transactions secure.

P2P transactions are small amounts of money. This creates a challenge to identify non-business. The advantages of P2P payments are that they are convenient and untraceable compared to traditional bank transfers. Like say, people in money laundering or terrorist financing would have moved to P2P platforms for transferring moneys. P2P payments can also be a vulnerability for fraudsters who scam individuals or start unauthorized transfers.

Why Monitoring P2P Transactions?

Monitoring P2P transactions is crucial, and monitoring peer-to-peer (PtP) payments ensures compliance with regulatory requirements. Without monitoring P2P payments, banks risk motivated cybercrime: losing millions and being fined by regulators for poor diligence.

Tracking Loan Disbursement Transaction

What is Loan Disbursement? The bank is responsible for overseeing these significant transactions. Banks monitor loan disbursals to ensure funds are used for the right purposes and prevent poor actors from using them for illegal activities such as fraud and money laundering. Second, banks also ensure proper monitoring to safeguard against turning into systemic risk materials and adhere to regular norms.

General loan disbursement transactions need to be dealt with, as they involve huge amounts of money. Careful handling is necessary with these funds, as they could be abused for illicit purposes, such as financing criminal activities or facilitating money laundering. Bank stands to lose large amounts of money. Fraudulent loan applications (where people lie about their personal details) can also expose banks to significant financial losses.

Why is Monitoring Loan Disbursements so important?

Banks monitor loan disbursements to see where the money goes, whether it is keeping a firm on buying real estate or for financing business activities as expected. This is also to identify any discrepancies during the transaction process.

Monitoring Account-to-Account or Commercial Fund Transactions undertaken by Staff

For banks, it is paramount that every transaction made must be secure. For example, whenever bank staff performs money transfer operations as from account to external or between two external accounts. By transacting through these means, one puts themselves at risk of fraud and unauthorized access or misuse by the bank. Thus, financial institutions should monitor the transactions of these staff-starting banks to prevent money laundering and other criminal activities, according to their internal policy, ensuring trust for them.

These staff have access to internal systems and confidential information. Left unchecked, they can abuse this access. Staff-related transactions risks:

Internal Fraud: Employees can steal from the business for financial gain. This may include unauthorized transfers, creating false accounts or otherwise changing records to conceal unlawful activity.

Conflict of Interest: Staff make buy for themselves, family etc to receive all the benefits in comparison with other users. It allows banks to be on the lookout and ensures that all activities of their staff are ethical (and aligned with bank policies).

Regulatory Compliance: Banks must follow well-defined regulatory guidelines that manage and record all financial activities, including those of the staff. Failure to monitor the activities of employees might cause a violation of related law such as (Anti-Money Laundering AML) rules, Bank Secrecy Act BSA or other laws.

Why is it necessary to monitor the transactions of staff running your project?

Banks using the solution can prevent internal fraud, identify conflicts of interest, and meet financial regulations by monitoring staff-starting transactions. Safeguarding the bank's integrity and avoiding legal penalties is important.

Issues in Transaction Monitoring

1. High Volume of Transactions

Millions of small to huge transactions happen on the bank side on the daily basis. Additionally, the Harvard International Review could focus on user conflicts of interest and highlight high utilization that leads to numerous transactions, triggering monitoring system alerts at a rapid rate. The possibility exists that warning devices would not timely alert on routine suspicious movements, enabling fraud or noncompliance to go undetected.

The volume of transactions will only rise as digital banking grows. Scalable monitoring systems that can handle large amounts of data, which also allow for sensitivity, are a necessity for banks. These systems are expensive to produce — a reality that may discourage smaller banks from getting involved.

2. Complexity of Financial Instruments the greater the complexity, rotten are these.

A Part of financial transactions may be very complex, such as securities or derivatives. They are multifaceted, comprising different components, such as underlying assets and market conditions that make them more challenging to track. The more complicated the transaction, when taken at a high speed, increases risks of fraud slipping though.

Banks need to possess sophisticated tools and expertise to monitor such complex instruments. For instance, derivatives often comprise multiple transactions across various parties, and banks need special algorithms to deconstruct these transactions in order to search for abuse.

3. Growing Fraud Tactics

Fraudsters will change tactics to beat additional security. The better the monitoring tools are of banks; criminals find different ways to exploit vulnerabilities. Consequently, banks are stuck in a never-ending loop of updating systems while new threats emerge.

New methods like synthetic identities and trade-based money laundering have supplanted the old-school simplistic account takeovers. There are smarter tactics being used to commit identity fraud. Banks require technology such as AI and machine learning to detect these.

4. Limited vs Full Long-Term support Regulatory Requirements & Permits

For international banks, compliance is an even trickier question, as different markets have different regulations. Of course, these rules vary across jurisdiction that they will be subject to a country's laws relating to anti-money laundering (AML), counter-terrorism financing (CTF) and sanctions.

5. Security and Customer Experience: Finding the Balance

The catch here is that, while robust monitoring is important for fraud prevention, it may also damage the customer experience. sensitive monitoring systems can cause legitimate transactions to be addressed as suspicious and this results in delays, which is a major issue leading up to accounts freeze. This leaves customers frustrated and breaks trust.

When these systems become too liberal and cannot detect fraudulent activities, they expose customers to potential risks. Balancing security and user experience is an ongoing challenge. Banks need to change their systems so that they can ensure both security and convenience for the customer.

6. You can integrate with Legacy Systems

Most banks continue to run on systems developed 20 or more years ago. These legacy systems may not have the full capability to perform advanced analytics and real-time monitoring that you need for tracking transactions in a modern way. Upgrading these systems can be costly, and it's challenging to incorporate new technologies.

Legacy systems lack effective monitoring and struggle to detect subtle fraud. Far more expensive to replace or upgrade, and they often require data migration expenses and reskilling of the staff. This six-stage model may be impracticable for banks, which often take a phased approach in bringing new technology into the environment to reduce disruption.

7. Data Security and Privacy Requirements

You will need to analyze millions (billions) of customer transactions, which means you are dealing with an enormous volume of sensitive personal information and account details. The data is valuable to potential cybercriminals. Bank and customer both stand to be damaged happen a breach.

Banks have an extensive set of data privacy laws that they must adhere to given GDPR in Europe. These laws place tight restrictions on how banks can gather, keep, and handle client data. Encryption and secure communication channels are necessary for banks to protect information from unauthorized viewing.

8. False Positives and Negatives

False Positives occur when the system incorrectly thinks that normal transactions are fishy. They result in delays, increased costs and angry customers. If fraud scrub solutions cannot catch these activities, we refer to the instances that they miss as false negatives. These are significant security risks to the bank and its customers.

Increasing frequency of sampling Verification can be burdensome for banks and they should calibrate their systems to decrease false positives while also not skip actual threats. This includes testing and improving algorithms, often through machine learning for increased precision. Balancing output remains challenging despite technological advancements.

9. Developing Technologies

Challenges created by new technologies, such as blockchain, cryptocurrencies and real-time payments, have to deal with transaction monitoring. Several solutions operate in decentralized, anonymous settings, posing challenges for banks to monitor and analyze.

For example, blockchain transactions are transparent but pseudonymous, which makes them hard to be linked back with any individual. Cryptocurrencies also enable cross-border transactions without requiring an intermediary or using traditional financial systems, making it easier to launder money.

This means updating banks' monitoring systems to new technologies' unique risks. That could mean creating various applications for tracking transactions carried out in cryptocurrencies, or teaming up with blockchain analysis platforms.

10. Restriction on resources

In terms of finance and human capital, the banks will need to invest a significant amount in ensuring establishing a robust system for transaction monitoring. Banks will have to invest in sophisticated technology, recruit compliance experts and train employees. Those investments can become too costly for smaller banks.

If resources are scarce, the vigilance to catch false transactions can wane. For instance, a bank cannot use the latest AI tools to counteract various kinds of fraud more advanced than counting one's carcasses. Banks with fewer resources will have to pick where they invest, doing so in the most risk-prone areas.

Global Efforts and Regulatory Push

AI in transaction monitoring is supported by regulators. In December 2018, U.S. regulators encouraged banks to use AI to combat money laundering and financial crimes. The banks were assured that conducting AI trials would not result in penalties if they complied with regulatory norms. This reflects an increasing embrace of AI to safeguard financial systems.

The European Central Bank (ECB) and the European Banking Authority (EBA) have been pushing for greater deployment of advanced analytics in financial monitoring as well. These groups st*ress the need for transparent systems that can be traced* and understood as required by regulations like GDPR, and to uphold public trust.

Industry Insights

Experts have well-established reports and opinions on the usage of AI in transaction monitoring.

McKinsey & Company:

> *They share that monitoring banks to AI has emerged an uplift of alert detection and operational efficiency. According to their analysis, AI can reduce false positives by as much as 80%, then lower operating expenses.*

PWC:

> *AI reduces false positives in transaction monitoring, freeing up compliance teams to investigate critical alerts. According to PwC, AI can achieve up to 90%*

improvement in accuracy that would allow compliance efforts to become more efficient.

Woodhurst:

This report highlights the shift in advice by regulators towards the adoption of AI for monitoring to reduce operational costs and increase detection rates. SharpQuant has built a sophisticated financial transaction system to detect complex transactions and is of the opinion that AI will have many advantages in monitoring global markets.

The adoption of AI in transaction monitoring presents opportunities and threats to banks alike. The utilization of AI can make operations more efficient; help cut costs and ensure better compliance. Rick mentioned earlier that while these initiatives and use cases are great, they must be executed within a regulatory framework that banks need to adhere to. Therefore, when using AI systems, transparency and alignment with global standards are crucial. From ATM and mobile transactions to trade finance or crypto currency, AI's role is increasing in all banking operations. However, AI ensures a more secure and efficient future for banks.

Transaction Monitoring Solutions for Banks

Banks must monitor transactions to detect fraud such as Wellston money laundering and market manipulation. With transactions intricate and frauds also becoming more sophisticated, banks resort to external self-learning solutions that use AI (artificial intelligence) in tandem with machine learning (ML) technology alongside monitoring

Systems. Important resolutions aid bank transaction monitoring improvement.

1. High Volume of Transactions

Solution: Feedzai

If a card is lost or compromised, the bank must promptly address the thousands of transactions happening each second in their respective businesses. Feedzai uses artificial intelligence that can track fraud during real-time operation and save itself from it. It leverages ML algorithms to find strange patterns and detect fraud. From Feedzai to do a huge amount of data processing and also reduces false positives, hence increasing monitor efficiency. Compiling scaling allows banks to process superior transaction numbers per unit time without compromising on safety.

2. The Complexity Of Financial Instruments.

Solution: NICE Actimize

For those types of instruments, NICE Actimize provides products for surveillance around complex transactions, including derivatives and structured products. The OfferPlex Platform Leveraging AI and ML to analyze elaborate transaction data, identify anomalies based on types of risk in real-time. NICE Actimize deconstructs complex financial instruments into its many parts and uses risk models to make out any potential fraudulent or market manipulation. That way, banks cover bankers from the most complex transactions.

3. Developing Fraud Tactics

Solution: Darktrace

Darktrace: An AI-based cybersecurity software that weeds out novel displays of fraud and threats on the cyber front. Instead, it is constructing a pattern of normal behavior for each user and system, setting in place notifications that trigger the moment any deviation erupts. It is a self-learning system to stop new frauds and make sense of the next trick before it hits.

4. I Regulatory Complexity, Jurisdiction Realities

Solution: FICO Falcon Fraud Manager Solution

FICO Falcon uses AI and ML to analyze global transactions in real-time, helping banks navigate complex regulatory environments and automating local and international regulatory requirements. FICO Falcon evaluates risk in line with unique regulations for each geography, enabling banks to comply without burdening the compliance teams. Banks can adapt to new regulations using the platforms' customizable rules.

5. Balancing freedom and security is necessary.

Answer: SAS Anti-Money Laundering

SAS Anti-Money Laundering — combating security for better customer experience. If any suspicious of fraudulent activities, its AI models will also be able to minimize the number of false positives and help clear legitimate flow transactions. Vast data processing algorithms enhance customer satisfaction and maintain security levels. Corpus-based learning frameworks tune these algorithms based on consumer trends with the help of SAS.

6. Adaptability to the existing legacy systems.

Solution: Palantir Foundry

Banks add modern AI tools to their older, legacy systems using Palantir Foundry Permits joining old and new data systems to improved monitoring. Banks don't need to replace their old systems to implement transaction monitoring in 2021. It offers Palantir Single Source of Truth which results make monitoring much faster to examine.

7. Security and Data Privacy Issues

Solution: ThetaRay

ThetaRay surveillance transaction including data privacy and security. This relies upon its unsupervised machine learning, which can detect anomalies yet keep user data private. With ThetaRay, control is maintained despite minimal data damage, thanks to encryption protection. This ensures that banks can also adhere to laws regarding data protection (like GDPR) and security.

8. False Positives and Negatives

9. Rapidly developing technologies–Chainalysis.

Banks use Chainalysis to monitor cryptocurrency and digital asset transactions. As blockchain and cryptocurrencies create new layers of complexity, the platform allows banks to track digital assets and identify illegal activity. It gives banks real-time intelligence on crypto transactions to help them understand and manage the risks. One of the earliest use cases for Chainalysis was tracking transactions involving Silk Road. 10. Restriction on resources–Jumio. Jumio is based on AI and helps banks verify identities and monitor transactions with minimal human effort. It automates the compliance and fraud detection tasks, allowing banks to maintain their high standards even with scarce human resources. The platform allows banks to have less need for mammoth monitoring teams. AI and ML external solutions are an essential enabling factor in transaction monitoring for banks. These tools allow banks to deal with complex regulation, high volumes of transactions, and new fraud strategies. As a result, banks can protect their custo8mers, play by the rules and maintain the integrity of the financial system. As FinTech keeps developing, AI and ML will help banks stay ahead of unknown risks and challenges.

Top 5 Bank Use Cases

1. HSBC

Use Case: Anti Money Laundering (AML) and Fraud Detection

Tech Used: Quantexa and Google Cloud AI AML CORA

Value realized: HSBC uses Quantexa and Google Cloud tools for real-time AML/fraud detection. The AI analyzes extensive transaction data, identifying intricate patterns that older systems may miss. This has enabled HSBC to decrease false positives and allocate its teams to suspicious transactions. This heightened HSBC ability to detect and prevent fraud, comply with global regulations and increase operational efficiency.

2. JPMorgan Chase

Use Case: Transactional Fraud Detection and Prevention

Solution Technologies: Ayasdi and SAS AI & Machine Learning

Impact: JPMorgan Chase could use Ayasdi's AI-powered data analysis along with the fraud management tools from SAS and monitor transactions more efficiently. This technology analyzes huge datasets to find possible fraudulent cases deranged among the noise. And by reducing false positives, the AI models resulted in faster transaction processing that also allowed better fraud prevention — this helped both serve customers well and prevent potential fraud.

3. Standard Chartered Bank

Case: Monitoring of Trade-Based Money Laundering (TBML)

Silent Night and IBM Watson trade monitoring

Goal Attained: Standard Chartered Powering Up on Tech To Keep In Line With Trade Finance Sanctions During The Pandemic Using AI from Silent Eight and IBM Watson. The system uses a multi-faceted approach to identify red flags and anomalies indicative of TBML activity. This automated process helped the bank identify criminal trades, comply with international AML standards, and address issues related to KYC and ultimate beneficiary ownership. It also improved operational efficiency and reduced the risk of financial crime.

4. Danske Bank

Example Use Case — Real-Time Payment Fraud Prevention

Leveraged: Feedzai AI and ML

This has caused Danske Bank to partner with Feedzai for a real-time fraud detection solution. Feedzai uses its AI to look at all the different transactions flowing through various channels (mobile banking, card payments) and detect fraudulent actions in real time. Prior to completion, Feedzai reduced fraud losses and blocked transactions. In addition, there were fewer false positives at Danske Bank, which had benefits from an operational point of view and from the customer experience, as it avoided unnecessary delays.

5. ING Bank

Use Case #2: AI-driven Anti-Fraud and AML Monitoring

Tech Used: NICE Actimize, Microsoft Azure AI

Result: ING Bank Combats Fraud and Money Laundering with NICE Actimize AI-Driven Monitoring on Microsoft Azure the AI monitors transactions in real-time to detect malicious activity and determine financial risk. ING Bank decreased false positives by 20 times, enabling more immediate actions and resource effectiveness. ING also received both the scalability and flexibility to meet changes in regulation or threat with its cloud-based solution.

Top 5 Asian Bank Use Cases for Transaction Monitoring,

1. DBS Bank (Singapore)

Scenario: Real-Time AML & Fraud Detection

Technology Used: SAS IBM Watson AI-Powered AML and Fraud Detection

Outcome: DBS Bank incorporated AI using SAS and IBM Watson for monitoring transactions on AML, as well as fraud in real-time. The AI will evaluate vast datasets to identify unusual patterns. This system reduced false positives, thus allowing the compliance teams to concentrate on high-risk cases, which lead to improved ability of DBS in preventing financial crimes and maintaining regulatory compliance.

2. ICICI Bank (India)

Example: Improved Transaction Monitoring, Fraud Detection

Technology Used: Feedzai Machine learning, AI

ICICI Bank used AI-based transaction monitoring with Feedzai to detect fraudulent behavior in real-time across mobile banking, internet banking, and card payments. It has lower false positives, reducing the effort taken by investigators and simplifying customer experience. The real-time system stopped fraud before it could harm the bank or its customers.

3. China Construction Bank (CCB, China)

Trade Surveillance Use Case — Trade-Based Money Laundering (TBML)

Methodologies / Technology: Silent Eight & FICO AI-Driven Trade Monitoring

China Construction Bank saw benefits from monitoring trade finance transactions for TBML with Silent Night and FICO The engine discovers outliers such as invoice anomalies, or atypical trade routes. In fact, this system led to a more effective detection of TBML and compliance with legislation at the bank level, taking some manual load off the monitoring.

4. Name: Mitsubishi UFJ Financial Group (MUFG) Country: Japan

AI-Powered Market Surveillance & Transaction Monitoring Solution

The collaboration between NICE Actimize and Microsoft Azure AI technology.
MUFG Adopted NICE Actimize AI on Microsoft Azure for Real-time Monitoring of Market Activity. It recognizes unusual transactions as finding insider trading or creating a market effect. With Hyperledger Fabric, MUFG was seeking a more secure and broader system that would facilitate the far-reaching supervision of financial transactions in Japan. The cloud-based system also offered MUFG the ability to respond to market changes.

5. Hang Seng Bank (Hong Kong)

Applying AI to Fraud Detection in Digital Banking

Tech Used: Darktrace LivePetail, Palantir Foundry

Hang Seng Bank integrates Darktrace's AI cybersecurity with Palantir Foundry for fraud detection. Real-time monitoring of digital transactions to identify account takeovers or unauthorized access This has made digital banking more secure, reducing occurrences of fraud and losses, the safety of transactions.

In the perspective of the modern financial landscape where traditional banks and new digital players (like Barbara) coexist, transaction monitoring has gained utmost importance. Banks are using AI and ML tools to fight financial crimes like fraud and money laundering. Banks need technologies that can process large sets of real-time data, identify suspicious activities, and maintain strict regulatory needs.

HSBC, JPMorgan Chase and Standard Chartered are among banks using AI to bolster security, compliance and efficiency processes. Revolut and Monzo, among other agile digital banks, also show their use of AI tools to avoid falling behind. With increasing financial crimes, signifying AI and ML in transaction monitoring will only grow. Banks who invest will be better able to safeguard customers and comply with regulations, as well as stay ahead of threats in the fast-paced financial landscape.

Reference – Further reading - Chapter 13

ComplyAdvantage Website: https://complyadvantage.com
Feedzai Website: https://feedzai.com
NICE Actimize Website: https://www.niceactimize.com
Darktrace Website: https://darktrace.com
FICO Falcon Fraud Manager Website:
https://www.fico.com/en/products/falcon-fraud-manager
SAS Anti-Money Laundering Website:
https://www.sas.com/en_us/software/anti-money-laundering.html
Palantir Foundry Website: https://www.palantir.com/what-we-build/foundry/
ThetaRay Website: https://www.thetaray.com
ACI Worldwide Fraud Management Website:
https://www.aciworldwide.com/fraud-management
Chainalysis Website: https://www.chainalysis.com
Jumio Website: https://www.jumio.com
Ayasdi Website: https://www.ayasdi.com
Silent Eight Website: https://www.silenteight.com
Featurespace Website: https://www.featurespace.com
RISK IDENT Website: https://www.riskident.com
Alloy Website: https://www.alloy.com
Socure Website: https://www.socure.com
Callsign Website: https://www.callsign.com
HSBC Website: https://www.hsbc.com
JPMorgan Chase Website: https://www.jpmorganchase.com
Standard Chartered Bank Website: https://www.sc.com
Danske Bank Website: https://danskebank.com
ING Bank Website: https://www.ing.com
DBS Bank Website: https://www.dbs.com
ICICI Bank Website: https://www.icicibank.com
China Construction Bank (CCB) Website: http://www.ccb.com
Mitsubishi UFJ Financial Group (MUFG) Website: https://www.mufg.jp
Hang Seng Bank Website: https://www.hangseng.com
Revolut Website: https://www.revolut.com
Monzo Website: https://monzo.com
Chime Website: https://www.chime.com
N26 Website: https://n26.com

FOURTEEN

Basic Chatbots to Intelligent AI Virtual Agents in Banking

Introduction

When we think back to over the years, 'chatbot' (until recently) has meant simple automated bots which took care of linear chat flows for customer support. Yet consumer engagement is flashing in the digital space and competitive financial institutions must keep pace with advanced technology offered by adopters. This is the chatbot that we will develop further through a series of tutorials, eventually turning it into an AI agent by combining two outstanding features: NLU (natural language understanding) and contextual information.

Understanding AI Agents

AI agent is essentially a digital assistant with advanced language models and natural language understanding (NLU) via ML-powered data analytics. AI agents differ from basic chatbots that rely on scripted responses and predefined keywords. Unlike chatbots, AI agents can understand complex questions, handle diverse user interactions and situations, and make autonomous decisions. These capabilities allow AI agents to handle various tasks, including customer service and financial advice, which are in high demand in modern banks.

AI Agents Trending in Financial Institutions

Better Customer Engagement: The ability to talk naturally makes AI agents capable of striking a rapport with people. Understand context and nuance to provide better (accurate, relevant...) answers. This is especially powerful in the financial sector, according to Gitlin, since personalization and trust are paramount.

Self-Sufficient: AI agents do not follow predetermined dialogue flows like most of the traditional chatbots, they can decide during their conversations. It also allows them to escalate more complex requests automatically or act as the first point of contact for ticket resolution.

Advanced Features:

Identify Entity Extraction:
We extract the important pieces of conversational useful bits. For instance, payment plan amounts, transaction details like this.

Intent recognition:
As AI agents, allow the seamless experience for your customers by knowing what they want, reducing their frustration levels.

Emotion Detection: AI agents can identify the feelings of customers — whether anger or frustration — offer tailor-made responses and add a binocular touch to every interaction.

AI powered third eye predicting the flow of conversation as output to that finally helps improve conversion by targeting human agents or sometimes experts and propensity Modelling: based on propensities, AI converts outcomes into actionable strategy details about how fastest "conversation helpers" continue with more informed decision making.

Using generative AI:
Integrating generative artificial intelligence can automatically summarize conversations for human agents, creating a good use case in integrating conversational summaries.

Scalable Training, Fast learning: AI agents use real data of past interactions for training, but they gradually learn more from users' protocols, leading to increased versatility. This kind of flexibility is crucial in a mercurial financial world.

The more advanced the AI agents become, then it may process and clarify different communications; voice notes in customer call logs or PDFs users downloaded from a website — fulfilling whatever your customers need.

The Future of AI Agenting for Data Management

Advanced Hyper-Personalization:
AI agents will analyze higher quality data and gain better customer knowledge; thus, they can provide more unique financial products even far beyond this way.

Financial well-being instant check:
AI agents will also take it a step further to the next level and monitor clients' financial health in real-time, generating fulfilment recommendations related to commodities trading or banking based on live data.

The Next Stage of Predictive:
As machine-learning algorithms continue to improve, so will the predictable capabilities of AI agents; they are predicting customer needs and behaviors in an ever-on model (e.g., call-to-action-anomalies) more pro-actively nudging us towards interventions and opportunities.

Increased Focus on Security: AI agenting would focus more towards the using of AI to detect and prevent novel security threats so that customer data is safe.

AI agenting in banks can massively disrupt the current way on how they handle their data that will improve customer experience and significantly boost operational efficiency and houses true innovation. With time and technology, banks can see AI agents as the very foundation of their strategies that move towards a world driven by data.

Here are some examples of the AI agents that banks possess:

Erica from Bank of America:

Bank of America uses Erica, an AI-driven virtual financial assistant that helps customers with all kinds of banking needs. Erica, powered by AI agenting and first launched in 2018, delivers personalized financial guidance/insights, automates customer service inquiries and enriches the overall banking experience. Erica is in the Bank of America mobile app and provides 24/7 support.

Erica is a virtual financial assistant that provides personalized financial advice based on clients' spending habits and financial goals. What it does is—it observes the transaction history, spending modes and account behavior to provide you with custom made advice/recommendation.

Erica can notify customers when they are hitting their monthly spend limit or remind them about upcoming bill payments. Should a customer go overboard in say dining category, Erica will notice that and recommend budgeting changes.

Erica can answer questions about recent transactions, account balances and other financial issues. Erica uses real-time customer account data to provide fast, accurate and secure responses. You should allow the customers to browse through manually in their app.

Customer: What is my account balance? If the guitar is still bothering you, Erica can quickly inform you about the cost on all your linked accounts - savings, checking, or credit cards.

Customers use Erica to pay their bills automatically, thus also saving customers from overspending. Customers can engage with Erica by speaking or texting commands to conduct transactions such as paying bills, transferring money between accounts and sending funds to external accounts. Automated process making it easier for transactions and helping customers save a lot of their time.

Customer as a query that "Pay to credit card bill." Erica Within seconds, Erica will confirm the balance and due date of a bill; process payment through funds in an enrolled account; don't have enough money?

Erica analyzes account activity with the help of artificial intelligence to proactively warn customers about potential issues before they occur, including rare transactions or low balances. This enables real-time detection of anomalies that help in securing and managing customer finances.

For example, Erica will notify a consumer of an out-of-pattern high-transaction and inquire if the entire transaction is suspicious. Then, Erica prompts the customer to confirm whether the transaction occurred, which allows for real-time resolution.

However, Erica will also assist users in obtaining access to their FICO credit scores and ways in which they can improve them. This can alert customers to the credit health they have and what steps are available for them so as not just hurt, but positively affect, their scores.

For example, Erica might see that a customer's credit score has taken a hit and prompt them to bring their credit card balance down or pay on time.

Both similarly tries to help customers set and track their savings goals, giving suggestions on how doing so using contextual insights based on the customer spending. It performs a cash flow analysis and suggests an allocation of funds to save.

Erica assesses a consumer's income and spending to recommend a monthly savings amount for their vacation goal. She also evaluates the progress towards reaching that milestone.

As she interacts with customers, Erica learns and develops. Over time, it predicts individual customer behaviors and habits in financial areas. When Erica analyzes spending patterns based on pre-defined rules, the responses become more accurate.

Erica improved the customer's experience by showing an overview of his transactions without being asked, something she learned from their first conversation.

KAI by DBS Bank:

We partnered with DBS Bank to deploy KAI, an AI-powered conversational banking agent. KAI, built by Kasisto, uses NLP and machine learning to provide customers with a seamless virtual banking experience. It can handle text-based and voice-driven banking tasks. DIA delivers greater customer engagement via an AI agent that can handle real-time help for repetitive banking inquiries and more advance financial transactions.

KAI engages customers in natural, conversational language to create an intuitive banking experience. Customers can ask questions and get things done in their own words. KAI responds with meaningful content or executes actions.

A customer could inquire about her account balance with a question like "

How much do I have in my wallet? or "Add $500 to my Savings." KAI responds to the request in on-the-spot manner give account balance or does fund move with no human adding-process involved.

The KAI allows you to make easy transfers of funds between accounts or make payments. This uses customer APIs to eliminate time and cost in routine banking activities by automating them as per customer commands.

Customer Says to KAI: Bill Payment Electricity KAI fetches the details of this bill, verifies the amount and pays. It can manage more complicated transactions as well, such as scheduling payments for the future or even setting up and paying recurring bills.

Using NLP to deliver a brand-new era of personalized financial advice and insights, courtesy of its customer data. KAI recommends how and with where to save, invest and budget by mining spending patterns, transactional history alongside the valuable data of account behaviors.

One question they ask us often is, how am I doing on spending. KAI breaks down their spending to see how they can save better — by—as an example— cutting back on discretionary expenses or creating savings rules.

Real-time retail account and transaction checking enables KAI to pick up any issues or anomalies, such as high-spending patterns or low balances. It proactively alerts the customers and helps them to be informed & secure.

KAI gently nudges the customer with a message alerting them that their account balance is under $100 and recommends they move some cash from another one to prevent overdraft charges. This helps customers manage their accounts in a better way.

Unlike other chatbots, it can integrate more sophisticated concierge-level customer inquiries. This AI is context-aware, intent aware and understands multi-step transactions, which then enables it to respond intelligently across a spectrum of queries ranging from basic questions to complex financial tasks.

For example, a customer may instead ask, "What type of loan is best for me? KAI assesses the financial condition of a customer and recommends the most appropriate loan products, if they are beneficial based on interest rates, payment terms or specific needs.

KAI learns from each interaction, honing its ability to understand how people want to interact with their bank. This allows the agent to learn and become better at responding to each bit of feedback it receives.

KAI is accessible on different digital platforms that DBS Bank uses, such as the mobile app and website. Since this information is accessible on all channels, customers can start a conversation on one device and continue it on another.

A customer initially discusses mobile app transactions with KAI but later wants to view detailed financial reports on their laptop without restarting the chat.

KAI can provide usage-based financial reports to customers and assist them in planning for saving or investing better. With AI-driven analytics, KAI helps customers learn about their financial health and shift strategies.

KAI, A Customer: Can you provide me a report of how much I save for the year? KAI creates a visual summary of their progress towards the savings goal and sends them hints on how to get there faster.

Eno by Capital One:

Eno is an artificial intelligence assistant created by Capital One. It sends customers notifications about their accounts, helps them pay off credit card debts faster, and gives them useful information based on their spending habits. Eno's Realtime help uses language processing and machine learning to assist customers with common tasks and enhance security by providing real-time notifications through proactive monitoring. Eno is a digital assistant within Capital One's mobile app and has additional capabilities on other favorite digital platforms, with 24/7 support.

Eno analyzes customer account activity in near real time to detect potential fraud signals, such as uncommon transactional anomalies or changes that can surface from modifications on an existing account. This early detection, preventive measure improves security and creates a way for clients to know more about their money — without the need to verify their accounts.

If Eno spots a transaction it doesn't expect — whether that is a large purchase or one in another country, etc — she sends the customer an alert to confirm. The customer can confirm it or mark it as fraud with a single click from within the chat.

For online transactions, Eno creates a virtual card number for the customer to use that would keep merchants from seeing their actual credit card. Finally, all virtual cards are unique and tied to a specific receiver, reducing the probability of fraud and identity theft.

A customer shopping online requests Eno to create a virtual card for his purchase. Eno then assigns a unique Card Number to that merchant, further protecting the customer's account if this virtual card number is compromised.

Eno by Capital One allows consumers to check their transaction history, and they get instant notifications for new purchases made as well as payments and account balances. It also offers spending insights through expense categorization that enables customers to monitor their finances and take decisions better.

The customer asked, "How much have I spent on dining this month?" What Eno does is scan the transaction history and then identify only food-related expenses, providing a simple overview of how much was spent in that category.

Eno allows customers to receive reminders prior to due dates on their bills and even pay the same via conversation. This automation eases finance management and also decreases the odds of missing a payment.

Eno alerting a customer of an upcoming credit card payment, due in 3 days. The chat empowers the customer to respond on-the-fly to your reminder and release payment instantly.

Eno features fraud-detection powers and can review transactions for signs of fishy business. Eno can spot possible fraud quickly through patterns of customer activity and spending, informing Citi to act right away against fraudulent charges.

Eno can detect when a series of above-average transactions are conducted one after another that do not match the client's standard spending profile and prompt them to verify. For any fraudulent transactions, Eno can buffer the account and let Capital One's fraud team know.

Eno gives customers tailored financial suggestions using their data, which can aid them in saving and investing better. Eno can offer advice on budgeting, warn customers about overdraft dangers, and teach you how to maximize your credit card rewards.

If a customer is low on balance in their account, Eno might recommend curbing any discretionary spending or College Lightning with Capital One.

Immediately informing the customer of each purchase made on their account with Eno, showing an up-to-the-minute snapshot spending. With this feature, customers can monitor their transactions on time and quickly detect any suspicious activities.

Once a customer purchases something at a retail store, Eno will send an immediate confirmation message with the transaction amount, and it also includes merchant details. The transparency of these types allows customers to closely monitor their spending, and the type of percentage rates vary as well.

Like an omnipresent customer-service agent, Eno fields questions concerning account balances, recent transactions, and fees for other banking matters. Eno works with text, so it can provide instant answers before a customer might have to wait for a human.

Customer: How much money do I have on my credit card? Eno immediately follows with the balance, available credit and payment due date — providing that consumer rapid access to critical financial information.

Eno takes what they learn from each chat and continues to improve its capability, whether it is in understanding user habits; behaviors regarding their finances; or communication style. Eno gets better over time at predicting customer wants and serving up more customized replies.

In this example, if a customer often requests information about spending, Eno can send weekly spend summaries or simply inform the user when they are approaching their budget limits.

Eno is vital to advance digital security and acts as a filter for transactions that look too suspicious or out-of-scope with normal spend patterns by customers. Eno can use machine learning to identify when something is wrong and act fast.

If a card is suddenly used for an unusually high number of transaction activities in quick succession or from the other side of the world, Eno automatically sends out alerts to ask if the transactions are legitimate.

MyKai by Kasisto:

A conversational AI designed for banking, MyKai, is developed by Kasisto. Debuted with DBS Bank, MyKai delivers a comprehensive suite of banking capabilities throughout natural language in what is becoming the most intuitive yet human experience for retail and commercial banking customers. You can ask several simple questions and receive advice or recommendations in response, through AI agenting capabilities.

Customers can access their bank accounts via texts on MyKai using natural language commands. Consumers can inquire with MyKai about their account balances, recent transactions, or start transfers between accounts. Use of the conversational agent removes customers through multiple screens or menus, so that they can move directly to and throws process.

A User asks MyKai a question, e.g. "My checking account balance? MyKai instantly retrieves the information and issues a response, eliminating the need for users to go into their banking app to see how much is left.

MyKai helps customers stay informed about their spending habits and offers suggestions to manage everyday expenses based on their trends. It segments costs, follows a certain way of spending and gives advice on how to save or stay in good finances shape. MyKai garners these insights by providing financial planning based on real-time data.

The user query is about their grocery spending last month. To provide this information, the customer is asked to consent for MyKai to scan their transactions. MyKai then identifies grocery-related purchases, allowing the realization of the total amount spent on groceries during the requested period.

MyKai performs banking activities like moving money from one account to another or paying bills, all with no human help. Customers can easily ask questions and complete transactions with no manual steps using MyKai, making the process smoother and enhancing the user experience.

An example would be if a customer tells MyKai "Move $500 from my savings account to the checking". The workflow on MyKai does, confirming the transaction within seconds.

MyKai provides financial advice that is custom to the user by analyzing customer data and providing insights. That may include savings plans — investment opportunities, or products like credit cards and loans that align with the customer's financial profile and goals. So they can make better financial choices. If the customer frequently overspends on dining, MyKai may advise creating a restaurant budget or recommending more effective ways to allocate income towards savings.

MyKai offers real-time alerts and notifications for account activity. These notifications include things such as possible overdrafts, reminders of future bill payments or alerts about abnormal account behavior. With MyKai financial alerts, the virtual assistant informs customers of critical events that can alert them to charges and set cash flow in motion all day long.

You know, play that simple incoming/outgoing service message game to send messages via SMS alert (e.g. Attention: Check low balance → Transfer funds from savings now)

MyKai is an advanced AI dedicated to tracking customer account activities and sniffing out anything suspicious as regards security. MyKai uses data analytics to monitor transactional behavior and identifies any deviations, which could hint at fraud — alerting the customer in real time. It can also provide freeze and report in real time an option of a suspected account.

For MyKai, something like a sequence of abnormal transactions in another state. With a positive confirmation, MyKai can carry out further safety measures regarding account security.

MyKai is built to learn after each interaction with a customer, thus enabling the assistant to more effectively understand varying individual preferences, financial behaviors, and communication styles. The learning, over time, strengthens MyKai in providing accurate responses and predicting customer needs effectively as a virtual assistant.

Example: The MyKai chatbot discovers a customer asks regularly about their monthly transportation usage. From there, it starts automatically offering a round-up of transportation charges at the close of every month requiring no explicit form trigger.

Digital channels: MyKai on messaging apps, websites and mobile app. Given this capability, multilingual banks cater its customers in various locations according to their preferred language. This approach guarantees you receive the same experience on all channels and devices.

For example, a customer can chat with MyKai in their bank's mobile app about account balances and pick up the conversation on the same desktop at mybank.com. MyKai preserves conversational context, which makes navigating across channels seamless.

Beyond answering questions about one's balance, MyKai operates as a sort of first-line customer-service agent for more complicated inquiries. This bot can answer questions on financial products (which many banks and credit unions already do), help explain banking fees, or even assist in loan applications that would allow human agents to focus on more valuable tasks.

Customer asks MyKai for Loan Application fees. It gives the customer a detailed analysis of many charges ranging from transaction processing fees to interest rates, enabling them to make wiser decisions.

Besides account management (in beta), MyKai offers financial wellness tools as well. It provides savings tips, tracks a customer's budget, and suggests achievable goals based on their financial behavior. So, credit & identity monitoring, balance and budget prediction are all nestled right into the banking customer interface—the way more effectively completes a total health for customers.

For instance, MyKai monitors a customer's goal of saving $10k for a house down payment in X years. It offers advice to reduce discretionary spending and sends reminders as the customer nears their target.

Sara by SEB Bank

SEB Bank Sara, the AI assistant at SEB helping with common banking queries and support. Sara, built using natural language processing (NLP) and machine learning, enables customers to do routine banking activities like asking for account details, etc. Also, be a personal bank assistant who can guide you/direct/help on-demand base as needed by Sara in real-time during the interactions (more than just an IVR). With automation of many interactions that would traditionally involve human agents, Sara is helping SEB Bank address both customer service and operational efficiency.

For her customers, Sara is there to answer all their banking questions–things like checking account balances or looking at recent transactions and bank services. Sara automatically performs these functions, minimising invasive human activity and providing rapid response time instead.

Example: Sara gets asked by a customer, "What is my account balance now?" Upon receiving the request, Sara instantly fetches and displays the balance of that customer, so he no longer has to navigate through his online banking account.

Sara also enables customers to perform regular tasks easily, e.g. transferring money between their accounts or paying a bill using a conversational user interface. This saves customers the time and effort of having to navigate traditional banking apps or websites.

Example: A customer says to Sara, "Please transfer 500 SEK from my savings account to my checking account." Sara confirms the request, ensures that the transfer is seamless and make user receive a notification right there itself.

Sara sends push notifications in real-time any time there is account activity (e.g., bills that are due soon, balances running low or unexpected expenses). Customers can easily monitor their financial situation without constantly refreshing or sifting through transaction history and balance inquiries. This helps prevent overdraft fees and missed payments, both of which can cause unnecessary trouble.

For example, Sarah sees a customer is close to their limit, and so she sends them an alert suggesting they make a transfer in order to avoid some overdraft charges.

Sara monitors customer accounts, watching for signs of any strange behavior. If a transaction appears suspicious, such as a large withdrawal or an overseas purchase that is not typical behavior for the cardholder, Sara will contact the customer via text to verify the transaction before proceeding.

For example, if Sarah sees a large buy in another country that was unusual for the customer, it is going to send out an instant notification asking them to verify whether this transaction was real.

Sara provides personalized financial advice, considering a customer's spending and saving patterns, as well as their future goals. By studying the transaction data of customers, Sara can suggest saving measures or financial products that suit them.

For example, a customer who overspends on entertainment. The result both Sara and other similar others have noted is offering a monthly entertainment budget to clients in order to track spending on this front, as well as alert the customer when they are close.

Sara assists customers with inquiries about SEB's medical products, credit cards, consumer loans, and more. Sara explains terms and answers different queries regarding fees, interest rates and the eligibility through which you can apply for these products.

For example: Sara inquiries about how to request a personal loan from a customer. Sara explains the loan options, interest rates, and the approval process, along with personalized suggestions based on a customer's financial profile.

Over time, Sara gets better and learns because of customer interactions with machine learning. Sara learns more about customer preferences and most asked questions — even individual financial behavior — ensuring she is pulling from the right information to provide a great experience each time.

For example, if a client consistently asks for end-of-the-month reports from Sara to gain insights, then as time goes on.

Sara can automate customer inquiries, allowing human customer service agents to deal with more complex tasks and leads. This not only increases operation efficiency, but it also decreases the time that customers who require more in-depth help have to wait.

Example: A customer inquiring into specific mortgage advice is directed to a human agent, however, Sara still deals with the repetitive bulletins such as account balance and transaction history requests.

Originally launched as a voice interface in 2009, and since made available on all digital platforms, including mobile apps (iOS & Android) as well web browsers — Sara is reachable for the bank customers any time they want to get help or apply for SEB products. With an omnichannel approach, continuity of experience is key to digital customer touchpoints.

For example, a customer talks to Sara about their mobile messaging app to view an account balance and then later opens Sara in the web browser, mirroring that same conversation history.

Sara provides customers with financial goal setting tools, alerts them when reaching savings milestones and offers timely advice that enables their long-term financial well-being. They recommend the best ways how you can start saving/investing regularly and as per your income or expenses.

For Example: A user who wanted to save for a vacation. Sara monitors the customer following their savings and provides with updates, advice areas where you can make more money to save by cutting off unnecessary expenses.

Kai-G by Garanti BBVA

Kai-G is an AI powered conversation banking assistant developed for Garanti BBVA in partnership with Kasisto. It provides customers a broad suite of banking transactions, investigation in conversational language enabling personalized financial suggestions and performs routine banking tasks autonomously. Kai-G offers personalized real-time service for the customer while also improving the operational efficiency of Garanti BBVA.

Customers can use Kai-G to check account balances, go through transaction histories and get their account statements effortlessly. By taking a conversational approach, which is far more natural and inclusive than the menu-drive alternatives still being used today by some financial services apps, it becomes easier for customers to engage with their accounts promptly.

Customer: What's my savings account balance (Kai-G) Kai-G pulls the balance of a customer's savings account and shares it with them in seconds—milli-seconds versus time to check manually through an app.

Customers can transact on Kai-G, from moving money between accounts to paying their bills or anyone else. Kai-G automates these daily processes, which means you do fewer handling of money and move faster with transactions.

Example: A customer tells Kai-G, "Move 1000 TRY from my checking account to savings." Kai-G acknowledges the request, carries out the transfer and provides real-time confirmation back to a customer, which is all very convenient.

Kai-G uses [AI] to provide tailor-made financial insights from customer's spending, saving habits, and their personal goals. And it can show how to cut costs, suggest products like loans or credit cards and give advice that is personalized for healthier financial behavior.

For example, if someone is spending a lot of money at restaurants, Kai-G can use the transaction data together with information about that individual (like their income and financial goals) to suggest they set themselves a budget for dining or propose savings plan.

Kah-G sends real time alerts on account activity, upcoming payment dues or low funds. Kai-G keeps customers informed of their financial position — real-time updates prevent overdrafts and missed payments.

For example, Kai-G sees one of your customers has a balance close to zero and sends an alert advising them to move money, so they don't go into an overdraft. This proactive step can prevent fees and offer the customer service team a better way to address disruptions.

Real-time detection of abnormal transaction Skai-G keeps an eye out for behavior beyond the norms If a transaction appears unusual, Kai can alert the customer right away and they have an opportunity to either confirm that it is indeed them or deny processing of the transaction, adding another security wall against fraud.

The breaching point is a large foreign transaction and Kai-G throws an alert asking the customer if there was any change in his spending pattern, and this usage to prevent fraud.

But Kai-G can also help you with more complicated queries too, like giving info on your loan options or explaining certain banking fees to even general investment-related questions. Kai-G saves human agents time by automating these interactions.

Example: "Terms for personal loan" asked Kai-G by a customer Kai-G not only educates the customer on loan interest rates, repayment periods and eligibility requirements but also provides comparisons in a simplified manner helping them understand which has a better option for their benefit.

Kai-G: Machine learning applied to customer dialogues It can then use this data to identify key trends in the customer's life identifying types of restaurants, brands and services which they commonly spend money on, so it will only provide accurate responses back.

Example: Kai-G realizes, after some time, that one of their customers does often view their expenses in transportation. At the end of each month, it offers a preview transport cost overview, and that is why Calling Card provides much appreciated convenience.

Kai also speaks multiple languages and runs across platforms in the bank's ecosystem — mobile apps for offline support, web portals etc., providing customers an ability to converse with their bank whenever they want. It is this flexibility that allows customers to have a seamless experience, whether they opt for online or in-person channels.

For example, a customer triggers the chat with Kai-G about recent transactions in their mobile app and then continues to engage on the web platform without losing context, which translates into "cross-device" experience.

Kai-G uses existing customer data to recommend personalized financial products. Kai-G provides personalized recommendations to customers for cash credit, loan products and investment based on customer financial profile factoring in the needs and preferences of everyone, which will further aid Garanti BBVA enrich their cross-selling opportunities.

Product Example: Kai-G might recommend customers with a rising liquid checking account balance consider opening an investment-oriented high-yield savings account or further their investing journey based on where they are in their pursuit of financial success.

At Kai-G, we help our clients start financial goals and follow the list to ensure they have a clear path to what saving for something would be or how debt can reduce. It helps show the customer how they can adopt new spending behaviors to reach these goals and gauge progress.

Scenario is a goal like the customers want to save 20,000 TRY for their summer holiday. Kai-G tracks their savings, gives them regular status updates and advice on increasing or improving the way they are saving in order to reach a certain goal.

Lucy by UBS:

UBS AI Lucy — A virtual assistant developed by UBS for wealth management needs on both the client side and financial advisor side. Lucy provides support with portfolio management and real-time market insights, uses AI agenting capabilities to provide tailored financial advice, enhancing customer engagement. Powered by AI, Lucy enhances operational efficiency at UBS with its ability to automate common tasks that allow financial advisors to concentrate on more strategic and customer-oriented efforts.

Lucy offers clients real-time insight into how their investments are performing and can help to manage strategies while providing personalized financial advice. Then, it can analyze the marketplace for recent trends and offer recommendations on necessary portfolio adjustments within those guidelines. It allows the customer to take intelligent decisions without manning above their heads.

A typical question for Lucy is from a client asking, "How did my portfolio do today?" When the user asks for an update on his/her performance, that is given through Lucy immediately retrieving and analyzing their portfolio information to report if gains or losses are being made as well as some suggestions of trades, they should make based on current market conditions.

Lucy provides clients and financial advisors with real time market data such as stock price, bond yields and multiple other financial instruments. Insight into market trends, breaking news and economic events that could be of benefit to a client's portfolio. With passaging time, it empowers timely decision-making and keeps clients informed on market components.

Sample: the client asks, what's going on in the stock market today? Lucy gave a quick rundown of market action: which stocks or sectors were actively trading in ways that might be germane to her client.

Lucy provides tailored investment suggestions depending on the financial profile, needs, and risk appetite of each client. Based on historical performance, market conditions and client behavior, Lucy will proactively propose investment opportunities thanks to a set of specific hints which allow clients to benefit from portfolio optimization tools towards their financial goals.

For instance, if Lucy sees a client who has mentioned some curiosity about sustainable investing, she might suggest that they investigate ESG

(Environmental, Social and Governance) funds more in line with their values and long-term financial objectives.

Lucy automatically sends status notifications on your portfolio's performance, market changes, or any key financial events. These notifications keep clients apprised of their investments, so they can strategically adjust in a timely manner. The moments when stock prices slip, or market trends change dramatically, Lucy keeps the customers in a loop.

Sample: Lucy realizes that a stock in the portfolio of customer dropped significantly. It will first explain what caused it and then send a notification telling you how to avoid that in the future or better navigate around its effects on your entire portfolio.

Lucy supports UBS financial advisors by learning and automating routine tasks; for example, generating performance reports, providing client insights, answering questions from clients. This frees up advisors to concentrate on strategic activities and enables them to deliver tailored advice.

E.g., a financial adviser asks Lucy for the portfolio performance report of a client, over last quarter. Lucy instantly produces the report, which identifies relevant metrics and suggests potential portfolio enhancements, preparing advisors for a well-informed conversation with their clients.

Lucy uses programs to calculate and track current asset allocations, helping clients manage their portfolio-level risks. It outlines areas of over-exposure to certain sectors or asset classes and provides strategies for re-balancing in order to better reflect a client's risk profile.

It learns from its mistakes and gets better over time through Machine Learning to get a deeper understanding of the client on "another level" than VC using more advanced clustering methods you won't. Growing with the system, Lucy becomes smarter at providing insights and recommendations that are unique to a client by learning from market changes.

For Example: An energy sector market news hunting customer. After a while, Lucy provides updates from the energy sector and insights on her own initiative, which improves the overall client experience.

Lucy works with clients to establish and monitor their long-term financial needs, including saving for retirement, paying for college, or securing property ownership. The technology provides customized approaches and recommendations that align with the goals of a plan, assisting individuals in keeping them on target with what they aim to achieve.

Instance: A client has the goal of saving for his child's college education. Lucy monitors progress communicates savings target status updates to the client and makes appropriate recommendations (in line with the view of changing market condition and expected return values) for investment strategy change.

The Lucy solution is available via mobile apps, web browser or integrated into the client's wealth management portal-EXTERN. Lucy Available on any Channel Clients can engage with Lucy via their preferred platform to get the same experience.

For example, a client approaches Lucy on their mobile app to review portfolio performance and then later picks up where they left off during discussing a desktop computer, missing no context.

UBS instructs Lucy to generate compliance reports regarding transactions, portfolio changes, and other investment activities automatically in order to comply with financial regulations. Lucy can deliver these reports to clients and financial advisors, while also complying with all relevant legal demands.

Sample: A financial advisor has requested Lucy to comply with their clients within the previous 12 months. Lucy compiles this report to make sure all trades and investments comply with regulations so that UBS can remain in compliance.

Bob by Ping An Bank (China)

Ping An Bank's Ask Bob is a personal account for the bank, acting as an AI financial assistant to customers的秉承这一理念，Ask Bob是平安银行旗下AI+智能机器人，并为用户提供保险、经济补偿与实时支持。The first is an automated support agent that can respond to customer queries in natural language, automate processes and deliver personalized financial notifications using machine learning techniques. Bob Empower Bank Ask Bob's agenting capabilities to help Ping And Bank improve customer engagement, service delivery optimization and operational efficiency.

Ask Bob helps customers by providing data and information about market trends, customer portfolios, risk profiles to make suitable investment decisions. The consumer gets customized suggestions based on his/her financial aspirations, which also considers the existing market scenario. This AI agent makes complicated investing trivial and enables customers to invest appropriately in their portfolios.

For example: A client question is, is it time to buy tech stocks? Ask Bob algorithmically examines the customer's current portfolio, determines their risk behavior and outlines an investment proposal on how to best invest in the tech sector. As one of a kind, dealer perpetuated robo-advisor for connective exchange with limited/handicap perspective. It also recommends diversification strategies to disperse the risk across different portfolios with varied return profiles.

Ask Bob keeps you updated on stocks, markets and finance in real time. Which makes it easy for users to query on Ask Bob and receive the market data; keeping them updated with their investments without even needing to search manually.

Example: Customer query How much is the market so far in Shanghai stock today? Ask Bob pulls live market data and provide an end of the day summary with any major moves that could affect your portfolio.

Ask Bob — to help customers understand and control their expenses, set budgets, save as a goal. It provides targeted financial advice based on transaction data to help users improve their day-to-day budgeting and refine saving plans. This provides an improved financial knowledge, and the customer might make better yet economic conclusions themselves.

For example, if a customer goes over budget to eat out. Ask Bob analyzes their spending and suggests a monthly dining budget. It also alerts them when they approach the limit and offers tips to reduce discretionary expenses.

These responses address common user inquiries related to banking, including account balance, transaction history, loan details, and more. Ask Bob functions as a customer service officer, always available to assist. It also helps with more involved tasks, such as product descriptions of financial products and support through the application process, relieving human agents' burden.

Sample query: What is the interest rate on a personal loan? Ask Bob shares an array of information regarding ongoing loan offers, interest rates being offered on loans, and repayment terms so that the customer knows their best fit with exactly what they want including personalization for an in-time human assisted personalized service responding to the pre-approved check offer without waiting for it.

Ask Bob maintains a constant surveillance on the recent activity of customer accounts, including sudden low balances or pending large transactions. It alerts customers to transactions as they occur, assisting them in monitoring their balances and stay abreast of issues like overdrafts or unpaid bills.

Ask bob, you can notice that customers' account balance is running low and send them the appropriate alert asking for a top-up from savings or give credit one to avoid overdraft fees. That means customers are less likely to blow their budget on a big payment the previous month. It sounds like good preventative customer service.

Bob checks customer transactions for fraud or other wrongful behaviour. It uses machine learning algorithms to identify out-of-the-norm patterns going in real-time and alert the customer, who can act on a potential problem (e.g. freeze account or report a fraudulent transaction).

E.g., a customer from out of country [not one without ID] makes an extremely large purchase. Bob notices the deviation, asks, and sends a fraud alert, prompting them to endorse. Should the customer reject, Ask Bob will automatically lock their account and tip off the bank's fraud department.

Ask Bob to help their customers with the customization of loan products based on individual financial profile, credit history, as well needs and support to foster a guaranteed process. This helps in automating the Form filling, document submission and eligibility checks etc which makes application process easier to fill faster & customer friendly.

For example, a customer wants to know "Can I apply for a mortgage?" Ask Bob qualifies the customer, present mortgage options available and assist them with submitting their application followed by helpful reminders for any required documentation to be submitted and confirming the terms given.

Ask Bob is a machine-learning platform that listens and mines the natural language customer interactions in real-time to maximize its responses by continuously retraining itself on new data. As this model continues to interact with customers, it networks in either adjusting or influence parameter. In the long run get more can interpret treatment class based on confounders rather than initial patient churn (or often both) if we're not necessarily truly interested in P-value kicked.

Example: A client calls frequently to inquire about what is going on with their investment portfolio. After noticing this behavior, Bob sends out updates to the portfolio, market news, or recommendations without being explicitly requested. You get hands-on service but personalized service with Ask Bob.

Through Ask Bob, we continue to increase financial literacy by educating our customers on different financial products and services. It responds to questions about banking, investments and savings and helps customers gain a clearer understanding of the complex nature of financial terms in order to make informed decisions.

Case in point: A customer asking, "How do mutual funds and ETFs differ?" Bob explains the benefits and drawbacks of both investment options, helping a customer choose an option that suits his or her financial objectives.

Ask Bob is an omni-channel enabled service, integrated into Ping An Bank's mobile app and website as well being able to post on their various channels in social media etc. It uses an omnichannel strategy — so Ask Bob will be where the customer is, and it seems like the same journey for them.

For example, a customer could start interacting with Ask Bob on the mobile app to inquire about account balances and then continue the conversation on the Ping An website regarding investment options, but the AI agent ensures to maintain all conversation follow-up across channels.

Eva by HDFC Bank (India)

HDFC: Eva (Electronic Virtual Assistant), the AI powered chatbot helps in servicing its customers 24/7 by assisting with Day-to-day routine banking services, providing personalized offers and real time information for customer queries. Eva manages millions of customer interactions, effectively promoting operational productivity and improved the consumer experience. The platform enables the bank to interact with customers through an array of digital channels by tapping NLP and ML capabilities, ensuring that customer banking experience is sub-servant.

Credit: Eva can manage all the way from customer balance or transaction history inquiries to information about its personal loan and credit card applications. By automating the questioning process, Eva minimizes human effort and helps customers get prompt responses, enhancing response times to produce high customer satisfaction.

Example: A customer says, "What's my savings account balance?" In real-time, Eva pulls the balance and communicates it back immediately to the customer, which is far more convenient for them than trying to find this information within their bank's mobile app or website.

Eva — Facilitating customers with information to apply for Credit Cards and Loans including eligibility, interest rates & terms. It also navigates users through the application, automating parts of document filing and tracking to create a seamless customer journey.

Any other example: The interest rate on a personal loan is......Eva shares the interest rates at the time and directs the customer on how to apply for loan, explaining the list of documents needed, etc.

Based on customer data, Eva provides individual recommendations to customers for various HDFC Bank services and products such as savings accounts, investment possibilities or credit-cards. At the time of analyzing customer behavior - spending patterns and goals for a specific period, Eva tells you what might apply to them so that it can align with their needs 3.

Case In Point: A consumer who travels the world over often Eva offers a tailored recommendation based on the boater's lifestyle, in this case an HDFC Bank card with travel perks like lounge access and reward points for foreign transactions.

Eva actively manages real-time monitoring on behalf of customers, alerting them to any suspicious activity/spam and taking proactive measures to prevent fraud by suspending accounts. Examples of such features include real-time alerts to the customer when Eva detects an out-of-pattern transaction and helps immediately with securing their account, e.g. by blocking the card or freezing transactions if there is a potential security risk at play…

For example, Eva notices that someone is making a big purchase from an unknown location and the customer receives this information via push notification. It asks whether the transaction was genuine, and if the customer denies it, Eva can then automatically freeze the account and help them with reporting their fraud.

Routine banking tasks, such as transfer of money from one bank account to another or paying bills and recharging mobile phones, can be done by Eva. Eva makes the entire workflow much more streamlined and user-friendly by dealing with these transactions in real-time.

Eva, transfer ☐5,000 from savings to checking for customer. Eva processes the transaction immediately, then wraps up that transfer in a few seconds, which makes it quick and comfortable.

Eva keeps customers notified of their account status with real-time updates for things like low balances, upcoming payments or large transactions. It allows you to keep track of your finances and prevent overdraft or a missed payment.

Use case: When a customer has their balance reaching low, Eva sends an alert, recommending them to move in money from another account or deposit cash into it so that no overdraft fee occurs. Eva can alert customers when their credit card or loan payments will soon be due to keep them from missing any deadlines.

Because Eva employs machine learning to get better and more effective at its conversations with customers. The more queries that Eva processes, the better it gets at comprehending customer desires and delivering congruent answers that are personalized as much for context. Its tailors to specific desires and lifestyles, which improves the customer experience.

For example, Eva discovers that one of her customers usually checks to see his balance at the start of each month. Eva can provide this point without intervention — more consumer ease, and therefore personal service.

Eva: Eva is a key chatbot that gives the covered insights for HDFC Bank items like protection plans, contributing choices and bank account. It allows to compare different options and track the advantages of each option so that consumers could decide which product suits them better according to their financial requirements and goals.

For instance, say a customer asks about insurance plans. Eva replies with a range of HDFC Bank insurance products it offers, explains how each product works, and eventually assists the customer in picking any plan (best fit) as per their criteria, e.g. Sum assured premium amount, etc.

Eva helps to direct more senior department employees at Zendesk for customers filing complaints or grievances. Eva prompts them through the process of escalating their issues to the departments. It also gives them the status of their complaints and solutions if they can.

Scenario: Someone complained about a service fee and said to Eva, "I would like to complain as possible the last charge on my account." Eva steps the customer through submitting their complaint, logs it and returns an expected completion date back to them.

Eva is also available on multiple channels like the HDFC Bank mobile app, website and even third-party messaging applications like WhatsApp. This version keeps the customer in mind, resulting is Eva everywhere and yesterday — a seamless experience across channels.

For example, a customer begins a conversation with Eva at the HDFC Bank website to know the loan options and carries forward it on mobile app to check account balance. Eva maintains the conversation context well on both those platforms.

Rita by Revolut (UK):

Rita is an AI-assisted chatbot of Revolut that helps customers to get instant feedback on account-related queries like balance, transaction info and supports with basic banking help automatically. Supports unprecedented automation of customer services for Revolut's global digital-only banking platform, enabling responsive real-time help and optimizing operational efficiency.

Rita — Enhanced Security Measures & Customer Support in Revolut users can conveniently view critical account details like current balances, transaction history and exchange rates. Customers do not have to navigate several screens with this automation, that makes mundane account-related queries easy for them.

Sample Use Case: — Customer says, "Rita What is my account balance right now?" Rita fetches the real time balance and gets back to customers immediately instead of checking their Revolut app manually.

Ever since Revolut presented one of its core business models — multi-currency accounts with cheap exchange rates — Rita has helped people to make currency exchanges inside their account. It delivers immediate currency exchange rates and easily converts currencies with a least number of steps.

Example: Customer asks "What is the current exchange rate GBP to EUR" Rita gets the new exchange rate in an instant and offers customer to make currency change inside of app.

Rita assists customers in transaction management, where one can view account transactions and review the history of individual transactions and confirm payment or flag any dispute on a transaction. Rita can help customers report a fraudulent transaction or explore account activity discrepancies.

Here is just an example: A customer opens their account and sees a charge they are not familiar with, so Rita asks, "What's this in my statement?" This allows Rita to iterate through the transaction details and suggests whether they should dispute a charge on that date as well, ideally making it easier for customers to solve any issues in the transactions.

Rita can provide spending insights tailored to the customer's transaction history. Rita analyses the patterns and helps customers take control of their money, such as saving suggestions/ budget setting or spending habits tracking.

Sample: Customer requests, "What did my dining spend for the month of last"? Using this transactional data as a basis, Rita delves into the dining expenses and shows you where's your problem area is in that segment of spending, among other insights.

Rita tracks account activity live, AKA she can alert you immediately if something weird or suspicious pops up in your transactions. When we have a potential fraudulent transaction detected, Rita goes CRAZY: warns the customer right of way and offers to freeze the card for those who really wants/escalates for human investigation.

For example, a customer uses your card: Rita triggers an alert. "Did you order this transaction? If the customer says no, then Rita locks the card and alerts Revolut's fraud team to investigate.

Rita helps send and receive payments in many currencies, a mainstay of Revolut's global banking platform. It also makes it easier to transfer money from one account to another and allows you to be able do the same with other users of Revolut in any currency.

For example, a customer asks, "Can I send 200 EUR to my friend in the US?". Throughout the entire process, Rita assists the customer, handles all currency conversion, ensures that the money is sent directly to receiving the lowest fees, and provides downloadable real-time updates from the IRS.

Rita offers instant transaction alerts and timely notifications to the customers, so they know immediately about any transactions in their accounts. These notifications also make it easier for customers to keep tabs on spending, payments and unauthorized transactions.

For example, Rita immediately sends a notification to customers with the sum of purchase and retailer geolocation right after the payment is completed. Even if the customer suspects it is a fraud, Rita provides dispute options on charge immediately.

Rita (Real Informational Transaction Assistant) Using struggle: Deposits/Transfers; Sends Bills, Via the Linked Bank Account Approved by the Customer Helps in freezing artistically or virtually a card to buy money, set how much, etc. This helps users to fully block their Revolut cards without having to ask for help from the customer support.

Example: A customer calls in saying, "Can you freeze my card?" Rita freezes the card on the spot and gives me a rundown of how to get it replaced so poor actors can't use my plastic for unauthorized activities.

Users can speak to Rita within the Revolut app round-the-clock, 7 days a week. Rita will deal with most of the queries, answering frequently asked questions and performing routine transactions with no need for any human customer service whatsoever — including during a peak hour when human CS may be less available.

Example: When a customer approached Rita late at night with the question, "How do I change my phone number linked to my account?" Rita could walk him through it, helping him to update the information in real-time and ensuring that the account remains secure and under the user's control. Rita becomes more effective at its job with each user interaction. It learns from each query and refines its responses to provide customers with more accurate and customized answers. Rita can be increasingly effective at solving complicated customer queries, as well as anticipating user requirements via predictive application based on behavior.

WeBot by WeBank (China):

The developers built and designed WeBot, an AI-powered virtual assistant, to give users a seamless experience in fully automated banking. Since it is the first all-digital bank of China, WeBank has real time logging bots (WeBot) to automate a variety of customer service activities — from account status enquiries and loan requests using state-of-the-art NLP and machine learning model. The WeBot levels up customer engagement, process efficiency and serves personalized financial advice at the speed of NOW!

WeBot allows a user to query for their account balance or recent transactions, as well as request statements on an ad hoc basis. WeBot speeds up the process of customer service interaction by automation these tasks.

For instance, a customer might ask WeBot "What's My Account Balance". Receiving the real-time balance instantly thanks to your WeBot, without you needing to scroll like a Dum Dum through mobile banking.

WeBot streamlines the loan application process by deploying automatic eligibility checks, a user-instructional method of prompting users through the system for applications and offers an immediate approval based on existing financial profile and credit history. Using the customer data, it analyses and matches loan offers which suit their financial requirements.

Customer asks, Do I qualify for a personal loan? WeBot assesses the financial situation of the customer and guides him or her to an appropriate brand financing offer. With all this, it offers instant approval to the borrowers, reducing the traditional loan approval time considerably.

A conversant chatbot using WeBot AI to gather information, analyse and display personalized financial advisory suggestions based on user data, including transaction history, spending pattern & savings goal. It advises on types of bank accounts and investment options or savings methods that are most relevant to the user.

For instance, a prospect wants to get better at saving. Based on review of the spending patterns, WeBot gives personalized financial advice and recommends a high-interest savings account or investment options that will give better returns to achieve specific saving goals.

WeBot serves customers with a range of basic and sophisticated queries going from general service-related questions to elaborate product specifics at WeBank. WeBot uses NLP which allows it to understand the question from its user and provide accurate, contextually relevant answers in no time reducing human intervention.

A customer asks WeBot "What is the charge when I transfer funds to international"? WeBot gives guidance on these fees, explaining what they are and how to avoid them by offering alternative methods of low-cost movement such as lower fee transfer services or changing currencies.

WeBot alerts you as soon as any abnormal or suspicious activity takes place on a user account. Whenever WeBot identifies odd transaction behavior or potential fraud, it sends the information to end users instantly via alerts. Users then have the choice of either freezing their account or initiating a charge dispute by profiling charges. This provides added security to customers, assisting them in securing their accounts.

For example, WeBot observes several large transactions within a short time frame originating from another country, which is not how the user usually behaves. The system notifies the customer and prompts if those transactions are accurate. WeBot freezes the account instantly shut, if the customer declines to allow activity.

The messaging app will help people complete everyday banking tasks — like paying a bill, shifting money between accounts or sending funds to another WeBank user. WeBot automates these bots, thus removing the frictions from managing finances and makes all transactions instant.

For example, a customer tells WeBot: "Transfer 2,000 RMB to my savings account." It works for you instantly to deal with the transaction, confirm a transfer and update your customer's account balance–all in one quick step.

In addition, WeBot sends proactive alerts for low balances, upcoming bill payments and when it detects any suspicious activity in the accounts. It also monitors the customer's finances by tracking his/her spending patterns and providing tips to create a savings plan.

Example: When a customer balance is low, WeBot will send an alert to the user, suggesting that they transfer funds or top up their account earlier to avoid potential overdraft fees. It recommends modifications to their budget, so they don't come up short in the future.

The WeBank service is only a click away for any customer so long as you have an account on its primary platform, WeChat — which many people living in China do. It makes banking more convenient because customers can use financial services and account management, as well as real-time help without having to leave WeChat.

Use case: a customer opens WeChat, says to Party A, "What is my last three transactions?" and Product B immediately provides the corresponding information in the chat interface of WeChat; Users can consequently realize side by side the complete economic services immediately for them via a platform they have become used to, only monetary amenities on tender.

Every interaction train WeBot to respond in a more precise and customized manner. Learn over users' preferences and behavior to provide more relevant services.

WeBot helps create automated KYC (Know Your Customer) compliance checks by taking new users through the onboarding process. It confirms the identity of customers by scanning over documents, running checks against collect databases in real-time and making sure that you are following financial or regulatory laws.

The New Customer wants to open an account. WeBot prompts the New

Customer to drop off the documents, perform facial recognition, and verify their identity. WeBot also confirms in real-time whether accounts have been created, which dramatically reduces onboarding time.

Final Words: AI Agenting Use Cases in Banking

The above use cases highlight how the banking sector is moving towards leveraging AI-powered virtual assistants to significantly improve customer service and operational efficiency. AI agents such an Erica by Bank of America, KAI by DBS Bank or Rita by Revolut assist customers in real-time and personalized manners while executing the machine level task like account management, transaction monitoring, etc. These AI agents create an end-to-end customer journey that helps customers navigate through complex financial processes–including loan applications, KYC compliance and even investments.

These AI solutions offer benefits, like enhancing the user experience. AI chatbots offer tailored and fast support, which speeds up response rates, elevates user engagement.

Operational Efficiency: Automating routine tasks frees human agents to focus on more complex issues, saving bank's money and increasing efficiency.

Better Security: Detecting fraud with AI agents for effective monitoring of transactions and precautionary alerts that enable customers to act quickly against unauthorized access.

Such AI solutions go through a learning curve that involves adapting over time, which makes them better and more personalized as machine learning is implemented.

AI Agents with Special Extended Features:

WeBank WeBot: The natural banking experience of the future, directly on top of the ubiquitous social platform of China — WeChat. With AI-driven proactive financial health monitoring and Fraud detection, the automatic KYC it is one of the best overall proprietary AI agents. It is one of the most convenient onboarding services in terms of execution, with users being able to consume full banking services from inside a known platform.

Bank of America: Erica: The most cutting-edge in terms of customized financial insights- customers get proactive alerts and help to manage your finances with Erica. This suite of functionality allowing account access, capability to see spending patterns and suggestions for budgeting strategies and real-time fraud detection is largely enhancing the customer experience.

Bob by Ping An Bank: the most sophisticated element about this chatbot is its integration with investment advisory, using real-time market data and customer profiles to recommend personalized investments. Comprehensive security and fraud detection is available as well, which makes that happy hour purchase data possible for anyone in need of to-the-minute investment stats.

Revolut: Rita stands out as one of the best at helping global clients care about multiple currency accounts, real-time cash exchange and cross-border transfers. Specifically, it supports near-instant international financial transfers which are optimised for Revolut's global user base to improve the digital banking experience.

Conclusion — AI agenting in banking is the future and has helped to bring banking services on our fingertips while serving customized, safe and faster alternatives. Agents like WeBot, Erica Ask Bob and Rita have become the bright lights that provide a peek into what futuristic customer experience can look like when tailored with cutting edge AI solutions designed to address precise needs in real-time; reshaping banking as we know it.

External AI-Agent Solutions.

A Bank and financial institutions also used 3rd party AI to increase the various processes. Banks and financial institutions can access AI agents trained by specialized companies during servicing. These agents incorporate bank systems and deliver a range of services like customer service, detecting frauds or examining data. Here are some examples:

Salesforce Einstein:

This is a platform integrated with the Salesforce ecosystem and powered by AI that provides banks with tools for CRM, predictive analytics, customer engagement, among others. Einstein acts as a virtual assistant, increasing customer service and workflow automation while offering insights from data analysis. Using machine learning and natural language processing, Salesforce

Einstein empowers banks to provide a tailored positive experience for customers at scale by automating workflows within their own business.

Salesforce Einstein applies customer data (transactional history, product usage and behavioral patterns) to forecast their needs and preferences. Beyond this, it uses these insights to provide personalized product recommendations which drive more powerful cross sell and up-sell for the bank. It also enables the relationship managers to understand their customers' behavior and financial need proactively.

For instance, if Einstein notices a customer has suddenly spent more on travel or dining out, powered by Salesforce can then surface campaigns offering incentives like airline miles credit cards geared towards customers who are new to those spending categories. Artificial intelligence-based personal recommendations for customers can allow relationship managers to get ahead of the curve and engage their customer these relevant, personalized views.

Account balances, transactions or product offerings (Einstein could field these queries and automate customer service). It leverages natural language processing to interpret and react to customer queries via chatbots or voice assistants. Einstein can also categorize and route more complex cases to the right teams-in real time for faster response times, and happy customers.

For example, a customer might say: "What are my last transactions?" For example, Einstein reads this information and replies immediately through the bank's chatbot. If it is more involved, such as a disputed transaction, Einstein sends the case to the right team with information needed to get them moving faster on resolving that issue.

Einstein leverages machine learning models to detect anomalies and potentially fraudulent activities on a real-time basis, as it monitors customer accounts & transaction data. Once the system detects anomalies, it sends alerts to customers and bank personnel who can act on them there and then preventing fraud risks.

For example, Einstein identifies several large transactions across geographically remote locations, and all occur within the same short amount of time despite this much to spend on a particular day such as shopping cannot match with customer profile. It then automatically flags these transactions and informs both the customer and their in-house fraud prevention team for validation.

Einstein helps relationship managers by taking the loading of such mundane tasks off their desks like document handling, customer on-boarding process and follow-ups. It can even direct high-conversions-leads at the top, so managers address their priorities in a more valuable way.

Example: Einstein alerts a relationship manager that a new client qualifies for high-end coaching services based on their financial history. Einstein creates a customized email template for the manager to use during outreach, which helps in automating this process and allows the manager to get back with the customer faster.

Examples of this include patterns that analysts can analyze to expect when a customer is at their riskiest for attrition through predictive analytics available in Einstein. These patterns result in decreased engagement and reduced product usage. Alternatively, this could spell potential reward for banks who can proactively manage such risks through proactive mitigation measures (e.g. special offers or red-carpet service) to offer targeted retention strategies aimed at enhancing customer loyalty circles that matter most in the eyes of their customers yet while doing so keeping profits up within acceptable parameters appropriate for deeper relationship among profitable pool segments.

Apply on this Example Einstein realizes after a customer stopped using one of the bank's products for several months. It sends it to the bank's retention team and recommends spending a loyalty bribe or proposal rate trying to win back that customer before they go elsewhere.

Einstein works with a variety of digital channels — from mobile apps to websites and email platforms. It guarantees the continuity of service and experience for all customers, independent of what communication channel they use.

Example: A customer begins a mortgage product inquiry on the bank's website chatbot and later calls in to talk with someone at customer service. By using Einstein, the chatbot conversation ensures that when the agent joins next time, he/she should have a full context from the previous December 5th chat so it will be a seamless transition to improve customer experience.

AI Banks Powered by Salesforce Einstein.

Salesforce Einstein aids up many global banks and financial institutions to improve upon their customer service CRM capabilities and operational efficiencies. Notable examples include:

Barclays (UK): Implements Salesforce Einstein to provide CRM and customer insights to increase personalized banking services.

Building a predictive customer engagement model for wealth management using Salesforce Einstein at Citibank.

HSBC (Global)–Optimize customer service workflows using Einstein and provide predictive insights to relationship managers.

Bank of America (US)–Leverages Salesforce Einstein for intelligent case management and more proactive customer service engagement.

Standard Chartered (Asia, Africa, Middle East) — uses Salesforce Einstein to deliver personalized customer email and help drive cross-sell/upsell opportunities.

The Role of AI-Powered Data Cloud in Banking: Snowflake

What is Snowflake: Snowflake is a data cloud service provider, provided by the Amazon Web Services with which banks easily stores and analyze all of their Big-Data. Snowflake is not an AI agent like Salesforce Einstein, but a platform which facilitates the execution of effective AI and Machine Learning models by storing data into secure storage areas in order to perform analyses on top. Banks can optimize their operations, detect fraud more quickly and easily around the world easily thanks to Snowflake's instant data sharing features combined with advanced analytics features which allow banks to provide a hyper-personal service while making AI-driven decisions.

Snowflake is helping banks collect, analyze and interpret at scale transaction histories, interaction behavior and information on product usage. By combining with AI systems, the Snowflake allows banks to launch personalized experiences, such as skin-nugget product recommendations and customer-servant interventions customized for every customer profile.

Example: A bank uses Snowflake for real-time analysis on customer records to spot direct debit and other payment services used a lot by certain customers The bank's AI agent uses these insights to recommend the most appropriate foreign transaction fee waiver or travel rewards credit card for that customer.

Snowflake, with its data-sharing and analytics power, helps banks in implementing the fraud detection in real time. Using data from multiple sources (transactions, behavioral patterns and geographical information), Snowflake makes it possible for machine-learning models to recognize signs of fraud quickly.

Example: A bank that uses snowflake to aggregate data across channels, for example ATM transactions, online banking and mobile wallets. The system uses AI models to analyze the data immediately, alerting on suspicious real-time activity such as transactions from far-apart locations or a high-speed withdrawal request from multiple accounts. The system will investigate and may put an account on hold.

By consolidating data from different departments, such as loan department data, mortgage department information and even credit card division findings into one centralized location through the Snowflake platform allows banks to have a 360-degree customer view. This comprehensive view of customers enables banks to deepen customer relationships by uncovering opportunities for cross-selling and up-sell their products.

I.e. A bank uses Snowflake to aggregate data and finds a customer has just paid off loan, with increasing savings amount the bank AI-agent offers the customers suitable investment products or premium credit cards which bolstered well into a financial experience and, subsequently, up-tick in revenue potential on for the banks.

This is important to a bank where they have very strict regulatory requirements such as Anti-Money Laundering and Know Your Customer. Banks that use Snowflake can keep customer data secure and compliant with regulations while providing it to AI models so they can assess risk, detect suspicious activity.

For example, snowflake store and analyze many transaction data as well customer wise. The Snowflake environment has AI algorithms that monitor transactions in real-time to discover those patterns, and subsequently prevent illicit money laundering activities. The system automatically triggers review by compliance teams for high-risk transactions.

Secure data sharing features of Snowflake enable banks to share the data with partners, regulators or among financial institutions near real-time without moving / duplicating it physically. This segment enables industry collaboration, better regulatory compliance, and customer service — banks can work together with third parties to boost offerings and services.

Real-world example: A bank leverages Snowflake data sharing to work with a FinTech online small business loan company. With Snowflake, one of those notebooks first orders a custom loan to be offered and then the notebook with the distinct approach for additional machine learning models will quickly guide both the FinTech partner and Bank about how any customer is performing in terms of financial health.

Banks use comprehensive data sets to signal the creditworthiness and underwrite loans. Snowflake use cases include providing data to AI and machine learning models that predict fraud and determine real-time approval processes on loan applications, among other things.

A bank that uses Snowflake to centralize data on financial and transactional information from credit bureaus, customer banking histories etc Such data processed in AI-driven credit scoring models through Snowflake prompts the system to provide a real-time risk estimation and result so that it can help the bank decide if they are going to approve or deny loan applications on-the-spot.

For Banks, this is an opportunity to improve customer service by combining data from various touchpoints using Snowflake. This data can be valuable to banks that are enhancing AI-driven chatbots or virtual assistants with response times, customer satisfaction, and a personalized service.

For example, a bank could combine customer interaction data sourced from emails, phone calls and social media with snowflake. Helpfully, the image created by this unified data finally pictures in one place all of a banker's travels through customer service and enables support that is more contextual, with future potential to be proactive.

Real-time information processing and advanced analytics capabilities from Snowflake enable banks to produce current financial plan projections that they desperately need. This enables them to take faster, data-driven decisions on asset allocation, capex and strategic planning.

For example, a bank might use Snowflake to create up-to-the-second financial reports that pull from many departments. Using AI to model this data enables the bank to predict forward performance and thus be more efficient at resource allocation as well gear its sails towards new economic winds earlier.

Banks Using Snowflake:

Snowflake is already used by many banks and financial institutions worldwide for its powerful data management, analytics capabilities.

Capital One (U.S.)–Uses Snowflake for cloud-based data storage and analytics to help power customer insights while alerting fraud detection.

With Snowflake, Western Union can centralize data and improve its AI-driven fraud prevention and compliance programs.

Citi (US)–Uses Snowflake to integrate diverse data sources in AI and machine learning models for delivering hyper-personalized customer experiences, as well as financial reporting

HSBC (Global) — Using Snowflake for Real-time Data Scenarios and Regulatory Mandates.

IBM Watson in Banking:

IBM Watson: This is the AI-powered platform from IBM, which gives banks advanced tools for customer service automation, decision-making and overall operational efficiency. Its talent in natural language processing (NLP), machine learning, and data analysis contains it to act as an intelligent agent, such as performing personalized interactions with customers' fraud detection or financial insights. Using Watson to power customer services and in back-end operations, banks can streamline processes, making banking faster and more secure.

IBM Watson acts as a virtual support system, responsible for managing customer queries and automating repetitive tasks such as balance checks or provision of transaction histories besides guiding customers through account opening processes. By integrating Watson into customer service platforms, banks can offer round-the-clock support without requiring human involvement.

Asks: What is my account balance right now? Through a chatbot or voice assistant, Watson will quickly recover and issue the balance. For more complicated queries, Watson can walk a customer through activities like applying for credit or raising a service claim.

Using Watson, the bank can tap into its wealth of customer financial data and behavior to serve up more personalized product advice — be it proposing better loans or credit cards or investments. For example, Watson can suggest credit cards or investment products that are based on what a user is looking for drawn from customer relationship management (CRM) systems in the bank itself.

For example, a customer who travels abroad often. Watson detects this and offers travel rewards credit card with no foreign transaction fees that will increase the stickiness of the customer's financial relationship, while providing cross-sales opportunities for the bank.

By utilizing IBM Watson's powerful machine learning algorithms, we can monitor and receive alerts on these. By utilizing IBM Watson's powerful machine learning algorithms, they can specifically design to process massive amounts of transactional data and detect anomalies that may show fraudulent activity. Any unusual spending behavior, uncharacteristic withdrawals or any patterns of activity that may show a security threat — Watson is there to help spot it first. Put, this gets ahead of security and helps in minimizing losses from fraud.

Banks are using Watson to simplify loan underwriting and credit scoring. Watson evaluates loan applicants in real-time, using data from credit histories and customer behavior and external sources for instant decisions or recommended study by the human underwriters. The data-driven insights from Watson enhance the accuracy of decision-making and results in reduced time to reach a loan approval.

Example: A customer applying for a mortgage. Function: Watson processes the credit information, employment and spending history of the applicant, producing quickly a risk score. Watson can recommend interest rate and terms to the bank processing a loan application based on its risk profile.

Watson allows banks to monitor transactions and customer activity so as not to violate Anti-Money Laundering (AML) or Know Your Customer (KYC) regulations. It studies vast amounts of data and recognizes patterns that need more inspection, preventing non-compliance.

Example: Watson reviews transactions looking for money laundering indicators, such as large deposits of cash, followed by a quick withdrawal. If Watson finds any such activity, it automatically creates a compliance report and sends it to the bank risk management team, alerting the end user of such activity, which helps the banks stay in line with regulatory standards.

Via Watson's NLP capabilities, banks automatically analyze thousands of documents, including loan agreements, contracts or compliance reports. For document processing / Watson helps to extract valuable information, identify discrepancies and even suggest changes, thus not only saving time but increasing the efficiency of documents processed.

For instance, a bank would have Watson review hundreds of loan applications It reads the documents from inception and finds unpopulated data points, error or missing signatures alert to human intervention by flagging those back for review while on an auto-pilot mode extracts key information essential for downstream processing.

For example, Watson assists banks with measuring customer satisfaction by analyzing interactions not just across email and chat but also the thousands of social media entries relating to a bank in one month as well using proprietary content from almost 100 million calls between customers and call centers. Watson detects customer sentiment and problems which are used to generate insights that improve service and bank-customer experience.

Watson–With the ability to interpret customer support chats, Watson could note what has gone wrong hundreds, thousands or (insert staggering number) times and recognize that a certain comment shows a negative sentiment. When customers take the time to say express dissatisfaction, it took me 50 blogs and zero humans on earth ever want that…which Watson will then red flag for follow-up so service teams can immediately jump in before the dam bursts?

Within Financial Services, Watson can even help Wealth Management clients analyze financial markets and predict trends to better inform their investment decisions. It offers portfolio recommendations under the customer's risk tolerance and financial goals, resulting in better performing asset allocation.

A customer asks Watson - "How can I reduce my risk by investing?" Watson dissects what the customer currently holds, examines how it stacks up against market trends and recommends a rebalance — i.e. switching stocks to bonds in order for them to reduce their current risk exposure.

Watson, for instance, aids banks in fine tuning their marketing strategy, focusing on the most effective ways to solicit from its customer base by analyzing target segment. Based on demographic and behavioral consumer data, the solution can also show to which customer segments, particular financial products, should be offered, diversifying conversion rates and consequently increasing sales.

For Example: A bank advertises a new credit card. Watson Reviews: Look at customer profiles to recognize those most likely to take up on offer and recommend marketing strategies that resonate with known consumer affinities; if something has brought younger people in for cash-back discounts, suggest offering increased rebates across popular spending categories similar as dining out or entertainment.

Banks Using IBM Watson:

HSBC (Global) — uses IBM Watson to automate other customer interactions, offer personalized financial advice and enforce regulatory compliance.

Royal Bank of Scotland (RBS) (UK): RBS-survive Puts in Watson for Customer Service And Sentiment Analysis From Various Online Channels

Citibank–a US bank that uses Watson to analyze internal and external data, manage customer relationships, and improve fraud detection capabilities. Société Générale–a French bank that uses Watson to improve client onboarding and compliance automation for AML and KYC.

JPMorgan Chase–another US bank that uses Watson for document and contract reviews, optimizing legal operations and eliminating manual times of processing.

Google Cloud and AI Solution:

Google Cloud offers two NLP and AI solutions helpful for banks: Dialogflow, a platform for creating conversational interfaces, and AI model to detect fraud. With the help of their AI model, Google also delivers pre-built models for unique use cases or tailored solutions, such as virtual advisory services. Banks can deploy virtual agents powered by Dialogflow to interact with customers, automate operations, and assist clients across digital channels. Powered by NLP, virtual agents can understand customer questions and respond with natural language or resolve issues without human intervention. In case of uncertainty, a virtual agent directs customers to a human advisor and passes the information already got, offering a seamless transition between a robot and human support. If a customer asks, "What is my credit card balance?" a virtual client assistant can instantly retrieve the customer's profile and provide the balance information. But if a customer files a claim for a specific transaction, such as "I didn't issue this purchase," the virtual assistant will forward the issue to a human advisor. Google's AI analyses extensive real-time transaction data and identifies abnormal patterns that signal fraud. It continuously learns to improve business intelligence and the ability to detect and prevent high-risk activities.

For example, Google Cloud's AI identifies if there have been withdrawals of large amounts from several locations within a short space of time. Once the transactions are flagged, the system sends the customer an SMS or email to notify them. It also halts any other transaction on this account until these two transactions can confirm that they are calling the owner of the registered mobile number than soon as possible, decreasing potential fraud loss.

Using customer data, such as transaction history and spending habits, financial goals etc., our AI solutions from Google Cloud analyses the info to suggest products very personal or relevant so Bank can benefit in cross selling/up-selling. The system also leverages machine learning algorithms to personalize recommendations for each individual user based on his or her financial situation.

E.g. a usual foreign traveler spends on travel and food, The Google Cloud-powered virtual agent notices this pattern and suggests travel rewards credit card — better positioning the bank in context of its product and services.

In various AI tasks now faced by it, the Google Cloud can be enlisted, for example, in analyzing customer financial data in loan underwriting and calculating a credit score as near to real-time. The system connects to machine learning models that determine the credit risk of certain individuals in a more accurate way. This leads to earlier loan approvals and improved decision-making at banks.

As an example: A customer is applying for a personal loan online. Google Cloud AI processes the customers' credit score, income history and spending patterns to come up with a risk evaluation in real time. Using these reports, the system will suggest whether a loan should be approved and which loans merit further scrutiny by human eyes.

Google Cloud NLP. can be used to process automatically fraud prevention and compliance documents, such as IDs issued by the government, utility bills, or tax forms. Machine learning and other AI technologies can enable banks to record identities automatically, as well as ensure they comply with relevant data regulations like Anti-Money Laundering (AML) norms.

E.g.: A new account opening user uploads his documents. The AI of Google Cloud extracts the information from documents by natural language processing (NLP) for identification and cross-references with government databases in search of compliance flags. By automating a usually manual and time-consuming exercise, the AI of Google Cloud reduces errors and speeds up customer on-boarding.

Banks can use Google Cloud's NLP to understand and analyze customer sentiment from multiple sources like emails, chat or social. Emotion-led, customer-centric thinking allows banks to understand where it hurts and fix the root of issues faster than competition — while also shaping a higher level of experience for consumers.

For instance, in an email, a customer expresses their dissatisfaction with the freshest incident through their feedback. Sentiment analysis also labeled the sentence as negative, which triggered Google Cloud's NLP to flag this conversation for a follow-up. This will then allow the bank to address what has gone wrong, preventing further churn and increasing satisfaction.

In its simplest form, Google Cloud AI will analyze customer shopping and demographic data to inform how banks issue targeted marketing campaigns. Segment customers and tailor offers: According to the data above, segmenting your engagement strategies is a great way for creating personalized experience based on customer preferences which will lead in high engage rates with applied dynamics (behaviors) of marketing messages that make it more inclined than before by reducing conversion time both.

For example, a bank may use Google Cloud AI to examine the transaction records of its customers and then find out who often makes purchases online. The system has a targeted marketing campaign to provide these customers with an offer on the new ecommerce credit card, driving more efficient ways of managing customer reassessments and increases in applications for the new cards.

Using Google Cloud data analytics, banks can produce real-time money reports and projections with the help of AI devises and Machine Learning models. The system supports banks in making data-driven decisions around asset allocation, investment strategies and liquidity management by analyzing past performance alongside recent market conditions.

Illustration: A bank processing its near-real-time financial data with Google Cloud to produce a liquidity report. These liquidity risk predictions help the bank reallocate its cash reserves based on market condition feedback from customers and earn a steady income without suffering financial distress.

Take the example from Google Cloud, you can use AutoML Natural Language to process reams of documents like loan agreements and compliance forms or financial reports automatically. Banks can take advantage of faster onboarding, reduced manual entry errors and smoother approval workflows by extracting the necessary information, as well as identifying variances.

Bank processes mortgages of thousands leveraging the Google Cloud NLP. This would identify if loan amount, interest rate and repayment period are in a few of cases and those fields which are missing or different from what was passed. This minimizes human effort while providing better response time and accuracy in the approval process.

Bank Use Cases Google Cloud AI & NLP Solutions

Several banks and financial institutions use google Cloud around the world for its AI, NLP capabilities, including:

HSBC (Global) — Leverages Google Cloud AI for automation in customer support and data analytics to improve air travel experience and regulatory compliance.

Spain-based BBVA–AI with Google Cloud: It has been implemented to provide tailored financial recommendations and improve the chat-bot facility in customer service.

ANZ Bank (Australia): leveraging Google Cloud AI to speed up customer onboarding and compliance processes, improving its operational efficiency.

Santander (Spain)–Uses Google solution for managing customer experience.

Microsoft Azure AI in Banking

Microsoft Azure AI provides Bank of the West with a complete solution, tailored towards boosting customer engagement and operational efficiency using advanced artificial intelligence tools, secured by cutting-edge security features as part of Microsoft's multiple offerings for banks. Azure AI programmatically executes workflows by integrating natural language processing (NLP), machine learning (ML), and cognitive services. With an AI-first approach, banks such as RBS are using top azure ai services like virtual agents for customer engagements and deep insights with analytics from enormous volumes of data & better decision making to enhance their operational efficiency.

By using Azure AI, banks can deliver an intelligent virtual agent that is driven by artificial intelligence (AI), which acts as a human-like brain deployed through the same technology of the Bot Service and powered by Cognitive Services control its deployment across different touchpoints automatically communicating with customers. These are virtual agents that can conduct account inquiries, recover transaction history and attend customers in real-time for any banking process you get them to do.

For example, a customer says to the virtual agent: "What is my credit card balance? The Azure AI-powered agent works quickly and finds the right data to automate your answer immediately. For more intricate questions like disputing a charge, the virtual assistant seamlessly conveys that context over to a live agent for even better help.

Machine learning models offered by Azure AI scrutinize massive swaths of transactional data in order to assist banks with real-time fraud detection. Such models keep incorporating learnings with historical data and increase its ability to catch anomalies in spending behavior or transaction patterns.

E, g., Azure AI notices that a user is completing multiple high-value transactions from various regions within close temporal proximity, whereas the usual behavior of the customer would not permit such activity (even when considering weekends) The system automatically identifies these transactions as suspicious and locks out new activity until the bank confirms it is a legitimate transaction and cuts fraud cases to zero.

By analyzing customer data - such as transaction history, spending patterns and financial behavior- Azure AI can provide personalized recommendations. Azure AI seamlessly syncs with customer relationship management (CRM) systems and helps banks offer products to each of their customers — for instance, a credit card or loan service or an investment product tailored for the individual.

For example, a customer who makes regular international transactions The Azure AI platform will infer the propensity of an existing customer to open a Forex account or take out a credit card with international travel rewards based on their actions; this would make cross-sell and up-sell opportunities more appropriate, resulting in higher success rates.

Using Azure AI, banks can also shed the cumbersome loan underwriting process of analyzing financial data and credit history for each lending customer in real time. The machine learning models of azure evaluate credit risk and return with an immediate yes or no loan decision, decreasing the time required for processing loans while achieving high accuracy.

For example, a customer is looking to apply for a mortgage. Azure AI takes an application and looks at the applicant's financial history, whether they have a job, and how good their credit is to give them a risk rating. Using this analysis, the bank can make personalized loan terms or demand additional documents for a high-risk profile.

For example, when a new customer uploads ID documents to create an account, Azure AI's document processing services extract the needed data and perform ID checks. They also go through AML databases to run background verification, reducing the output time. This automation of compliances comes at a much lower cost compared to the usual manual KYC process.

With Azure, AI banks can measure customer sentiment for things like email, chat interactions, social media and surveys using text analytics (Sentiment analysis). Azure AI reads customer emotions that lead to frustration, which drives more churn and uses sentiment analysis to determine why the customers are dissatisfied.

For Example: Customer writes feedback because of late service delivered causing displease. Analyzing the message, Azure AI discovers it is expressing a negative sentiment and red flags this for immediate attention by the customer service team. This proactive method enables banks to address issues quickly and increase customer retention.

Models are developed in the Azure AI suite, and these models can analyze how customers behave now so that their behavior six months or a year down the line can be estimated — allowing for targeted marketing such as offers made when open an app bank via your mobile phone. Predictive analytics solutions can help banks predict which customers are more likely to go elsewhere for their financial services and understand the right-timed incentives necessary to reach those consumers with offers personalized.

For instance, using the customer example above — and if Azure AI has detected a concerning lack of activity in their checking account for several months while they have not engaged with any bank services at all. The AI system will then give you a retention strategy idea, such as providing them with a cashback reward or personalized savings plan to help keep the customer engaged.

Azure AI allows financial institutions to process documents automatically at scale, including the organization of loan agreements, compliance forms, or even customer contracts, using Form Recognizer and Optical Character Recognition (OCR). Azure AI simplifies document processing by automatically extracting crucial data and detecting discrepancies, making your process more efficient while decreasing human errors.

Example: A bank has to process out thousands of mortgage applications. From the documents, Azure AI's Form Recognizer automatically pulls key information such as loan amounts and interest rates—whilst alerting if sections were incomplete or signature is missing for action—to speed up approval.

Banks can now generate real-time financial reports through Azure AI, a platform which enables the analysis of large datasets and offers predictive insights for more accurate financial planning. When used alongside the existing AI models in Azure, banks can predict liquidity requirements and market movements in order to make instant decisions using data.

For example, Azure AI parses real-time data collected from different departments in the bank and produces a timely financial health report which observes trends related to cash flow, overall market conditions as well predicted liquidity deficits. This tool provided decision-makers at the bank with ways to adapt asset allocation or investment strategies rapidly in real-time.

Microsoft Azure AI — Main image Several businesses in the banking and finance sector worldwide incorporate Microsoft Asure Artificial Intelligence to automate their processes as well improve consumer experience.

Standard Chartered (Global)–Leveraging Azure AI to power virtual customer service agents and real-time ML for anti-fraud efforts.

BNP Paribas (France) — Uses Azure AI for better customer engagement by rendering personalized services and virtual assistants.

ABN AMRO (Pays-Bas):

HSBC (Global)–Builds on Azure AI to automate KYC and compliance workflows with improved operational efficiency and regulatory compliance.

Deals with external AI solutions for agenting in banks.

External AI solutions like Salesforce Einstein, IBM Watson, Google Cloud AI, Microsoft Azure AI, and Snowflake have transformed banking by automating customer service, improving fraud detection, and streamlining operations to generate real-time data analytics. Not only the top global banks like HSBC, Citibank, and Standard Chartered, which I previously wrote about, but also hundreds of Tiers-2 and -3 banks around the world are employing these solutions. Powered by AI, these platforms empower banks to deliver best-in-class service and security features, accelerating adoption of cutting-edge AI capabilities throughout the financial industry.

Every single solution provides several uses, but the following major use cases highlight their breadth:

Salesforce Einstein–Lead and Account Scoring with in order to generate highly personalized customer recommendations that drive cross-sell opportunities (for Barclays).

IBM Watson: Automates KYC checks for enhanced compliance (Employed by HSBC)

Google Cloud AI: Uses advanced anomaly detection models to catch fraud in real-time (as done by BBVA).

Microsoft Azure AI for customer service automation.
Virtual agents (in use by Standard Chartered)

Snowflake: Cloud-based data warehousing and collaboration for rich decision-making (Capital One use case)

These AI solutions support large banks, as well as smaller ones, to streamline operations and give integration cost benefits while providing of customer-centric secure smart services. Banks of all sizes can remain competitive as they adapt to a rapidly changing financial services environment with the help of these technologies.

The financial industry has strategically moved onward from plain chatbots into AI agents. The finance sector can be benefitted from the use of AI agents at large, mainly by generating a better investment option for customers and gaining cost efficiency. As new tech motors ahead, Artificial Intelligence will allow AI agents to truly revolutionize the way customer service is done in banking and change operations permanently.

The banking services at which AI agents now excel have gone from simple chatbots to supporting a variety of tasks, all intending to augment customer service and operational efficiency. Using natural language processing (NLP) and machine learning, these advanced AI agents do not just deliver scripted responses — they personalize in response to customer behavior automatically escalating opportunities or issues.

Reference – Further reading - Chapter 14

Accenture: Trend 2 - Meet my agent: Ecosystems for AI
https://www.accenture.com/us-en/insights/technology/technology-trends-2024?c=acn_glb_accenturetechnogoogle_14070970&n=psgs_0124&gad_source=1&gclid=CjwKCAjwzIK1BhAuEiwAHQmU3q10PXSftKyBK2Rnfy7oHp1JYfqVYoZVKEZvu9vOlZoJwkz4hICCPxoCLOoQAvD_BwE&gclsrc=aw.ds#block-meet-my-agent

AI in Banking a usecase of Erica by Bank of America
https://www.linkedin.com/pulse/ai-banking-usecase-erica-bank-america-suyash-bhatt-ph-d-/

Case Study: DBS Bank's Billion-Dollar AI Banking Dream
https://www.forrester.com/report/case-study-dbs-banks-billion-dollar-ai-banking-dream/RES180780

Capital One's Intelligent Assistant: Why We Built Eno's NLP Tech in House
https://medium.com/capital-one-tech/capital-ones-intelligent-assistant-why-we-built-eno-s-nlp-tech-in-house-8c0007c3c102

Meet Einstein Service Agent: Salesforce's Autonomous AI Agent to Revolutionize Chatbot Experiences
https://www.salesforce.com/news/stories/einstein-service-agent-announcement/

How To Build AI Assistants and Chatbots on Enterprise Data with Snowflake Cortex AI
https://www.snowflake.com/thankyou/how-to-build-ai-assistants-and-chatbots-on-enterprise-data-with-snowflake-cortex-ai-2024-07-30/

watsonx Assistant
https://www.ibm.com/products/watsonx-assistant

Vertex AI Agent Builder
Build and deploy enterprise ready generative AI experiences
https://cloud.google.com/products/agent-builder?_gl=1*tebnx8*_up*MQ..&gclid=CjwKCAjwzIK1BhAuEiwAHQmU3lFPPr1QYaRK1lufJ6yL8AldZUcGCUx44KrV7-BwkRxsfm7RcACRkxoCNtwQAvD_BwE&gclsrc=aw.ds&hl=en

FIFTEEN

Advanced Customer Segmentation with AI

1. Introduction

The digital transformation in the banking sector has brought about profound changes in how banks implement customer segmentation. Previously, customer segmentation involved a process of manual analysis based on demographic, geographic or transaction details that were both time-consuming and lacked accuracy. Today, introducing artificial intelligence (AI) and machine learning (ML) has made this process way more granular and flexible by allowing us to look at a plethora of parameters to segment the opportunities from each other. It dives into technology, being such an enormous factor in digital segmentation, the origins of data and different data that businesses used to create more targeted experiences for their customers and ultimately deliver better results.

2. How to Get Batman-Level of Customer Segmentation?

Artificial Intelligence and Machine Learning allows banks to process more factors than they could in any other case. These parameters are more than the traditional demographic and transactional data, it also involves entry of psychographic and behavioral data. By including these additional data, organizations gain a deeper insight into what their customers really need or want.

Internal Data–Traditional data sources, such as age, income, transaction history and product usage. The first step in the ref arability process is collecting internal data: understanding customer behavior; If you are a consumer finance company, knowing how healthy your customers are financially.

External Data: The importance of external, and typically unstructured, data integration is only increasing. This can be anything from the social media activity to online browsing behavior to public records and out of house 3rd party consumer data. Social media interactions can give away sentiment, likes and dislikes of the customers while browsing behaviors may show interest in a particular financial product or service.

Third-Party Data Providers: Acxiom, Experian and Equifax are companies that offer rich datasets with credit histories, purchase behaviors and lifestyle indicators. This data complements the internal data that banks already possess and offers a more holistic perspective for each customer.

3. Benefits of Unstructured Data

Text, video and social media posts are all unstructured data that can also provide a lot of information not found in structured data. AI and ML models can decode this unstructured data as this data contains insights which provide the customer opinions, preferences, and requirements. For instance, NLP techniques can reveal how customers feel and provide a context with a wealth of information from customer reviews or comments on social media, including identifying potential problems.

Sentiment Analysis — Analyzing customer reviews on the bank's mobile app or social media post shows what customers think about that banks' products and services. The easiest way to understand it is by finding new trends or potential solutions.

Behavioral Analysis: We can also analyze customer behavior by referring to this unstructured data. Those might include visiting a type of website often or searching repeatedly for financial advice—a sign the customer may be interested in a particular product offering.

4. A Complete Guide to Customer Segmentation Using Machine Learning

Given the rise of big data, businesses are increasingly turning to sophisticated advances in tech to glean insights into consumer patterns and predisposition. It is one of the most powerful tools — machine learning (ML), with more advanced techniques to dissect customer data and find such unique segments. Being able to do these is very important because it allows you to custom make marketing strategies, improve the customer journey, and eventually boost your business.

5. Customer Segmentation and machine learning

Customer segmentation is dividing your customer base into segments of consumers who are like one another. In the past, businesses would mine data to see trends; this was all a very manual process. But machine learning has automated, improved, and scaled solutions to new heights that cannot be achieved with traditional methods.

6. Where AI/ML enables us to focus on customer segmentation

1- Product Development:

Based on the information gleaned from segmentation, better understanding of the customer needs and preferences can develop new banking products. Examples include analysts being able to identify a segment of green buyers based on transactions, demographics, social media, and browsing behavior. Machine learning models can analyze all these data points to detect little clues about customers who are interested in investing 'green'. Banks can then create targeted products, be it ESG funds, green bonds or sustainable ETFs.

2- Risk Management:

It also allows the institution to evaluate and manage distinct risk profiles with companies of varying sizes. For example, we might think that young customers with non-regular income are riskier. Age, income stability, employment status, and credit history are examples of features that machine learning models can train on to determine the level of risk. They self-improve over time, allowing banks to sharpen their estimates and deploy countermeasures like requesting more collateral or teaching basic financial education.

3- Pricing Strategy:

Tier your pricing strategies: Breaking pricing down by assets and transaction volumes allows banks to segment customers. In this way, banks can grant lower prices on top of the base price to more valuable customers, who either have higher assets or transaction volumes, thus increasing customer satisfaction and loyalty.

4- Customer Retention:

Analysts use machine learning to analyze churn patterns and uncover what might cause one customer segment to exit. For instance, if a segment is churning because of high fees, banks can bolt-on services that drive retention via fee offset.

Behavioral Segmentation: Make sense of customer behaviors such as spending (transaction patterns) and usage of services, also to understand which products or services are most prized by different segments. Online banking power users may particularly focus on cutting-edge digital innovation and convenience, whereas more traditional customers could prefer in-branch services that better suit their personal needs.

Age, income, location and life stage: demographic segmentation is one of the biggest factors that will detail how customer needs vary. This valuable data can help banks to cross-sell, offering products and services at the moment of important moments in life (for example, mortgage loans or retirement planning).

7. Customized Messages and Promotions

Personalized Marketing: Segmentation helps banks design personalized marketing campaigns catering to different consumers. This could lead to high conversions and retention rates — such as offering student loans & credit cards for college students, or travel-related products for frequent travelers.

Personalized Offers–Based on the spending patterns and financial goals of each segment, banks can offer personalized offers and rewards. For example, people who are identified as financially disciplined are likely to respond well to high interest savings accounts or even investment opportunities.

8. Enhancing Customer Experience

Omni-channel integration: It starts there, comes over all digital and physical channels. By segmenting customers according to how they like to engage will allow banks to deliver better service experiences.

Feedback and Adaptation:

As banks, you get various customer segments sending feedback by taking feedback from different customer segments might help in identifying the areas for improvement that customers are looking out for. As a result, banks can adjust their offerings to more closely meet the needs of customers, improving retention.

Proactive Engagement

Churn Prediction Models — Machine learning models are used to make predictions about which customers are likely to churn by analyzing their data. This allows banks to identify these segments at risk and to limit attrition by proposing stay offers or higher service quality.

Loyalty Programs: Boost customer retention by creating loyalty programs that return the favor to customers who stick around for the long haul. Enterprises can customize these programs regarding their segmentation data in order to cater to them towards the customer type they are targeting.

9. Cross-Selling & Up-selling

Recommended Products: By gaining insight into the common characteristics of each segment, banks can cross-sell the right products or services for each person within the same group. This benefits the customer as well, as they see this added value and it encourages them to stick with the bank.

Cross-Selling and Up-Selling banks can use banks to identify opportunities for cross-selling, shop around for potential lending candidates. For example, banks may target a niche group of high reciprocating credit card users and offer them reward cards such that give extra benefits.

Upselling involves encouraging customers to purchase a pricier item or upgrade, while cross-selling encourages them to buy additional items. With the right segmentation, one can predict meeting customers who are likely to upgrade their services from now on.

Value-Based Segmentation: This is an example of segmenting customers based on their value to the bank. This enables banks to focus their up-selling efforts on those most receptive to high-value offers, such as private banking or select investment products.

How It Can Be Better: Customers that are high-volume users of a lightweight product may be ripe for an upsell. The example that springs to mind would be for heavy travelers with regular credit card experience to sign up for a premium card with travel benefits and insurance.

Feedback & Surveys: Customer feedback and surveys responses give you an idea about customer satisfaction and their intention for up selling. To illustrate, we might point to high touch customers with a desire for better service to premium banking phone lines that receive faster customer support.

10. Branch Strategy:

Banks use segmentation to determine where to open new branches or ATMs, the services that might work in each location. One example is a heavy density of small businesses in an area, which suggests the necessity for a business banking service focused branch.

Transaction Analysis: based on the types and frequency of transactions carried out at branches, banks can know what needs to be suited by them for a better customer experience. 6.

Customer Demographics: Data on the demographics of customers who prefer a branching model can help banks to understand the specific demands of those groups.

Service Utilization: Traffic to decide which services are more used in branch, such as loan consultations and cash withdrawal, show the value of the physical interaction?

Client Acquisition: Insight into the most profitable or with high-growth potential customer segments to target acquisition strategies and operations efficiently. Banks can run a campaign for young professionals, which is a good demographic to go after and has plenty of future growth potential.

The above examples show how customer segmentation powered by machine learning can enable banks to create more targeted products, services and strategies — which help drive business performance.

11. Digital Channel

Financial institutions can gain a deeper understanding of their digital customers by monitoring engagement metrics such as login frequency, visit duration, and usage of online services like bill payments and mobile check deposits.

By collecting and analyzing customer feedback on digital platforms, we can detect areas of dissatisfaction and open up new user experience opportunities.

Cross-Channel Behavior gives you insights into how your customers are using "digital and physical channels" so that you can examine customer preferences from a more holistic standpoint.

Cash account for about 16% of all transactions in the USA, which is significantly higher than in Asia and other countries. South Korea, and Singapore.

12. Top Heavy and Bottom Out Strategy in Banking

The banking strategy focuses on retaining profitable clients and efficiently managing less profitable ones through digitalization or phasing them out. This strategy divides the customer base into the top 35%, a core 50%, and a bottom 15% segment.

The wealthiest segment of customers profits from page views by visitor, top 35%.

These are customers who bring in good revenues through the high amounts they maintain, the frequency of transactions, and premium services. This segment represents a contribution that is very important to the bank's profits and, as such, it is essential to maintain this part of the book. Such customers often account for 80% of the profit in many banks, focusing on corporate products, investment banking, trade, capital markets and financial marketing or portfolio management. Several of the global banks to fall under this category.

Core 50% (Average Value Customer)

This segment considers 80% of the bank's customers. While not nearly as lucrative per click as the more expensive terms, they add up in revenue.

To keep them engaged, offer a variety of products and services that meet their needs, provide excellent customer service, and utilize technology for convenient banking solutions. There may also be opportunities around cross-selling and up-sell within this segment as well.

Banks are typically more retail products oriented, i.e. credit cards, auto loans, mortgages and enormous sum fixed deposits.

Bottom 15% (Non-Profitable Customers):

Some of these customers may have low balances on their accounts, engage in low transaction frequency, or require primarily cost-intensive services. The revenue attributed to them may not cover the costs borne by the bank.

Management Strategies: The bank might want to explore opportunities for a lower cost-to-serve in this segment, either by incentivizing the usage of digital channels or providing basic low-cost services. If retention is not possible, tactics could involve pushing self-serve or moving them to digital only services.

Accurately segmenting customers using data analytics and machine learning based on profitability, behavior, potential value. This enables banks to execute targeted strategies for each within a group.

For instance, the top 35% among Internet surfers value heavily localized wealth and private banking services or exclusive investment opportunities. Targeted marketing campaigns and loyalty programs can stir the remaining 50%, the core, into activity. For the bottom 15%, we might focus on cheaper digital tickets and clear service information. There are digital-only bank products that serve those segments.

By streamlining operations and encouraging digital adoption (especially among the bottom 15), we can significantly reduce costs. It involves urging ATMs, internet banking, and mobile ambitions.

It is necessary for strategies to be reviewed and adjusted from time to time, if they still cater to customers, if profitable and respond accordingly in the market. This contributes to the fact that the bank does not waver from its strategic directions, which are close to business and customer needs.

Advantages of using machine learning in customer segmentation:

1. Manual segmentation takes a long time, and it is almost impossible. After all, ML algorithms can process vast amounts of data to identify intricate patterns and correlations. This velocity and accuracy help businesses to make real-time data decisions using marketing strategies and Highland's customer satisfaction.

2. The business landscape and customer behaviors are ever evolving. To maintain the relevancy of customer segmentation, businesses should keep ML models with new data. This flexibility is essential for businesses that must remain nimble to changing market conditions and consumer demand.

3. The ability to scale with your business as a company expands, so does the amount of data they need storing and, in more complex ways,

Scalability: ML models scale and lose efficiency as the data you contain increases. A cloud-based infrastructure, which permits rapid integration and deployment of ML models in various environments, often supports this scalability.

4. Accurate Segmentation — Identify the right Number of segments deciding on the number of customer segments is an unsaid prerequisite for effective segmentation powered marketing. A few common examples of such methods include the use of the elbow method in k-means clustering. There are several ML techniques available that provide systematic ways to identify the most meaningful segments. This improves the accuracy of targeting and allows for the effective allocation of the marketing budget.

13. Machine Learning algorithms for Customer Segmentation

We can place machine learning algorithms into 2 major groups — supervised and unsupervised learning. Unsupervised learning, which deals with clustering and customer segmentation, is more common in real-world scenarios because it has to deal with unlabeled data.

Popular Clustering Algorithms

1. K-Means Clustering K-means clustering, one of the most popular clustering algorithms that partition the data into k clusters, each of which contains the Dana Point resembling to its 0cluster center. You can use it to find customer segments based on behavioral data: purchase history, website activity and more.

2. Agglomerative Hierarchical Clustering This works by building a hierarchy of clusters. It makes the clusters merge and/or split apart as needed. Behind the scenes, this helps organizations that may need to segment their customers based on a single criterion, whereas they segmented them.

3. EM clustering is a used technique in statistical models to find maximum likelihood estimates of parameters, often for clustering. In particular, it can be helpful with data that has a lot of variation in structure, which would not otherwise fit well with the simpler models.

4. Here, you can identify the clusters based on the density or number of data points in the region, which is useful for datasets with clusters of different sizes and shapes.

5. Mean-Shift Clustering mean-shift is a centroid-based algorithm, updating centroids to the mean of points in its region and therefore supports flexible clustering. — it is centroid based as such does not specify any upfront number of clusters.

14. Implementation and Use Cases

There are multiple steps to implement ML based customer segmentation, from data pre-processing to model training and evaluation. Here is what the typical process could look something like:

In Data Collection and Pre-processing, we can collect customer data from different sources, like transaction records, website analytics, and customer feedback. We ensure the consistency of data cleaning and normalization.

Model Selection & Training–Select a suitable algorithm based on data characteristics and business requirements Adjust parameters while training the model on your dataset, to optimize its performance.

Model Evaluation: Inertia (k-means) / Silhouette Score / Gap statistic to evaluate how good or bad the clustering was and check for cluster count using the Elbow Method

1. Visualization and Interpretation: Using tools like Plotly, Matplotlib visualize the clusters what are groups having which properties. This step is one of the most important ones because when you translate your findings into actionable business strategies, it results in beefing up your data capabilities.

15. Banking Industry:

In financial institutions, ML models are used to separate clients into groups of common characteristics and to offer an individual experience when buying financial products or services. Banks, as an example, are using customer transactions data to pinpoint the segments which may be interested in loan, credit card or investment opportunities. Segmentation: — It helps in detecting fraud by finding odd behaviors regarding transactional data.

Banks such as HSBC are focusing on using artificial intelligence and machine learning to develop intelligent customer segments, making customer banking experience more personalized.

Personalized Customer Experience — HSBC leverages AI to analyze transactional data to spot spend patterns and saving habits of their customers. The data lets HSBC offer personalized financial insights to its customers that would include bespoke budgeting tips or warnings about how they are spending their money. Capital One has added a "Budget" tool to its mobile app, built with Personates, that categorizes what customers spend their money on and provides them with personalized recommendations.

HSBC conducted a survey of Hong Kongers' spending and saving in December last year. They interviewed 1,244 adults across Hong Kong aged from 18 to 64 between June 6 and July 18. It was a broad cross-section of the population banking in the city, in terms of age and gender. But only 37 percent have set up a monthly budget, which is the essential first step to financial planning.

Better Customer Service: HSBC has introduced AI solutions to make its call center operations more efficient. They use Google's AI technology to automate the call center (CC) interaction review process, looking for areas where they can improve their customer service. This tool goes a long way toward showing where agents might need coaching and is an excellent means of ensuring quality service across the board.

Bank of America Bank of Already uses AI and machine learning to segment its customers, allowing the bank to use targeted marketing and deliver personalized services. This includes detailed customer profiles created by analyzing transaction, spend and interaction data. Bank of America uses segmentation to personalize its product offerings, such as credit cards and investment services. This is done by tailoring them to individual customers' needs and preferences, to increase customer satisfaction and loyalty.

JPMorgan Chase: JPMorgan uses AI-based segmentation to enhance financial risk management and customer-centric strategies. With k-means clustering or any machine learning techniques, the bank can determine some clusters of customers with their financial behavior. This can help with targeting at-risk borrowers who are likely to default on loans or potential customers in need of new financial products. This segmentation enables the bank to manage risks before they arise and provide customized services like, loans packages tailored to specific needs or specialized financial advice.

Wells Fargo: Wells Fargo is using AI to segment clients based on their engagement with digital channels and transactional patterns. The bank uses this segmentation to customize its customer experience design in its digital touchpoints, such as personalized financial products and service offerings that are mapped based on individualized needs. How Wells Fargo uses AI in sentiment analysis for customer feedback and sentiment, which helps to improve customer service and effectively manage grievances.

16. Banks across the globe are using AI and machine learning to segment customers to offer personalize services, enrich customer engagement. Here are a few important examples:

1. Banking Clients: Aspire Systems is an expert in helping banking clients through AI and machine learning from customer segmentation, etc. Banks use them to analyze customer profiles and behavior to provide customized services. Banks can segment customers on different variables like income, demographics and behavior and help themselves in predicting the service needs of a customer and can improve their service deliver.

2. Datrics: developed Machine Learning to segment payers and help banks automate such processes as LTV of customers. Banks can then focus on understanding the financial behaviors of their customer segments and develop their marketing strategies. For example, a leading European bank used Datrics to automate LTV computations, which empowered them with enhanced customer segmentation, enabling more precise strategic planning.

3. Quantzig: Quantzig is engaged in offering analytics services, such as customer segmentation, that allow banks to tailor their marketing strategies and resource allocation. They help banks with insight into customer preferences and behavior, facilitating targeted marketing and product development. This method ensures that one can leverage the maximum cross-sell and up-sale opportunities, uphold customer satisfaction and maintain a continuous communication with them. You can get more information about this on their website.

4. H2O. ai: H2O provides powerful AI and machine learning-based customer segmentation solutions. Using an expansive set of data, from browsing behavior and purchase history to third-party household data, their platform helps businesses identify microsegment within their customer base. Such detailed segmentation allows for more granular marketing and customer personalization. H2O focuses on democratizing AI for businesses in all industries, including financial services, to improve customer engagement and drive growth.

5. Accenture's Solutions. Solutions, all of which are enabled by AI: Accenture has an entire suite of AI-driven tools called "Solutions. Customers can provide billing and order inquiry through the first application selected under the AI umbrella that targets customer engagement and service. They leverage info from multiple customer interactions to constantly feedback on and improve their segmentation approaches. They allow companies to expect customer demands, improve their marketing efforts and elevate the customer experience by providing tailored services and support across all channels.

6. Visionet Systems (AI-driven solutions for the insurance and finance industries focusing on data integration from internal and external sources); Focusing on potential fraud, their AI includes machine-learning algorithms to identify patterns and trends within large data sets using transactional data and external market movements for better customer segmentation strategies. It enables organizations to discover new patterning trends rapidly and update their strategies in line with developing customer behaviors, improving both customer retention and acquisition strategies.

7. Rinf. tech: Rinf. IQ tech are experts in customer segmentation using AI and ML solutions. Their platform helps companies to identify customers in different segments as well by using the technology of both supervised and unsupervised machine learning. This also lets you gain access to real-time insights into customer behavior. For businesses that are trying to grow their operations and improve both their marketing and product development strategies, this is key.

So, finally, we can conclude that in the banking sector, AI and machine learning have changed the customer segmentation up to a great extent. The approach is inherently granular because of new data type besides the classical demographic or transactional view with a higher dynamic as we see many more features moving away from pure markets into customer view (incorporating things like behavioral, psychographics and external sources). It is this evolution that allows banks to provide extremely tailored experiences, develop better products and assume more risks with finer degrees of accuracy.

There are ample benefits to using an AI powered segmentation. AI enables the banks to tailor their products and services to their customers' needs, predict churn, improve bank customer retention rates and further optimize the marketing strategies. On top of this, machine learning models provide scalability, efficiency, and real-time adaptability that make them invaluable in the rapidly changing market landscape of today.

Banks can adopt segmentation to improve pricing strategies, customer retention initiatives and cross-selling opportunities and extract more value out of each segment. Banks can maintain the loyalty of high-value customers by providing good analogous experiences, while they can reduce cost loss for less profitable segments by managing them digitally.

AI-driven segmentation also benefits the banking sector by tapping into unstructured data sources, such as social media, improving customer insights with sentiment analysis and fraud detection using behavioral analysis. Banks such as HSBC, JPMorgan and Wells Fargo are already using the technology to segment their AI for better risk management and customer service, as well as tailoring product offers for different groups.

In a nutshell, AI-supported segmentation is an impressive way banks and financial institutions can continue to stay ahead of the competition while optimizing their operations and ensuring that customers receive highly personalized services. By utilizing robust machine learning algorithms with accompanying flexible infrastructure, the above mentioned is how we can truly leverage customer data and continue to power progress within banking.

Reference – Further reading - Chapter 15

HSBC Taps Google Cloud AI to Optimize Customer Service
https://brainstation.io/magazine/hsbc-taps-google-cloud-ai-to-optimize-customer-service
Artificial Intelligence at HSBC – Two Use Cases
https://emerj.com/ai-sector-overviews/artificial-intelligence-at-hsbc-two-use-cases/
HSBC Reveals two AI Use Cases for Banking
https://thenorth.ai/2023/06/13/hsbc-reveals-two-ai-use-cases-for-banking/
How K-means Clustering is Transforming the Banking Sector
https://www.datrics.ai/articles/how-k-means-clustering-is-transforming-the-banking-sector
Customer Segmentation in Banking: Examples
https://vitalflux.com/customer-segmentation-in-banking-machine-learning-examples/#google_vignette
https://www.quantzig.com/case-studies/customer-segmentation-banking-sector/
Navigating AI-driven Retail Testing Revolution 1
https://resources.aspiresys.com/collections/65f7d9ca8528711f70c23964/a/65d43aeb2b58f0029189bd84
https://www.aspiresys.com/
Accelerate Your Financial Services with Intelligent AI-Powered Growth Solutions
https://www.datrics.ai/financial-services
H2O.ai
https://h2o.ai/platform/danube/

SIXTEEN

AI-driven Underwriting: The Future of Risk Assessment in Banking

Introduction

In the global banking sector, there is a growing focus on AI and machine learning. Celebrating underwriting — overseeing who gets credit and at what cost, as a fundamental part of banking, is experiencing the most disruption from these technologies. Analysts forecast the global AI in the banking market to grow at a CAGR of 33.6% and exceed $64.03 Billion by 2030, up from $41 Mn in 2019. In 2020, the technologies have reached a market size of $3.88 billion! This rapid expansion underscores the increasing reliance on AI and ML to automate underwriting — services vital to banking operations that require a boost in efficiency, accuracy, and scalability.

So why AI is essential for underwriting?

Risk management underwriting is the process in which credit analysis of the applicant and various terms of loan agreement are affected. By incorporating AI and ML into your underwriting, you can adopt a systematic data-driven approach that speeds up decision-making and enhances risk evaluation.

By utilizing AI and ML algorithms, insurers can analyze large volumes of data during underwriting to identify patterns and correlations that human workers has overlooked. Which, in today's turbulent financial sector, can make all the difference between a sound decision and no decision at all. It could also translate to sounder, and more aim underwriting by diminishing potential human error or even bias — which AI can ease.

Conventional Underwriting vs AI/ML Assisted Underwriting

This is a paradigm that defines most underwriting processes, especially those using limited data sources like credit scores and financial statements merged with whatever information the applicant shares. Those efforts were all manual and subjected several individuals into an often-tedious process of trial-and-error — especially because they were using stoic data sets. On the flip side, manual reviews and approvals of traditional underwriting can take days, if not weeks.

AI and machine learning powered underwriting can utilize transactional data for enhanced accuracy. Additionally, it can analyze social media activity and other online behaviors to identify potential red flags. Therefore, when banks can better analyze the most significant risk they face, from a data perspective, they can also have more effective information used for decision over loans. Twisted Worlds created a machine learning model that can detect new or unseen risks, such as subtle shifts in shopping habits that impact overall financial stability. This is crucial for assessing credit extension, which depends on maintaining stability.

They learn by giving AI and ML models more data to chew on until they get better at predicting. It determines how it wants to learn something, choosing which deposits to select or not select. This is adaptive learning, unlike traditional underwriting where the rules and criteria were set statically a couple of years ago and have not caught up with new market conditions.

AI, ML to Revolutionize Underwriting in Banking

1. Speed and efficiency: One of the biggest advantages that AI and ML offer in underwriting is their ability to process data. Where such things used to take days or even weeks, today's new technologies realized these within minutes if banks use these so they can reply to loan applicants soon. And this increase in efficiency allows banks to better serve customers and process applications at a faster rate, enabling scale growth.

2. More accurate risk assessment: It uses AI and ML algorithms to analyze complex data sets (for example, patient histories) that would otherwise be difficult for clinicians to navigate. This data can be structured, such as customer information, credit history, or employment records, as well as unstructured consumer activity on social media platforms and other sources.

This reporting would give a fuller measure of the financial strength of applicants and enable better decisions on whether to extend credit. The AI models search for surrogate markers that show a possible defaulting vaccine. These markers may include a decline in bank account balances or a sudden change in payment behavior.

3. Powered by AI, the latest underwriting enables lenders to offer loans tailored to an individual's financial profile. Loan terms are determined by AI models of data, such as income and spending habits, credit history. Personalization enhances the likelihood of loan approval for FIs and better customer experience since it brings to them tailored (preferred) products.

4. Eliminate Bias and Error — Even when the human underwriters act in good faith, their future predictions are subject to a variety of cognitive biases. As AI and ML algorithms pass judgment using data, they are likely to have less bias. They will compare among sources to determine so many from the most current information. This objectivity is essential for the lending process to run fairly.

5. For example, artificial intelligence & machine learning has a potential to learn from new debs and even decide based on the same. In theory, the more data that passes through these models, the better they get at predictions. It's a continuous learning curve and an ongoing battle for banks.

6. AML can help improve the underwriting risks-based solutions for effective interdiction of frauds. Live fraud check Live-Fraud-Check checks the transaction data model in real time for patterns that characterize deception and reveal a potential attempted fraud. As an example, a service could use an AI model to find potential scourges in transaction patterns not seen before from the applicant, i.e., random large withdrawals or transfers. When the bank receives early notification of potentially fraudulent activity, it can save everyone money and protect people from fraud.

7. Regulatory Compliance Meeting the regulatory requirements is a concern banks have when underwriting. With the help of AI and ML, banks can conduct automated compliance checks to ensure loan decisions are conforming to operational laws or norms even amidst a haze of regulations. And the value of these technologies providing audit trails and documentation to substantiate compliance is paramount when some manner of regulatory scrutiny is imminent.

8. Implementing AI/ML with current underwriting frameworks will require advancements to API technology and cloud computing. AI-driven tools enable the banks to work side-by-side with their current systems instead of against them. This helps in a gradual journey towards new technologies, along with freeing up nodes in and around the banking sector. Approachable: Banks can maintain their existing underwriting streams and use AI in such a way that they do not undergo any disruption.

Underwriting to get a fresh Risk Seat with 3rd Party Tools & AIML Innovations

The banking sector has seen emerging new tools and platforms aimed at improving underwriting, besides the rapid advancements of AI and ML. They make use of tech capabilities like NLP, computer vision, predictive analytics to provide in-depth insights into the risk profile of prospective applicants.

Banks are now on the verge of using natural language processing (NLP) to mine their treasury body of loan applications, customer emails, and social media posts. This permits NLP algorithms to process large volumes of textual data, and act on what is relevant for taking underwriting decisions. A different application example is using NLP to examine an applicant's prior conversation logs for potential red flags → i.e., if they might be in financial trouble or lost their job.

Some companies have taken to computer vision technology for adding verification to old ID methods in the underwriting space. For example, an AI algorithm can compare a document with the images and videos used to create it to verify its authenticity. Such a quirk can even crop up in the underwriting for use, and document tampering, and forgery detection adds a benefit to this one.

Prediction of risk scores using AI and ML models.

AI and ML models used in predictive analytics tools analyze an applicant's financial history and behavior, along with third-party sources like social media. This analysis helps generate a risk score for the applicant. Banks use these scores to make informed decisions about the likelihood of a person defaulting in their loan. Predictive analytics may also find trends and patterns that could show a future risk of mitigating, allowing banks to adjust their underwriting rules.

Using the power of Cloud computing, developers can develop AI platforms banks integrate with its existing infrastructure. These platforms provide AI tools for underwriting, such as real-time data processing, model training, and risk assessment. As you know, customer traffic is changing, so banks require a working solution that can scale up or down with cost-effectiveness, which Cloud-based AI platforms provide.

Explainable AI (XAI):

We cannot overstate the importance of transparency in the decision-making process. Explainable AI tools give banks insight into what is happening in the decision-making part of their AI model, allowing them to understand and trust the results. It also helps banks to comply with the regulatory requirements, as it provides plain reasons did you choose this over that for each underwriting decision.

The banking industry seeks underwriting, especially in an industry known for lacking agility. Incorporating AI and ML into this fundamental practice is cutting-edge. Increased efficiency, personalized lending to customers and identifying fraud through more sophisticated patterns are the major benefits of these technologies. Enterprises can use AI and ML to manage banks with artificial intelligence in the future, adapting to changes in the economy.

Leveraging such AI tools helps expedite the approval process and reduce the time to grant loans with more accurate and personalized underwriting. AI will enable banks to unlock about 60% of underwriting capabilities that are untapped, delivering years of growth and profitability — expanding the AI in the banking market.

Top 5 Bank Case studies of Underwriting using AI & ML Use-cases

1. JPMorgan Chase is using AI & ML to supercharge underwriting

For example, JPMorgan Chase has incorporated AI/ML into its underwriting process to deliver a more precise credit risk analysis, allowing the bank to maintain loan approvers ongoing. The bank leverages AI tools to analyze extensive data, including limited payment transactions and social media usage. This allows them to predict credit defaulters, going beyond traditional loan applicant profiling.

Technology: JPMorgan Chase worked with underwriting platform Zest AI to develop the method. Zest AI uses machine learning models for credit risk evaluation at an individual level and goes beyond traditional credit scores using 300+ variables per applicant. Every time that data changes, that new data point is a chance to hone our models, which are learning to predict.

JPMorgan Chase has seen tangible results with its use of Zest AI. These include characteristics like speedier approval of loans, more robust risk evaluation and expedited underwriting. This resulted in 25% reduction in default rates and loan approval turnaround by as much as up to 40%, leading to a positive customer experience and thus higher profitability.

2. Wells Fargo: AN AI UNDERWRITING & DECISION-MAKING PROCESS

Wells Fargo: For small business loans, Wells Fargo started using AI/ML models in the underwriting process as well. Its primary aim was to speed up loan approval, while simultaneously making faster and more accurate decisions without human error or bias.

Technology: Wells Fargo uses FICO's decision management, powered by AI, to develop FICO-based credit risk models that are scored by machine learning algorithms. Wells Fargo integrates FICO's AI-powered decision management platform with its existing infrastructure and uses historical data for analysis.

Value Realized: FICO has simplified the loan application process for Wells Fargo customers, reducing it to just one or two steps. This is a departure from the traditional, more complex methods. It doubled approval rates for applicants without or limited credit history, more than any other technology at 30%, and has halved loan closing times. The lender has also been helping customers who operate small businesses and expanding its home equity lending portfolio, according to Wells Fargo.

3. HSBC — Mortgage for automated underwriting

Example: HSBC has applied the same capabilities as AI and ML for its mortgage underwriting process Real World Application. The bank wanted to improve the accuracy of its credit risk evaluation and offer personalized mortgage products for its customers.

Tech: HSBC partners with AI vendor Kabbage (a provider of an AI-driven underwriting platform) (American Express gains Kabbage). The Kabbage platform uses 2,000 variables to assess credit risk for applicants, including income sources, spending habits, and local real estate market conditions.

With Kabbage's AI-powered underwriting, HSBC recorded a 20% increase in risk assessment accuracy—resulting in decreased mortgage default rates. The mortgage unit also made "enhanced competitive" rates available to more eligible borrowers, in a bid for a bigger piece of that lending pie.

4. Bank Of America: AI-Driven Small Business Underwriting

Just take Bank of America, for example, which was looking to change how its processes to underwrite small commercial loans around speed and accuracy. The bank used AI and ML technology to evaluate unknown data types for small business applicants.

Features: Bank of America uses the AI Upstart AI lending stack on an Artificial Intelligence oscilloscope. As with its performance on the personal lending side of the product, Upstart's machine learning models are used to predict which small business loan applications are creditworthy. By examining over 1,600 elements, including payment history and cash flow, Upstart's machine learning models predict creditworthiness in small business loan applications.

Result Achieved: Bank of America is now also using Upstart's AI platform to speed up and more precisely approve small business loans. New loan approvals have increased 30%, and applications are now processed in a quarter of the time. This strategy has increased the number of small business customers Bank of America can win, and its lending activity.

5. Citibank: AI powered underwriting for consumer loans

Citibank used AI and ML to underwrite consumer loans, surpassing competitors in assessing credit risk and dominating the money lending industry.

Tech Deployed: Citi teamed up with the AI-powered credit scoring platform LenddoEFL. Machine learning powered LenddoEFL algorithms look at a variety of factors, such as social media behavior, mobile usage and even psychometric data. These reports help to create credit scores for non-traditional credit file applicants.

LenddoEFL's AI empowers Citibank to reach out to individuals who could not access banking services because of growing up in rural areas of the Philippines without identification. With an AI-driven behavioral scoring system, the bank can assess the risk of each individual, resulting in higher loan approvals and reduced default rates by 35%. This has allowed Citibank to expand into underserved markets and promote financial inclusion.

Use cases — Top 5 Asian Banks underwriting using AI & ML

1. DBS Bank, (Singapore) -AI Driven Personal Loan Underwriting

DBS Bank: Auto-underwriting personal loans using AI and ML to orchestrate automated business processes for faster credit assessments. TenFold. Bank needed to enhance their digital lending platform, an instant loan approval variety with little human touch.

Credit scoring platform using AI: FinScore Grab: DBS Bank. FinScore partnered with the vendor of AI. It uses extra data streams or other information that is outside of ordinary credit scoring. For instance, it might incorporate cell phone information, social media action and advanced impressions. FinScore collects non-traditional data points and uses machine learning algorithms to process them, providing a full credit score for every applicant.

Impact: Introducing its AI technology, the DBS Bank slash approval time for loan from days to fractions. This translated into the bank increasing their loan approval by up to 50% and decreasing default rates within the range of 30%! AI-driven underwriting has allowed DBS Bank to target more customers with zero or limited credit history and capture new market share.

2. ICICI Bank (India) — SME Loan Underwriting using AI

For example, ICICI Bank used AI and ML technology to upgrade its underwriting system for SME loans. It aims at improving risk evaluations and faster loan approvals.

Tech Stack: ICICI Bank had partnered with an AI driven FinTech company, Crediwatch which provides a wide range of business and predictive analytics via machine learning algorithms to create full credit profiles in terms of business. For every SME applicant, Crediwatch analyses a purview of the data including credit and financial statements, transactional and other industry trends.

The Result: Since implementing Crediwatch's AI platform, ICICI Bank has diluted its SME loan sanction cycle times by 40%. The bank noted that using this tool; it was 20% more likely to predict credit risk over other methods and increased its control over loan delinquencies. ICICI Bank provided more loans to the SMEs now with better assurance which will lead small business in India to new horizons of growth.

3. China Merchants Bank (China): AI for Consumer Lending

Case: China Merchants Bank (CMB) — CMB introduces AI into China consumer credit products by using machine learning to enhance its underwriting quality. The bank sought to overhaul its credit decision process and offer tailored loan products to clients.

Tech Stack CMB collaborated with Ping An Technology, which is an artificial intelligence technology provider. Alex, an AI platform that uses deep-learning and natural-language processing, extracts data from sources such as transaction history, social media behavior, or financial statements. This allows for complete customization on a company-by-company basis. The Bank can thus underwrite individual loans based on the platform's real-time credit scores and risk assessments.

Results: Through Ping An's AI platform, CMB slashed down the underwriting time by 60% and increased risk assessment accuracy. This slashes the percentage of customer deposits that are non-performing in half, delivers a 40% enhancement to cost structure and another $50 million from incremental revenues. Match your loan products as per the Customer Needs — The bank has a very personalized range of loans and nails it here. No one can beat them. This has even helped to keep the good customer stickiness rate.

4. Mitsubishi UFJ Financial Group (Japan) — AI-Enhanced Underwriting for Corporate Loans

To underwrite corporate loans at MUFG, AI and ML were also used to help streamline the process. From their own corporate clients, they knew that loan approvals that took less time led to a lot of discrepancies- the process for risk assessment needed to change.

Tech Used: This is where MUFG partnered with an AI vendor called AIDA

Technologies that provides AI-based solutions for risk management. AIDA utilizes machine learning and AI to analyze historical loan performance data, market trend indicators, and key corporate financials (such as balance sheets and profit & loss statements). This enables AIDA to provide transparent and real-time risk assessments for corporates seeking loans.

Integrating AIDA with a large Japanese bank, MUFG, decreased the corporate loan approval time by 50% and increased risk assessment accuracy by 30%. As a result, the bank could reduce loan defaults and is now in position to offer loans on better terms for its corporate clients. This AI-enabled method has also solidified the bank's status as among Malaysia's best in corporate banking, both the most efficient and reliable ones.

5. Siam Commercial Bank — Thailand: AI -Enabled Digital Lending

Siam Commercial Bank (SCB): Siam Commercial Bank (SCB) deploys advanced AI and ML technologies in its personal loans, as well as micro-loans digital lending program. To help them in making faster & accurate credit decisions automatic its Lending Process.

SCB used the Ai platform Kasisto to power the platforms. Kasisto can analyze a vast amount of data, including mobile exclusive customer data like purchase history, social media behavior, and digital breadcrumbs. Analysts will one day treat this data with reverence when judging credit.

Kasisto's AI platform reduced loan approval time, providing a significant advantage for SCB. This improvement also led to better utilization of data and increased potential for marketing by cross-selling products, resulting in improved NIM. The bank, however, has said that loan approvals are 45% up and credit losses are down by 20%. Utilizing data and targeting potential marketing, such as cross-selling products, has improved customer experience by using AI in underwriting. Now, the bank provides customers with instant feedback on their loan applications and recommends personalized loans to each individual based on their profile.

Small or Virtual Banks using Artificial Intelligence & Machine Learning — Use Cases

1. N26 (Germany): AI-based Consumer Loans

N26: Case Study: A leading European digital bank using AI and Machine Learning to underwrite personal loans! The Company highlighted the initiative of providing instant loan approvals with minimal human involvement through its digital platform.

N26 Tech Jewels: The bank did embrace with some cloud banking nations like Mambu Mambu uses machine learning models that take in customer data relating to transactional behavior, credit history and spending patterns. AI models assess the creditworthiness of applicants for loans, enabling immediate smart decisions.

Results/Impact Examples: N26 has reduced the time to be approved for loans from days to minutes by integrating Mambu's underwriting AI tools. The bank has since lifted its loan approval rate by as much as 60% and cut default rates by over 40%. Speed and accuracy of the loan decision made it possible for N26 customers to have immediate access to funds through the process.

2. Monzo (UK): AI Supported Underwriting Providing an Overdraft Facilitation

Established in 2015, Monzo is a Digital Bank based out of the UK that has extended its capacity by incorporating this model using Artificial Intelligence and Machine Learning. Its purpose was to assist banks to increase the debounce of credit graffiti and provide individualized overdraft limits to their customers.

Tech implemented: Monzo has integrated with the AI platform Comply Advantage to conduct real-time financial risk screening. The model, based on machine learning, examines consumer data, including transactional analysis, affordability checks, and income source classification to predict the likelihood of individuals using their overdraft.

Monzo: By leveraging AI technology from Comply Advantage, Monzo could cut the approval time of its overdrafts in half. By utilizing AI models across all their overdraft products, they achieve a 30% improvement in default rates. This is significant considering the potential vulnerability to commoditization and underpricing because of limited risk assessment diligence. So, this has made Monzo introduce new limits on over drafts so it can manage its larger user base better.

3. Revolut (UK) — AI-Based Credit Card Underwriting

Revolut (United Kingdom)–Leading global FinTech neobank adopted AI and ML to speed up their credit card issuance process. The bank was looking to offer real-time credit card approval right to reduce the default risk of the customers.

Solution:

TrueLayer, which is an open banking platform that provides AI power credit scoring capabilities technology adopted: Data ingestion from FinTech partners like Revolut brand This data about account history, credit and financial transactional data by leveraging machine learning algorithms. Revolut can decide on underwriting at lightning-fast speed thanks to machine learning driven risk scores, meaning the platform is now generating credit scores.

Benefits Realized: The business has reduced the time to process credit card applications by 70%, using TrueLayer´s AI tools. AI advancements in credit risk scoring now have efficiency like that exhibited by missing a default on a credit card application. Revolut offers golden ticket credit card approval in an afternoon to rocket customer numbers and market share skyward in the competitive FinTech market.

4. Chime (USA): AI-Assisted Credit underwriting for loans

Data problem:

A leading neo bank in US (Chime) may improve underwriting for personal loans with the help of AI/ML Collection applications but we wanted to put together an end-to-end solution, and provide a credit scoring model, which can complete and elegant and not as bloated as these sentence above.

Chime recently integrated with Varo Money for AI underwriting, as reported by TechCrunch. Varo's platform uses machine learning models to assess traditional financial data and non-traditional sources like mobile phone usage, social media activity, and digital footprints. Hence, these AI models provide you with a full risk profile for every loan applicant.

H2: Integration of Varo AI platform has reduced the turnaround-time for personal loan approvals by 55% at Chime. The bank further said improved credit risk assessments now make it 35% less likely that people will default on its loans. Chime's ability to diversify its underwriting mix would allow it to offer loans to a wider range of customers, including those with limited or no credit history. By employing AI, Chime could significantly increase loan appreciation for these customers.

5. In the UK with Starling Bank–Augmented AI Underwriting for SME loans

Use case: UK digital bank Starling used AI and ML to strengthen their credit analyst of business loans that are tailored for Small & Medium-Sized Enterprises (SME) The aim of the bank was to have both quick loan approval at high credit assessment accuracy.

Starling Bank and Funding Options partner for alternative SME finance. Funding Options uses machine learning algorithms to analyze business financials, transaction histories, and industry-specific risks. This helps create detailed risk profiles for SME loan applicants.

Funding Options AI technology helps Starling Bank reduce approval time for SME loans by 60%, resulting in shorter application and approval processes and successful adoption of the outcomes. The new AI-powered underwriting has even boosted loans approvals by 25% and the number of running defaults. Our team launched the Credit & Risk DocVerifi to fix this. We can provide insights into the status of your accounts and the potential consequences if a creditor were demanding repayment of their credit facilities. Starling Bank has been crucial in helping the much-maligned SME market during these rocky financial times. Lenders have had to be progressive and agile, offering multiple channel choices.

Neobanks and virtual banks have used AI/ML technology to enhance credit risk underwriting, replacing manual decision-making at traditional institutions. The banks partnered with AI players to reduce loan amounts, credit risk, and improve loan approval decisions. These banks have improved operational efficiencies, reduced risk, and enhanced the customer experience. This puts them ahead in the competitive digital banking game, ensuring long-term success.

Banks employ this artificial intelligence (AI) and machine learning models for underwriting operations. They are transforming credit-risk analytics advancement, error resolution, and operational efficiencies. AI-based capabilities have revolutionized the banking industry, allowing the company to create personalized financial products, faster loan processing, and more precise default risk management. These advancements apply to banks of all sizes, from those with tens to hundreds of thousands of employees.

They might have third-party models that can process significantly sized data using advanced technologies with no physical barriers. By utilizing this, they can uncover unseen patterns and make data-driven decisions that impact customer satisfaction, leading to increased sales. These innovations can revolutionize the customer experience by providing faster and fairer quicker, personalized, financial services while also enhancing operational efficiency.

As AI and ML mature, the technologies will translate into meaningful applications, leading to greater investments from banks seeking an edge in a competitive financial terrain. More importantly, banks lay the foundation for meeting the demands and embrace the opportunities of a strengthening financial world while delivering even more value to customers than in years past. This evolution keeps on reinventing the importance of AI and ML in banking to be considered not as differentiation anymore; this is minimum requirements today, to enable profit under cuts while remaining competitive.

Reference – Further reading - Chapter 16

Zest AI Website: https://www.zest.ai
FICO Decision Management Platform Website:
https://www.fico.com/en/products/fico-decision-management-suite
Kabbage Website: https://www.kabbage.com
Upstart Website: https://www.upstart.com
LenddoEFL Website: https://www.lenddoefl.com
FinScore Website: https://www.finscore.ph
Crediwatch Website: https://www.crediwatch.com
Ping An Technology Website: https://www.pingan.com/en/technology/
AIDA Technologies Website: https://www.aidatech.io
Kasisto Website: https://kasisto.com
Mambu Website: https://www.mambu.com
ComplyAdvantage Website: https://complyadvantage.com
TrueLayer Website: https://truelayer.com
Varo Website: https://www.varomoney.com
Funding Options Website: https://www.fundingoptions.com
AI in Banking: Trends and Predictions
https://www.forbes.com/sites/forbestechcouncil/2023/07/10/the-future-of-ai-in-banking-trends-and-predictions
How AI is Transforming the Banking Sector
https://www.mckinsey.com/industries/financial-services/our-insights/how-ai-is-transforming-the-banking-sector
The Role of AI in Modernizing Underwriting
https://www.ibm.com/blogs/financial-services/2022/01/12/modernizing-underwriting-with-ai/
The Impact of Machine Learning on Credit Risk Management
https://www.deloitte.com/us/en/insights/focus/cognitive-technologies/ai-and-risk-credit-risk-management.html
AI-Powered Credit Scoring Systems: Benefits and Risks
https://www.weforum.org/agenda/2021/08/ai-powered-credit-scoring-systems/

SEVENTEEN

Contract Management in Banking — A blend of AI & Smart Contracts

1. Introduction

AI and smart contracts have brought a significant change in the way modern-day organizations handle their contracts. Powered by NLP, ML and blockchain, these technologies combine to automate the most mundane workflows and support strategic decision-making in standardizing contract management to make it more agile.

2. How AI Plays a Role in Contract Management

Electronic contract lifecycle management is an old guard practice repackaged with AI capabilities for the drafting, review, and management of contracts. This automation spares company time and energy to spend on other, more strategic activities. AI allows organizations to extract and analyze important information from contracts, helping them identify crucial obligations or terms that directly impact risk assessment and decision making. By 2026, Garter reports that more than half of contract management work will automate, reducing the time spent on lengthy processes and minimizing common mistakes.

3. Advantages of Using AI in the Contract Management

AI has a lot to contribute to contract management, such as better visibility, risk management, and much more. By utilizing AI-enabled systems, it becomes possible to manage every agreement effortlessly and with no extra human resources, as the systems can track their status in real-time. AI can also well detect variances and contract hazards, which helps in preventing risks proactively. With the aid of AI, businesses can analyze extensive contract data to stay ahead of the competition and adapt to the constant changes in the modern business world.

4. Smart Contracts for Beginners

Smart contracts are a huge leap forward; by using blockchains, these contracts allow for automation of execution and enforcement of agreements. A smart contract is a self-executing contract with the terms of the agreement between buyer and seller being directly written into lines of code. With automation, the process has become faster, and mistakes are less likely to be made; which means there will also be a lot fewer arguments. Industries use smart contracts, Finance, Real Estate etc to secure and deploy faster transactions. According to a report by MarketsandMarkets, blockchain is expected to drive the growth of the global smart contracts market. A report by MarketsandMarkets projects that the global smart contracts market will experience growth, with the market size rising from $300M in 2020 to $345 million by 2023.

5. Smart Contracts and the Place of Blockchain

Smart Contracts: how blockchain fits in. It offers a safe and immutable environment for transaction execution and storing the transactions. Chains in the interoperable distributed ledger provide transparency and immutability. The system ensures that, once a transaction is recorded, it cannot be changed or removed. This transparency establishes trust between parties and eliminates the need for intermediaries, as well as mitigates fraud. Smart contracts execute once the conditions are met on other blockchain's decentralized characteristic, along with pre-agreed terms, streamlining the process and reducing costs.

6. AI & Smart Contracts Integration

Bringing AI and smart contracts together promises to be a game changing new way of doing contract management. Organizations can expect cost reductions and better risk management by using AI's data analysis power to execute smart contracts automatically. They can manage massive pieces of data; they can let us see potential dangers because then a wise contract supported by AI can see bits of emerging proof. That gives them visibility of their obligations so they can solve problems as they arise and negotiate contract terms for superior outcomes. Together, AI and smart contracts will reinvent contract management by automating intelligence and agility.

7. Improved contract analysis and due diligence

This is one reason AI-based tools are changing contract analysis, thanks to powerful algorithms that can quickly review many contracts with great precision. This would help in extracting specific clauses, analyzing risks and giving some guidance which can be helpful for due diligence efforts. AI can help organizations in driving trends, optimizing contract negotiation and contractual obligation from analyzing historical contract data. AI analysis of historical contract data can optimize contract negotiation and obligation fulfilment by identifying trends and ensuring accuracy and consistency, surpassing manual review processes.

8. Predictive Contract Modelling

AI algorithms can analyze historical contract data to predict outcomes from now on. These algorithms identify patterns and trends to forecast potential disputes and recommend the best types of negotiating strategies. By using predictive modelling, companies can effectively manage risk well in advance and optimize contract terms, ultimately contributing to better and smarter decisions.

9. Custom Contract Suggestions

AI-driven platforms enable advancing contract customization by allowing creating personalized templates and recommendations. Using historical data, industry standards or the bite-sized contracts still prevalent in many organizations does their best to serve up just what is needed. Having a contract creation workflow that is personalized to the requirements of individual proposals can help simplify drafting and negotiation, making contracts better align with strategic goals and regulatory guidelines.

10. Implement contract automation and compliance in execution.

They are self-executing contracts with the terms of the agreement between buyer and seller being directly written into lines of code, which automates enforcement. This secure and transparent execution of contracts is further guaranteed by the blockchain technology, which works as a tamper-proof ledger of transactions. It is the automation that lowers top end administration and builds upon expedite business relations with greater trust and active authenticity.

Only with an AI-powered system can your organization achieve real-time monitoring of contracts, allowing continuous analysis against those important matrices. This type of systems tracks milestones, commitments and deadlines issue alerts when the stakeholders are out of line or late. With an AI-powered system, you can analyze against those important matrices. This type of system tracks milestones, commitments, and deadlines, and issues alerts when the stakeholders are out of line or late. It empowers you to hold others accountable and tackle problems, eliminating any concerns about what is broken and instead motivating you to take action and fix it.

11. Compliance & risk

Artificial intelligence algorithms help verify compliance by scrutinizing contracts for consistency with requirements stipulated in the law or other regulations. Organizations can correct course and mitigate risk as these algorithms flag potential violations. With automation, AI-powered systems make compliance checks easy and help to eliminate any potential for legal disputes or financial consequences.

12. What Are the Upcoming AI And Smart Contracts Trends?

Progressing AI and the increased utilization in services offered through blockchain-based smart contracts will define this future of contract management. AI will strengthen to provide even more advanced features as an improved natural language understanding and predictive analytics. In the new world of digital transformation, AI and smart contracts will be integral to guiding efficiency, transparency, and trust in an intelligent enterprise. A report from Deloitte suggests that implementing AI and smart contracts in businesses can lead to a 20–30% drop in operating costs by 2025. This highlights the transformative power of these technologies in their respective industries.

AI, when integrated with smart contracts, is changing the face of contract management and providing a world of benefits that are centered on timesaving, improved accuracy, and mitigation of risk. Companies that use these technologies will have a clear advantage in today's ever-changing business world, leading to innovation and automation that will pave the way to success.

Smart Contracts for document and Contract Management (case study)

1. HSBC — Using AI and Smart Contracts for Streamlined Trade Finance

HSBC, a financial giant and one of the largest banking and financial services organizations in the world, has integrated AI & smart contracts to change its traditional trade finance operations. Integrating the blockchain-powered smart contract with AI, HSBC can now automate verifying documents and trade agreement execution. It has reduced the time to process trade transactions, ensured increased accuracy, and helped to maintain compliance with regulatory requirements. AI systems extract, validate, and verify data from trade documents with smart contracts to execute transactions based on preset rules under agreed conditions, lowering errors and the cost of fraud.

2. JPMorgan Chase–Automatic Contract Management

JP Morgan Chase developed an AI-driven contract management application named COIN (Contract Intelligence) that enables machine learning and NLP technologies to sift through legal documents and extract critical data. Smart contract has further enriched this system, especially in derivatives trading. JP Morgan automated, enforcing its voluminous complex financial agreements using JPMCoin, combining AI and smart contracts. This helped reduce document review time for legal experts and increased financial enforcement rates when terms are fulfilled. This has enhanced our operational effectiveness and decreased the exposure to legal risks because of manual contract management processes.

3. Santander Bank:

The bank of Santander in Brazil has incorporated AI and smart contracts into their loan processing and management workflows. The main purpose of blockchain Santander Bank is to ensure the security and inalterability of lending agreements. AI algorithms analyze the contract data to discover risks and compliance problems. Smart contracts also facilitate transferring chunks of money and ensure that repayments are made on schedule. As a result, the loan approvals are faster and there is a lesser administrative cost involved, and it also brings more transparency & trust into the system (for both customers & bank).

4. Automated Derivatives Contracts with Barclays Using AI Technologies

Barclays implemented AI-driven smart contracts for automating managing derivatives contracts. The blockchain stores these contracts, ensuring their transparency, secureness, and tamper-proof nature. AI systems constantly monitor these contracts in real-time and, if they detect any discrepancies, breaches, or risks, they start an automatic response, such as margin calls or contract termination. Barclays' legal and compliance teams noted that such automation enabled them to cut time away from the job and decimate human errors, thus improving derivatives management's overall quality.

5. Digital Identity Verification and Contract Execution with Deutsche Bank

Deutsche Bank uses AI and smart contracts for its digital identity verification and contract execution pipeline. Deutsche Bank uses AI for compliance with KYC regulations and quick verification of clients. Smart contracts execute agreements like agreements on account opening or transaction processing. This eliminates any fraud possibility and also improves onboarding time with new customers.

6. BNP Paribas: Private Company Financing with AI and Smart Angels

BNP Paribas and Smart Angels companies partnered to develop a platform that would digitalize securities release and management for private companies. The platform ensures a secure, unchangeable, and transparent ledger that describes any transaction involving these securities, minimizing the need for executives and reducing costs.

Executing smart contracts is a key role in automating the transactions. Once the pre-defined conditions set in the contract are met, the smart contract should perform the next steps. These actions which can be securitisation and paying dividend or transferring shares from the issuer itself. This allows not only a faster transaction lifecycle but also enables eliminating human errors with computer-automated compliance to regulations.

Contract Management in Banking

A fusion of AI & Smart Contracts explains how the traditional contract management had developed with incorporating artificial intelligence (AI) and blockchain-based smart contracts. This chapter brings out how AI using NLP and ML makes the contract lifecycle more efficient in use cases like automated contract drafting, analyzing, risk assessment in a contract. Not to mention, automation saves time on manual process, gets rid of errors and paves a way towards better compliance and risk management.

Smart contracts allow for self-executing agreements to be built directly into code, which brings more transparency, security, and trust, as described above. These contracts act as intermediaries that can automatically execute transactions without human intervention, which should (theoretically at least) reduce fraud and costs. This chapter illuminates use-cases, such as the rise of AI-and smart contract enabled banks like HSBC, JPMorgan, Santander, Barclays, Deutsche Bank and BNP Paribas optimizing processes in trade finance derivatives management, liquidness facilities and custody agreements loans processing digital identity verification esoteric financial instruments securities lending Etc.

However, the AI and smart contracts amalgamation holds great potential to lower costs, increase accuracy, and make businesses more efficient. A predictive model, AI-driven contract recommendations, and continuous contract monitoring all contribute towards helping organizations address risks before they arise. AI-enabled systems provide companies with a means of gaining a competitive edge in the changing marketplace of digital transformation by automating both execution and compliance checks.

The chapter concludes by discussing how the introduction of AI and smart contracts stands to reshape contract management across banking and beyond. These technologies are a firm foundation for more efficient operations, creating robust data infrastructures that can handle compliance and risk mitigation, leading the way towards smarter, agile contract management systems. I suggest that banks and financial institutions that effectively use AI and blockchain in their business strategy will be well-equipped to succeed in a rapidly strengthening digital world.

Reference – Further reading - Chapter 17

What is AI for Contract Management?
https://ironcladapp.com/journal/contract-management/ai-contract-management/

AI-Based Contract Management Guide
https://contractpodai.com/news/ai-contract-management/

What are smart contracts on blockchain
https://www.ibm.com/topics/smart-contracts

The Role of Data Analytics in Contract Services
https://tassgroup.com/uncategorized/data-analytics-and-predictive-modeling-in-contract-services/

HSBC Launches Document-Free Trade Finance Tool TradePay
https://www.pymnts.com/accounts-receivable/2023/hsbc-launches-trade-finance-tool-tradepay-so-businesses-can-improve-working-capital/

JPMorgan Chase's COIN (Contract Intelligence) System
https://www.gabormelli.com/RKB/JPMorgan_Chase%27s_COIN_(Contract_Intelligence)_System

EIGHTEEN

AI and Automation Have Transformed Letter of Credit Issuance - Future of Trade

Introduction

Letters of Credit (L/C): international trade goes to the natural care "net" performance between buyer and seller arrangements for payment in a critical role. The manual, error-prone process has been cumbersome and time-consuming for the business, which is increasingly leading to delays in acquiring images and rising operational costs. As tech innovation progresses, it has created new solutions for L/C issuance streamlined processes. They use tools such as OCR, RPA, AI &ML to serve the solutions. This allows financial institutions to automate the entire process end-to-end that increases efficiencies, accuracy, and compliance as well. This article goes through the automated L/C issuance process, talks about OCR-RPA-AI-ML technology integration and gives examples of leading banks that have deployed these solutions in practice!! We'll look at the dangers of automation and show you how to approach that transformation benefits more than it hinders.

The automation on L/C issuance via OCR-RPA, AI & ML is about building an end-to-end solution by combining multiple technologies around the process that automates it and guarantees for accuracy, compliance and time-efficiency. Here we will provide a step-by-step workflow that covers the complete procedure, from scanning of documents to make final SWIFT payment message.

Automated L/C Issuance: A Workflow

1. Read in and pre-process the documents

Scanned documents corresponding to the L/C Utility (e.g. client contracts, outdated L/Cs, reinforcing records)

Engine: ABBYY FlexiCapture or Kofax Capture

Image Enhancement: AI enabled Given Ongoing Neural Networks (GANs) to fix the issues with document quality.

Then, we feed the new system with scanned documents or digital copies.

Through preprocessing algorithms, the document undergoes cleaning, removal of noise, and enhancement of image quality to allow for better accuracy with OCR.

2. OCR and Data Extraction

Solution: ABBYY FlexiCapture integrated with UiPath for automation.

Machine Learning Models: CNNs (for text recognition) & LSTMs (for sequence prediction)

Process: Then, the OCR reads information from the documents (yes; we are talking about key fields such as customer name, contract terms, amount or letters and specific conditions).

Based on the extracted data, AI algorithms verify it using predefined templates or business rules.

3. L/C to be matched with contract and Previous L/Cs

Tech Stack: Machine Learning (ML) models (NLP based models, Transformers) to map the Extracted L/C details with other customer contracts and their historical L/Cs.

ML Models: NLP and vector embeddings, similarity detection via AI

Path: when the RPA bot is invoked, it triggers a ML model that compares current L/C details with the customer contract and prior L/Cs.

The system reviews contract consistency for both commitment and payment degree, also L/C's issues and it is matching. The system directs any discrepancies or matches that require resolution, either for automatic approval or manual review, under the organization's configured policies.

4. Automated L/C Generation

Technology: RPA Tool: UiPath for Workflow Automation.

AI MODELS: RULE-BASED AI FOR L/C GENERATION & TEMPLATE SELECTION

Steps: RPA Bot creates the L/C draft in pre-defined templates from the validated data and matches. An AI checked the draft for adherence to internal policies and regulatory norms. If the checks all pass, then we are going to complete and approve that L/C.

5. Accounting Entry Creation

Technology Platform: UiPath, Core Banking system (CBS) & Trade Finance System integrated with each other.

APIs: — APIs for attaching with accounting software and CBS.

However, the process by which the RPA bot creates the accounting entries in trade finance system and core banking system based on L//C details. The bot, using APIs which allows a real-time synchronization between systems. Our team does automatic reconciliation and error checking to ensure the entries are correct.

6. SWIFT Payment Message Generation

Technology: Robotic Process Automation RPA Tool: UiPath used for sending swift messages

SWIFT API- Integrated API for the generation and sending of SWIFT messages.

The RPA bot checks the content of L/C and creates SWIFT message format like MT700, with terms mentioned in L/C.

The SWIFT message comprises the name and address of the issuing bank, the beneficiary bank, the payment instructions and any condition pertaining to the transfer. When SWIFT API activates, then it sends the payment message to related banks. The system picks up the confirmation of a log for an audit.

7. Approval sought in the trade APP by the Trade officer/ Relationship Manager

Category: Technology and process: Mobile App; internal chatbot, checking Fx rates, clauses + approval, etc.

8. Document Dispatch and Client Communication

Its use-case: Automating Email and Document Dispatch Technology: RPA Tool: UiPath

Document Management System (DMS): DMS integration for document storage and sharing.

The sender uses email or a secure document dispatch system to send the final L/C document to the customer and other relevant parties.

The DMS stores copies as a measure for future reference and compliance.

9. Iteration and Feedback Flow

Techniques: Machine Learning: machine learning models which keep on getting trained from new data to increase accuracy scan of OCR and matching the algorithms.

Workflow: It is a system that keeps track of all transactions, errors and exceptions to learn from it.

We use this data to re-train ML models and enhance accuracy in subsequent L/C issuance flows.

Workflow Summary

Chatbot to End-to-End Automated Workflow for L/C Issuance using a perfect mix of OCR, RPA, AI & ML organs. This integration ensures that it takes scanned documents in text format, matches them with contracts & past L/Cs and finally processes them, reducing manual intervention and errors. AI strengthens the Matching and validation part, and RPA makes automating Accounting Entries, Generating SWIFT messages, communicating to customers simple.

Integration OCR-RPA and use of AI

Since OCR integration with RPA is a common practice, organizations can achieve an end-to-end automation where data-intake from document is digitization (BOT) as well as automate the process further. The Top OCR RPA Integrations Across Industries.

1. Integration with ABBYY FlexiCapture and UiPath

ABBYY FlexiCapture has Superior OCR for Data Extraction: ABBYY FlexiCapture is one of the top OCR solutions for extracting data from structured and unstructured documents. When used with UiPath, IQBot lends itself and allows automating document-centric processes such as invoice processing, contract management, and customer onboarding. The UiPath bots now will understand the data extracted from ABBYY FlexiCapture and can use it to fill it in on some systems, thus continuing into further processes.

Use Case: Invoice data extraction and payment processing in the ERP system for accounts of payable automation

2. UIPath with Kofax Capture

Advantages of Integration: Kofax Capture provides the best for OCR, can support many documents. Some may be difficult to convert into an electronic version. Integration with Automation Anywhere: When merged with Automation Anywhere, it automates tasks such as document classification, data extraction and then inserting the extracted data into databases or ERP systems.

Practical Application: Capture and process enormous volumes of trade documents to automate trade finance processes, e.g., LC issuance.

3. Tesseract OCR with UiPath

With integration benefits: Tesseract OCR engineered with the AI models becomes an open-source and flexible Optical Character Recognition solution. Users can use UiPath to automate operations such as text extraction from scanned documents, images, and PDFs, along with RPA automation, by integrating Tesseract OCR engineered with AI models.

Who does it: Government services of healthcare what it does automates data extraction of scanned forms and enters the info.

4. Form Recognizer Guide with Power Automate — Microsoft Azure Form Recognizer

Container benefits: Form Recognizer (Preview) AI extracts text, key-value pairs and tables from documents. Integrated with Microsoft Power Automate, which allows building automated workflows involving document processing (e.g. data extraction from forms and routing it to the departments or systems)

Example use case: Automatic data extraction to serve more customers better and faster.

5. UiPath Activities for Google Cloud Vision

OCR with Google Cloud Vision Capability Type: Image, PDF Benefit: The OCR capabilities of Google Cloud Vision are among the most accurate of those within our stack at extracting text from a range of formats. When combined with UiPath is available an end-to-end automation templates document classification, extraction and automatic actions based on extracted information.

Example: Planning, extracting text from photos / images and an automatic categorizing and reviewing process for content moderation.

6. Blue Prism (For Adobe Acrobat OCR)

Adobe Acrobat Features: OCR technology designed for document conversion and text extraction tasks that are necessary for integration among disparate systems. The addition of ABBYY tools to Blue Prism capabilities, examples include the automation of document centric workflows where Blue Prism can process scanned in text turning it into structured data for use within digital forms or databases.

Example use case: creating legal document management using text from legal contracts.

7. One of our valued partners is Automation Anywhere.

Pros of Integration: OpenText Capture Center is one of the best options if you need corporate-grade OCR capabilities for processing high volumes. Automation 360 is Automation Anywhere's powerhouse platform can automate document-heavy processes like large-scale data entry or customer service workflows, integrated with Automation Anywhere.

Insurance Use Case: This use case automates the process of key information from claim form and updating claims systems.

8. Hyland OnBase with UiPath

Seamless integration with UiPath: OnBase by Hyland packs powerful OCR capabilities that also synergize well with UiPath. The integration provides automation of document management tasks, including data extraction, workflow routing, and archiving.

Application: Processing and extracting information from the application forms of new student admissions in educational institutions.

For OCR-RPA integrations, the OCR (Optical Character Recognition) and RPA (Robotic Process Automation) processes both use different AI Models to improve their accuracy, effectiveness, and the role performed by them. Examples of AI models incorporated in some of these integrations are:

1. CNNs (Convolutional Neural Networks)

OCR engines such as Tesseract, Google Cloud Vision, and ABBYY FlexiCapture (Optional) use this model.

CNNs — Convolutional Neural Networks for image recognition and processing. For recognition of text from an image or scanned document, CNNs are used in OCR by identifying the patterns and shapes facilitated by characters present in the visual data.

Applications: Read complex documents, recognize handwriting and text extraction in images.

2. Residual Neural Networks (RNNs) / Long Short-Term Memory Networks (LSTMs) frame it as steps for Image Processing and Deep Learning

In: Some advanced OCR systems, such as ABBYY FlexiCapture or Google Cloud Vision.

The use of RNN and LSTM is common for time-series data and sequence prediction. OCR also helps to understand the order of characters in a line which is very useful for handwriting and text generation tasks.

Applications: Handwritten text recognition, natural language processing for textual data, and accuracy extract text from sequential information.

3. Transformer Models

Use Cases: OCR combined with NLP tasks for Google Cloud NLP APIs, or in Olive and UiPath AI capabilities.

The goal of transformer models (e.g., BERT, GPT) is to understand human language and also be able to create it. You can process the context of the extracted text to enhance data classification, entity recognition, and sentiment analysis.

Use cases: document classification, named entity recognition & intelligence, context understanding with text extracted to automate processing.

4. Attention Mechanisms

Usage: Modern OCR tools, AI-based document processing platforms.

Objective: Attention mechanisms focus on parts of the source data, such as regions of a document or an image, to enhance text extraction accuracy. They are robust in extracting information from documents of mixed layouts.

Use cases: Improving OCR performance in multi-section, table or image-based documents by only OCR'ing areas of interest.

5. NLP (Natural Language Processing) Models

Used In: Post-OCR processing in tools like UiPath, Automation Anywhere and Microsoft Power Automate

Use-case: NLP models help in processing, interpreting and producing human language data. However, OCR solely extracts text, and then it uses the extracted text as input for NLP models to classify, summarize, or analyze the text for subsequent steps in automation.

Use cases: categorizing extracted text, extracting specific entities (such as names, dates, amounts), and document processing workflow automation based on textual content.

6. This recurrent variational Bayes framework relates to a recent work on generative adversarial networks (GAN).

Examples of Uses: Sophisticated preprocessing for OCR, like for image sharpening in Google Cloud Vision and other niche OCR use cases.

Target: The goal of using GANs in OCR is to create crisp images — whether newly generated or enhanced — that will have a direct effect on the accuracy of identification.

Applications: Pre-processing low-quality scanned documents or images to optimize it for OCR processing and enhance text extraction accuracy.

7. Supervised Classification Machine Learning Models

Pain solving- Goes in document classification, data extraction workflows like ABBYY FlexiCapture and Kofax Capture.

Use case: Viewpoint models for document classification and data extraction field selection, paper vs. imaging, workflow assignment.

Use cases: Automatic classification of invoices, contracts or forms and extracting specific data fields based on the document.

8. Optical Flow Models

Applications: Video OCR (e.g., Google Cloud Vision)

Objective: Optical flow models can help in tracking the movement of objects (or text) through frames in a video and be able to perform OCR on content recorded from moving images or scenes with dynamics.

Application: Embedded live text extraction or dynamic environment front-to-back office.

The AI models developed as part of the vision quest address one or more OCR-RPA integration using shortcomings of existing technologies in enhancing text recognition and data extraction to enable intelligent automation of document processing tasks.

5 Leading Banks that Started OCR-RPA, AI and ML based Automation for L/C (Letter of Credit) Issuance achieving 99% Straight through Processing (STP) Process. After each use case, it describes the technology used and the value that resulted.

1. HSBC

Tech Utilised: OCR: ABBYY FlexiCapture, RPA: Blue Prism, AI/ML: Bespoke AI models for document matching and NLP for contract analysis

HSBC implemented a robot to automate issuing L/C, based on ABBYY FlexiCapture for OCR. They used Blue Prism RA together with RPA to notify document processing and entry automatically. The AI and ML models map the L/C details to customer contracts and previous L/Cs, aiding in checking consistency and compliance.

Advantages: 99% straight through processing (STP) rate. Cut L/C processing time from days to hours decreased errors and manual intervention improving cost-effectiveness and efficiency. Better compliance with the regulatory aspects of automation of checks and validations. Justice delivered.

2. JPMorgan Chase

Tools Used: OCR: Kofax Capture, Digitruaizing on Cognitive RPA (UiPath), AI/ML-based similarity detection and document classification machine learning models

Example Use case: JPMorgan Chase used Kofax Capture for processing the high volume of trade finance documents. Kofax Capture scans the documents and extracts data using OCR. UiPath bots then process the extracted data by matching the L/C with historical data and customer contracts using AI models for accurate and consistent processing.

Benefits: 95% STP rate for improved accuracy in L/C processing

Reduced Turnaround time for L/C issuance, which in turn enhances the customer satisfaction

Productivity gains freeing staff to take on additional, higher-value responsibilities.

Reduction in operational risk by automating manual tasks that are difficult to complete.

3. Deutsche Bank

Technology Used: OCR (OpenText Capture Centre) RPA (Automation Anywhere).

AI/ML: AI for contract modeling, ML for predictive analytics

Deutsche Bank: Deutsche Bank automated the process of issuance L/C using OpenText Capture Center with Automation Anywhere. Silicon Valley's Airbase Bank uses AI to analyze and match L/C information with contracts, and as well use previous transactions. ML algorithms predict potential risks and enforce regulatory supervisions.

Benefits: Wanting to get close to 95% STP and hence reducing data entry errors and associated processing times.

Reduced operational costs because of less manual work.

Improved accuracy and compliance that leads to better audit readiness.

This shortened processing period resulted in a faster turnaround to customers, which improved client satisfaction.

4. Standard Chartered Bank

Tech used: OCR: ABBYY FlexiCapture, RPA: UiPath, AI/ML: NLP for contract matching and ML models for process enhancement.

The exampled of use case; Standard Chartered bank implanted ABBYY FlexiCapture and UiPath to automate their end-to-end L/C issuance process. In addition, this included the AI and ML models, along with contract analysis, Historical L/C data used for sorting of candidate document data extraction and matching, both leading to Automated Document generation and processing part.

Benefits: 96% STP, which lowers the need for manual processing.

Efficiently scaling to meet a growing L/C volume.

Improves L/C matching accuracy with contracts, minimizing the risk of mismatches.

Automated checks leading to greater adherence to global trade regulations.

5. Citibank

Technology Used:

OCR: Google Cloud Vision

RPA: UiPath

AI/ML — AI for automated document analysis and ML to learn from historical transactions.

Use Case: Citibank has deployed an end-to-end OCR-RPA solution that utilizes Google's Cloud Vision for text extraction and UiPath for automating the workflow of L/C issuance in the bank's sender system. The AI models match L/C applications with trained contracts. Here, ML algorithms come to the aid as they learn from historical data and keep updating their rules for decision.

Benefits: Fully automated to 95% STP, elimination of manual errors and processing time.

Added assurance in L/C to customer contracts matching the customers, reducing compliance reporting risks.

Improved customer satisfaction and retention through prompt issuance of L/C.

Automation increases productivity, freeing people from mundane operational tasks to focus on driving the business.

Benefits across all banks:

Efficiency: Automating the L/C issuance process has reduced processing time and a manual workload for these banks.

Improved Accuracy: Using AI and ML makes the data capture more accurate, which means fewer errors or discrepancies in document matching.

Cost savings: A decline in manual labor, as well as the risk of error and money spent on rework, has dramatically reduced through automation.

Risk Management: Automated checks and validations, like all regulations to be met, reducing the chances of non-compliance.

Customer Satisfaction–They can speed up most of the process and raise the accuracy, which at the same time increase customer satisfaction delivering excellent results for all involved sides.

By using advanced technology to automate the process, these banks are at the forefront of L/C issuance - they accomplish almost 99% of transactions without human intervention.

(Disclaimer: this example of use case can be a different stage in bank, the above information is based on provided information's)

A breakthrough in the financial industry is OCR, RPA, AI and ML work together to automate L/C issuance. They provide advantages, including decreased process duration, accuracy, cost savings and regulation adherence. As shown by the likes of banks like HSBC, JPMorgan Chase and Deutsche

Bank over the years, these technologies can support close to 100% straight through processing rates, which also means minimal human intervention. Yet, it is important to be aware of the possible side effects and constraints that automation can bring, like for example, the need for AI models as a source or concerns around data quality. With strong error-checking mechanisms in place, along with continuous monitoring and keeping AI models retrained regularly, we can mitigate these risks. This will ultimately allow us to bring an even more efficiently and future of L/C issuance one step closer (across the board, in broader range) to a wider scope of adoption throughout the financial sector.

Reference – Further reading - Chapter 18

Workflow for Automated L/C Issuance

https://community.sap.com/t5/enterprise-resource-planning-blogs-by-members/letter-of-credit-import-process-issuance-trade-finance/ba-p/13494066

Enterprise-scale document automation, powered by AI
https://www.abbyy.com/flexicapture/

Kofax Capture - Capture Paper Documents for use in Applications and Workflows
https://csa.canon.com/internet/portal/us/csa/products/details/software/enterprise-office/kofax-capture/kofax-capture-capture-paper-documents

UiPath® Task Capture is a process discovery tool
https://docs.uipath.com/task-capture/standalone/2022.4/user-guide/introduction

Microsoft Azure Form Recognizer with Power Automate
https://sannidhisiva.medium.com/azure-form-recognizer-dacef053e5f6

OpenText Intelligent Capture
https://www.opentext.com/en-gb/products/intelligent-capture

Blue Prism - Introduction to RPA
https://www.tutorialspoint.com/blue_prism/blue_prism_introduction_to_rpa.htm

Printed in Great Britain
by Amazon